To Dr. Mark McColloch —

With sincere thanks

for your help.

Cynthia A. Repinski

9-24-91

THE *Univex* STORY

Universal Camera Corporation

by

CYNTHIA A. REPINSKI

Library of Congress Catalog Card Number: 91-071477

ISBN 0-931838-17-7

With much love and respect,
I dedicate this book to my mother,
Barbara Repinski,
and to the memory of my late father,
Edward F. Repinski, Sr.,
who passed away on February 17, 1988.

TABLE OF CONTENTS

PREFACE 6

INTRODUCTION 9

CHAPTER I: 1932-1936 11
---------- "A JEWEL OF A CAMERA"

CHAPTER II: 1936-1938 35
---------- "NOW MOVIES COST LESS THAN SNAPSHOTS"

CHAPTER III: 1938-1941 61
    PART I - "THE CAMERA OF TOMORROW"
    PART II - "THE UNIVERSAL 35MM SINGLE LENS REFLEX PROTOTYPE"
    PART III - "NOW EVERYONE CAN AFFORD A CANDID CAMERA"

CHAPTER IV: 1941-1946 113
    PART I - "THE UNIVERSAL OPTICAL SHOP"
    PART II - "THE UNIVERSAL BINOCULARS"

CHAPTER V: 1946-1948 170
    PART I - "ESPECIALLY DESIGNED FOR COLOR"
    PART II - "FOR PICTURES THAT CLICK...CLICK A UNIVERSAL"

CHAPTER VI: 1948-1952 200
---------- "THE TREND IS UNIVERSAL"

CHAPTER VII: 1952-1964 225
---------- "THE FINAL YEARS"

CONCLUSION 238

APPENDICES 241
    A: OFFICERS AND MANAGERS
    B: FACILITY LOCATIONS
    C: PATENTS AND TRADEMARKS
      I- U.S. DESIGN PATENTS
      II - U.S. LETTERS PATENTS
      III - U.S. TRADEMARKS
      IV - UNIVERSAL PATENTEES
    D: NET SALES AND PROFITS
    E: CONDENSED CHRONOLOGICAL PRODUCT HISTORY
    F: PARTIAL LISTING OF UNIVEX 8MM FEATURE FILMS
    G: GENERAL ELECTRIC AND SYLVANIA PROJECTION BULBS FOR
      USE IN UNIVERSAL PROJECTORS
    H: COMPREHENSIVE RECORD OF UNIVEX PRODUCTS WITH
      COLLECTIBLE RATING GUIDE
    I: UNIVEX ASSEMBLY PLANS

BIBLIOGRAPHY 264

INDEX 268

PREFACE

My interest in the Universal Camera Corporation and UniveX cameras evolved somewhat unexpectedly in 1974. At that time, I knew almost nothing about photography. Anxious to learn some of photography's finer points, I enrolled in several classes, one of which required the use of a 35mm camera with adjustable aperture and shutter speed settings. Not only did I lack possession of such a camera, I was totally unprepared at the time to make a knowledgeable decision regarding the purchase of a new 35mm camera. In answer to my problems, my father disappeared from the room, returning a few moments later with a small box in hand. Inside the box was a camera I had never seen before — it was, to say the least, quite peculiar in design. At first glance, I was utterly fascinated. The camera was a Universal Mercury II and its unusual design proved to be the conversation piece of my photography class. With that camera, I learned the principles of photography.

Much to my surprise, I discovered that the Mercury II camera was familiar to many people. It was not unusual to be approached time and again by curious observers on the street. One day a gentleman commented that he, too, owned a UniveX Mercury — "the prewar model", he said. Further elaborating on the subject, he explained that his Mercury required the use of a special 35mm filmload, unobtainable since the company went out of business years ago. The idea of a "twin" Mercury camera sparked my curiosity and several days later I began to explore the possibility of locating a UniveX Mercury I camera.

My knowledge of photography continued to grow and I eventually decided to purchase one of the new SLR cameras on the market at the time. As the months and years passed, I found myself devoting less and less time to photography, all the while becoming more and more preoccupied with the prospect of collecting cameras — more specifically, UniveX cameras. Since that time I have acquired a substantial collection of UniveX photographica consisting of nearly every known camera, projector and accessory item ever manufactured or marketed by the Universal Camera Corporation. When I first became involved in collecting UniveX cameras, I eventually discovered, as had many other camera collectors before me, that information relating to the Universal Camera Corporation and its products was extremely limited, with many apparent discrepancies. The need for a book pertaining specifically to the Universal Camera Corporation was self-evident.

I should like to take this opportunity to thank the many kind people who contributed information or assistance during the development of this book. In an effort to present the facts as accurately as possible, each and every contribution, no matter how small or insignificant, received painstaking consideration. Over the past several years, countless hours were spent gathering and organizing the research material compiled in this book — a project that, in the end, entailed much more time and effort than I had ever imagined.

From the very start of this endeavor, my friends and relatives provided me with an overwhelming sense of enthusiasm, encouragement and, most importantly, concern and understanding. My cousins, Thomas and Catherine Egan, were especially helpful during this project. I would like to extend my appreciation to both of them and also my assurance that their efforts will not soon be forgotten. While residing in the Washington D.C. area, Tom obtained copies of Universal-related material, all extremely essential to my research, from the Library of Congress, the National Archives, Security and Exchange Commission and the U.S. Patent and Trademark Office. Cathy was responsible for transferring my entire manuscript, originally written on an Apple computer, from Apple format to IBM format. Essentially, this transfer of information expedited matters greatly for those at Centennial Photo Service because they work exclusively with IBM compatible computers. I am quite certain that Jim and Joan McKeown of Centennial Photo Service are as grateful as I am for Cathy's efforts. My sister, Rosalinda Repinski, offered to type on a number of occasions when various health problems made it impossible, or at best, quite difficult for me to do my own typing. Finally, I am extremely grateful to my very close friend, Sharon Schmidbauer, for her continuous support and assistance throughout this four year undertaking. On many occasions, Sharon visited several Wisconsin area libraries with me to help collect information pertinent to Universal. As my chief proofreader, she offered constructive criticism when necessary and provided some very valuable suggestions that were eventually incorporated into the final manuscript.

Jim and Joan McKeown of Centennial Photo Service deserve special mention for getting the initial project off to a good start by providing me with all the information contained in their file on Universal. In addition to their generous contribution, I would like to acknowledge and thank the following people for their untiring persistence in locating and contributing critical documentation and/or artifacts: Mary Ann Abuisi, City Clerk, City Hall, North Adams, Massachusetts; Nathan T. Butcher, collector of military binoculars, Milton, Florida; John F. Buydos, Science Reference Librarian, Science and Technology Division, Library of Congress, Washington, D.C.; Ralph Kripner, Historical Office Director, Department of the Army, Rock Island Arsenal, Rock Island, Illinois; Lorraine Leonard, Librarian, The Transcript, North Adams, Massachusetts; Dr. Mark McColloch, United Electrical Archives, University of Pittsburgh, Pittsburgh, Pennsylvania; Morris G. Moses, Photographic Historian, Albany, New York; the late Walter Orr Roberts, President Emeritus, University Corporation for Atmospheric Research, Boulder, Colorado; Larry Tieger, collector of military binoculars, Pittsburgh, Pennsylvania; and Daniel T. Whiteman, Museum Director, Department of the Army, Rock Island Arsenal, Rock Island, Illinois. Additional research material was generously provided by the General Electric Co., the Girl Scouts of the U.S.A. and S.F. Spira, formerly associated with Spiratone, Inc. There were many other contributors, far too numerous to mention, that offered significant bits and pieces of information, all of which proved essential toward the development of a more precise and exact history of the Universal Camera Corporation. To each and every one of these contributors, I am extremely indebted.

Most finally, I wish to extend my deepest appreciation to former Universal employees Philip J. Brownscombe, the late George Kende, Joseph David Marks, Joseph Pignone, Steven I. Robinson, Simon Weil and all of the other people formerly associated with the Universal Camera Corporation who were kind enough to provide firsthand information through mail and/or telephone correspondence, questionnaires and personal interviews. I would also like to express my heartfelt gratitude to Mrs. George Kende for her concerned efforts in seeing that I received all of the remaining Universal-related documentation that her late husband, George Kende, Universal's Chief Engineer from 1935 to 1948, had intended to send me before he passed away on November 30, 1988. Without Kende's files, preserved for more than fifty years, many interesting aspects of Universal's history would have remained in total obscurity; instead, much of the material contained in his files has finally been brought to light — accurately documented and fully explained for the first time in any published book.

Whether on a personal or professional level, Kende was highly respected by all who knew him. It is my fondest desire that "The Univex Story" be looked upon with enthusiasm and approval by all concerned, making it a fitting memorial to George Kende, the man predominantly responsible for the most successful and memorable years of the Universal Camera Corporation.

Fig. 0-1 The Universal Camera Corporation, 28 West 23rd Street, New York City, 1938-1952. (Courtesy: Municipal Archives, Department of Records and Information Services, City of New York)

8

INTRODUCTION

The story of this American photographic manufacturer began in the early 1930's and spanned more than three decades over one of the most memorable periods in 20th Century American photographic history. After just one year in the camera manufacturing business, Universal Camera Corporation had managed to put inexpensive, easy to use, cameras into the hands of millions of people previously unable to afford a somewhat costly recreational activity. As a general rule, photography had always been a hobby limited to the well-to-do or affluent — at least until 1933, when Universal emerged as part of the photographic industry and began introducing its line of affordable photographic equipment.

Despite the financial hardship of the early 1930's, the demand for Universal's amateur photographic products continued to grow until "photography" became a common household word. Universal's instant success was largely due to the ingenuity and diligence of Universal's two top executives, Otto W. Githens and Jacob J. Shapiro. In all actuality, these two men were nothing more than novices to the camera manufacturing business. In the early 1920's, Githens founded the General Finance Company, one of the first automobile financing concerns in Indianapolis, the city where Githens was raised. After a few profitable years, the company folded for unknown reasons and Githens lost his entire fortune. Not long after, Githens was once again back on his feet, innovative and industrious as he was, rebuilding a lost fortune — though this time, as an executive for a New York loan company that handled taxicab operations in Chicago, Indianapolis and Philadelphia. Githens' new business proved quite lucrative until the depression struck. About 1930, Githens got together with a former business associate, Jacob Shapiro, an agent for a taxicab insurance company. Shapiro was remarkably talented in sales and public relations matters and wanted to discuss the possibility of starting an amateur camera manufacturing business together. By 1932, the depression had definitely taken its toll — Githens, 38 years old at the time, and Shapiro, 35 years old at the time, were firmly convinced that their next fortune awaited them in the amateur camera business — and so they organized the Universal Camera Corporation.

In 1932, Universal listed its first place of business as 521 Fifth Avenue, New York City. In the following year, the company moved to 32-46 West 23rd Street, New York City, where it remained until 1938. By that time, Universal had prospered beyond all expectations and lack of office and factory space had definitely become a major problem. As a result, Universal was forced to relocate once again — this time to the adjacent 12 story brick loft building at 28 West 23rd Street, New York City *(Fig. 0-1)*, where the company remained until 1952. Universal's executive, engineering and sales offices occupied the entire sixth floor, with additional space on the twelfth and second floors being used by the manufacturing department and customer service office. On January 26, 1933, under the laws of the State of New York, Universal became a New York corporation. Several years later, on October 1, 1937, Universal elected to dissolve its New York corporation, opting instead for the formation of a new corporation under the laws of the State of Delaware.

Through the years many of Universal's amateur photographic products have, in one way or another, escaped the formidable trash basket to become part of a growing market of photographic collectibles. A small number of Universal cameras, projectors and accessory items are still being seriously used today, although many others continue to collect dust in attics and basements across the country. One Pennsylvania man explained that he had received a Universal Cinemaster camera in the mid 1940's as a wedding gift. He used it regularly for nearly 20 years until 1962 when he decided to purchase a new turret camera. Until just recently, he continued using the Cinemaster as a "backup", or second camera, on vacation trips. His story is not an isolated one — many other owners of Universal products have told similar stories. Interest in photographic collectibles has grown considerably during the past 15 years — much greater than the average person would ever imagine. Many of Universal's unique prewar designs have maintained their popularity throughout the years, becoming prized collectors' items much sought after by collectors the world over. Indicative of the growing interest in photographic collectibles, books relating to various photographic manufacturers and their products have been steadily appearing, one by one, on library and bookstore shelves. Until now, Universal Camera Corporation was a subject dealt with only briefly in photographic books of a more general nature.

The pages of this book contain a concise and conclusive study of the Universal Camera Corporation — the company, the people and the products. Every known Universal product is chronicled and reviewed. In addition, many common misconceptions generally associated with Universal have been brought forth and discussed in detail. The majority of the chapter titles appearing in this book were selected from actual Universal sales slogans, each one clearly representative of a particular period in Universal's history. To date, this is the most accurate and complete story of an unforgettable American photographic manufacturer — the Universal Camera Corporation.

All photos not otherwise credited are by the author.

CHAPTER ONE

1932-1936

"A JEWEL OF A CAMERA"

Universal Camera Corporation was the creation of two innovative businessmen who shared the presumption that what America needed most was a photographic line of products "affordable to everyone". Otto W. Githens, President of Universal and Jacob J. Shapiro, Vice President, accentuated that claim in October 1933 with the introduction of a small, inexpensive amateur photographic product — the UniveX Model A Camera *(Fig. 1-1)*. Constructed of durable General Electric Textolite, the Model A camera incorporated a simple spring shutter and a hand-polished lens imported from Germany. Priced at just $.39, the Model A became an overnight success.

A sudden deluge of orders forced the company to step up production efforts. Within a few short months, Universal was maintaining a production schedule of 20,000 Model A cameras a day! Sales figures indicated that an astounding 2.6 million Model A cameras had been sold in 1934 alone, essentially confirming the fact that Universal had finally provided America with "perfect photography at a new low cost". Despite the simplistic design of the Model A, on a bright day with the sun at the correct angle to the subject, the camera did indeed produce surprisingly "perfect" pictures.

Suspicion and controversy reportedly surrounded Universal almost immediately following its introduction into the photographic business. Late in 1932, Githens and Shapiro contacted Norton Laboratories,

Fig. 1-1 The UniveX Model A Camera.

Inc., a company involved in the manufacture of synthetic plastic products. Norton Labs, located at 1035 Mill Street in Lockport, New York, agreed to design a cheap, simple camera that could be easily and inexpensively mass produced. Carl H. Whitlock, Vice President of Norton Labs, designed a camera which was "T-shaped" in appearance and constructed of General Plastics' new synthetic material, Durez. The camera employed the use of a direct vision viewfinder frame, a spring shutter and an American-made lens. Oddly enough, after Githens and Shapiro had observed the plans for the camera, sources claim that a dispute developed between Norton Labs and Universal. Supposedly, Norton Labs had already finished the dies and was ready to begin production of the camera when, in October of 1933, the UniveX Model A appeared on the market as a patented Universal product with Githens claiming sole inventorship. Astounded by this sudden turn of events, Whitlock submitted patent applications covering the ornamental design, construction and mechanics of his camera. In December 1933, the Norton Camera *(Fig. 1-2)*, retailing at \$.50, was introduced in an effort to

Fig. 1-2 The Norton Camera.

12

recover a seemingly lost investment. Due to the fact that the Norton and UniveX cameras were so much alike, Universal spared little time attempting to cloud the issue with public accusations of patent infringement and threats of legal action toward manufacturers and retailers involved in the sale of any similar type camera. Comparatively speaking, the only major difference between the two cameras was the distinctly different film spools that each particular camera utilized. The Model A required a special UniveX film spool having a "V"-shaped notch at one end: the Norton camera, on the other hand, required a peculiar six exposure filmroll manufactured by Eastman Kodak with the film wind knob affixed as an integral part of each spool. At a cost of $.15 per roll, Eastman Kodak supplied film for the Norton camera up until the beginning of World War II.

Even though Universal was generally credited with the introduction of America's first all-molded plastic miniature camera, many in the photographic and plastics industries suspected that Norton Labs had contributed much more to this photographic achievement than anyone would ever realize. A 1940 article in Modern Plastics magazine panned the history of molded plastic cameras and, interestingly enough, in doing so managed to slight Universal and its cameras entirely. Some of the camera models featured in the article included the Falcon Junior, the Falcon Press Flash, the Namco Midget, the Argus C, the Bull's Eye Six-20, the Baby Brownie Special and the Vokar. Plastic photographic accessories such as exposure meters, daylight film winders, slide viewers and film developing tanks were also featured. The UniveX name was left out completely; instead, credit was given to Norton Labs for introducing an all-molded plastic camera selling for only $.50 — described as "one of the earliest inexpensive miniature cameras ....literally opening the flood gates for a surge of molded models to follow and remain today".

Three different versions of the UniveX Model A camera are known to exist. (Fig. 1-3) The original Model A design featured a molded pattern on the front of the camera which had the appearance of "sunburst rays" emanating from around the lens opening. The earliest "sunburst" Model A cameras had no light steps in the lens openings and were assembled with plastic film

Fig. 1-3 UniveX Model A Cameras — the original "sunburst" version (left), the second and more common "sunburst" version (center) and the later "geometric" version (right).

13

wind knobs. Later "sunburst" Model A cameras had light steps in the lens openings and were assembled with more durable metal film wind knobs. A distinctly different variation of the original "sunburst" Model A appeared on the market in the spring of 1934. this variant Model A was designed for Universal by James D. Milne of Pittsfield, Massachusetts, after which time Universal applied for and was subsequently granted a design patent on the camera (U.S. Des. Pat.# 111,986). Milne's variant Model A had a molded "geometric" pattern, not as deep-set and bold as that of the original "sunburst" Model A. Less than one year after the original Model A was first introduced, this variant Model A was being featured exclusively in Universal's 1934 advertisements and was readily available in stores everywhere. Reasons warranting this change in ornamental design remain somewhat uncertain. The following explanation, although purely speculative in nature, does seem to shed some light on an otherwise unexplained subject.

Several months after the introduction of the Model A, it was a well-known fact that millions of UniveX cameras had been sold — an undeniable success for Universal! About the same time, a Los Angeles manufacturing firm, the Pacific Coast Merchandise Co., decided to share in Universal's newfound wealth by marketing a novel invention which employed the use of two "sunburst" UniveX Model A cameras. Introduced in the spring of 1934 and distributed by G. Gennert, Inc. of New York City, the Duo-Vex Camera *(Fig. 1-4)* was the epitome of inexpensive stereoscopic photography, designed to

Fig. 1-4 The Duo-Vex Camera — one version (illustrated) has the "Duo-Vex" marking, the other version does not.

Fig. 1-5 A 1934 Universal advertisement, including strict warning against the infringing use of Universal's patented Model A camera design, taken from the "American Druggist", July 1934.

15

introduce the amateur to a specialized style of photography never before possible at such a minimal cost. In all likelihood, the Duo-Vex camera was the primary reason for Universal's sudden alteration of the already popular "sunburst" Model A design. A close inspection of the "sunburst" and "geometric" Model A camera styles reveals something more than a simple change in ornamental design. Universal cleverly repositioned the film wind knob on the "geometric" Model A, essentially rendering the camera incompatible for use with the Duo-Vex bracketing device. In addition, the shutter release was moved to the opposite side of the camera body on some of the "geometric" Model A cameras. A design patent covering the original "sunburst" design of the UniveX Model A camera was granted to Universal on May 16, 1933. Under the terms of U.S. Des. Pat.#89,888, in any of the seven years that followed, it would have been a direct violation of Universal's patent rights for any person or company to manufacture, use, or sell any such "T"-shaped camera bearing this patented ornamental "sunburst" design without Universal's prior consent. Shortly after the Duo-Vex was introduced to the public, one particular Universal advertisement appeared in various trade publications emphasizing, quite clearly, the company's firm position regarding any infringing use of its popular UniveX Model A camera *(Fig. 1-5)*. Publicized warnings of alleged patent infringement, coupled with the prompt distribution of Universal's variant Model A camera brought production of the Duo-Vex to a sudden halt, explaining the relative scarcity of this particular camera today.

The Duo-Vex Camera Set *(Fig. 1-6)* originally retailed for $2.95 and consisted of a Duo-Vex camera, a Realism viewer and a package of 12 die-cut mounting cards. Not long thereafter, certain photographic distributors were offering the entire outfit for as low as $.89! The Duo-Vex consisted of a special metal bracketing device, finished in black enamel, designed to position and secure two UniveX Model A "sunburst" cameras side by side — one camera right side up and the other camera upside down. With the two cameras in this position, both shutter releases faced inward: a sliding metal component part linked the two shutter releases. Each time this metal linkage was pushed up or down, the shutters fired simultaneously. Two versions of the Duo-Vex camera are known to exist — one marked "DUO-VEX" on the upper bracket and the other marked with the manufacturer's name only. The Realism Viewer was a very simple two piece device, unmarked and all metal

Fig. 1-6 The Duo-Vex Outfit included the Duo-Vex Camera, a Realism Viewer, 12 Mounting Cards and instructions.

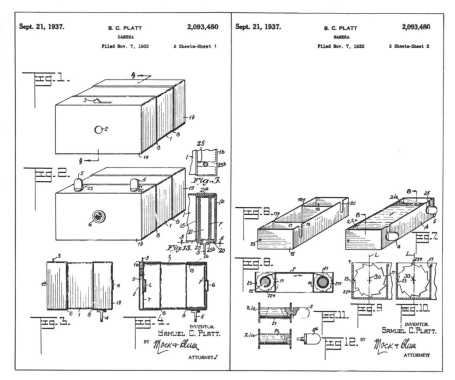

Sept. 21, 1937.   S. C. PLATT   2,093,480
CAMERA
Filed Nov. 7, 1932   2 Sheets-Sheet 1

Sept. 21, 1937.   S. C. PLATT   2,093,480
CAMERA
Filed Nov. 7, 1932   2 Sheets-Sheet 2

Fig. 1-7 A simple box-type camera and nonstandard film holder, depicted in U.S. Pat. # 2,093,480, invented by Samuel C. Platt.

in construction. Finished in black enamel, the viewer provided two glass lenses for magnified viewing. After inserting a pair of stereo pictures in the precut slits of the mounting card, the mounting card was then ready for insertion into the card holder portion of the viewer. With the mounting card in place, the picture was easily focused while viewing by sliding the two sections of the viewer in and out.

Githens and Shapiro had apparently given much forethought to the Model A camera and, in doing so, they ingeniously devised a way to collect an immediate return on their initial investment into the business. The Model A was designed to use a film spool with a "V"-shaped notch at one end — a special patented film spool that only Universal could provide. When inserted into the film chamber, the "V"-shaped notch on the film spool engaged directly with a similarly shaped metal key attached to the camera's film wind knob. Consequently, for each and every UniveX Model A camera that was sold, the company could expect significant profits directly related to the continuous sale of film for these cameras. A total of 15 million UniveX rollfilms were sold by Universal in its first three years of business. The "V" symbol found on the end of each UniveX film spool was fast becoming known the world over as the Universal Camera Corporation trademark.

For Githens and Shapiro, the notion of using non-standard film loads was not an idea solely limited to the design of the UniveX Model A camera or the Norton camera. The following Universal patent seems to indicate that Githens and Shapiro had originally intended to make non-standard filmloads

17

an important part of the Universal camera business. The earliest known public record relating to the Universal Camera Corporation was U.S. Pat. #2,093,480 filed by Samuel C. Platt of New York City on November 7, 1932. The patent was originally handled by the law firm, Mock & Blum, until September 14, 1933 when Platt transferred power of attorney to Morris Kirschstein, Universal's patent attorney. The patent related to a small and simple metal box-type camera *(Fig. 1-7)* consisting of three main parts: a hollow main center section, a front cover piece carrying both the lens and shutter assemblies and a rear cover piece carrying a non-standard film holder and a film counter window. The front and rear cover pieces fit tightly over the front and rear flanges of the center housing section, making it impossible for light to enter the camera except through the lens opening itself. Interestingly, the camera required a rather unusual non-standard filmload — a film holder, or cartridge of sorts, something similar to the 110 or 126 cartridge films in widespread use today. After the film was completely exposed, the film holder containing the exposed film was removed for processing and a new pre-loaded film holder was inserted into the camera. If, for some reason, Universal had not brought the UniveX Model A camera to market, the company might have attempted instead to manufacture this simple box camera with its unusual film holder. One might stop to wonder — would Universal have fared so well had it manufactured this simple inexpensive camera instead of the Model A camera?

Universal decided to contact the Gevaert Company of Belgium regarding the production of its non-standard UniveX films. Gevaert accepted the job and, in doing so, became the sole producer of Universal's special films. Inside Gevaert's manufacturing plant, each Univex film spool was loaded with precut lengths of film and paper backing, then wrapped securely in foil paper and covered with the UniveX label. Several years later, Gevaert

Fig. 1-8 UniveX Ultrapan #00 Rollfilm. An original store display box containing 48 rolls of UniveX film.

began packaging UniveX filmrolls in small boxes, the likes of which are more commonly found on today's collectibles market than the earlier examples of foil-wrapped UniveX film. The first UniveX rollfilm available for use with the Model A camera was UniveX Ultrachrome, priced at just $.10. This fine grain orthochromatic film, designated UniveX #00, was sold in six exposure lengths, producing negatives 1½x1⅛" in size. Universal was convinced that the short length of these filmrolls would eventually pay off in greater film sales for the company. In 1939 Universal offered one other UniveX #00 rollfilm — UniveX Ultrapan *(Fig. 1-8)*, a new and faster fine grain panchromatic film priced at $.15 and recommended for use in adverse light conditions. In addition, Universal began offering the original Ultrachrome in a new emulsion

Fig. 1-9 The UniveX Photocrafter — an amateur film developing outfit.

Fig. 1-10 The 1933 and 1934 Norton "Century of Progress" Cameras.

speed which was 50% faster than before. For the young photographer, Universal offered a home developing outfit called the UniveX Photocrafter *(Fig. 1-9).* The outfit included all the chemicals and equipment necessary for developing and printing pictures at home from UniveX #00 rollfilms. Norton Labs also offered a similar outfit that included the following items: a Norton camera, film, photographic paper, chemical solutions, a plastic measuring beaker, plastic developing trays and a small photo album for displaying the finished prints.

It was during the 1933-34 Century of Progress Exposition in Chicago that Universal attracted world-wide attention with its $.39 marvel. UniveX Model A cameras identified by a 1933 or 1934 "Century of Progress" decal are considered a rare acquisition for today's collector. Equally rare is the Norton camera marked with a 1933 or 1934 "Century of Progress" decal *(Fig. 1-10).* Despite an attendance of 38.6 million people, successful promotion of the Norton camera was rather difficult since most people considered the camera somewhat of an impostor to the more popular, and less expensive, UniveX Model A.

Undaunted by this lack of public appeal, Norton Labs remained firm in its efforts to gain patent protection for the Norton Camera invention. Applications for design patents covering the ornamental design of the Norton and UniveX Cameras were filed respectively by Whitlock of Norton Labs and Githens of Universal, with Githens being the first to file on February 23, 1933 (U.S. Des. Pat.# 89,888) and Whitlock following suit on October 30, 1933 (U.S. Des. Pat.# 91,228). Whitlock and Githens also filed separate patent applications covering the constructional and mechanical aspects of their cameras, but certain features common to both the Norton and UniveX cameras prevented the U.S. Patent Office from granting these particular patents to either party at the time. In a situation such as this, whenever two or more parties claimed substantially the same invention in their patent applications, the U.S. Patent Office declared an "interference". In the specific case of Norton Labs and Universal, interference proceedings were conducted to determine which of the two inventors, Githens or Whitlock, should be regarded as the "first" inventor. Much in Githens' favor was the fact that Universal had already brought the Univex Model A to market by October 1933, with high volume production of the popular camera continuing on a daily basis thereafter. Norton Labs, on the other hand, had yet to file its initial patent application on the Norton Camera, not to mention the fact that the Norton Camera did not appear on the market until December 1933. Undoubtedly, these factors weighed heavily toward a final decision by the Board of Interferences. Although Whitlock might have originally conceived the invention, in situations similar to this one, the U.S. Patent Office has consistently determined over the years that priority of invention should be awarded to the first party filing a patent application and also successfully reducing the invention to actual practice. Unless an invention's "true" date of conception can be proven by submission of corroborative evidence such as witness testimony, signed and dated documents, drawings and/or written descriptions, the U.S. Patent Office has generally considered the date of conception to be the same as the date of patent application. In the matter of Norton Labs and Universal, patent records clearly indicate the final decision reached by the Board of Interferences was in favor of Githens, with U.S. Patents #2,029,474, #2,029,475, and #2,029,476 being issued and assigned to Universal shortly thereafter on February 4, 1936.

Exasperated by the outcome of this matter, Whitlock decided to retain the one patent granted to him on the Norton Camera, U.S. Des. Pat.# 91,228, but resolved to sell and assign to Universal all other patent material relating to the Norton Camera. Additionally, Norton Labs made a decision to sell its entire inventory of finished Norton Cameras and home developing kits to Universal.

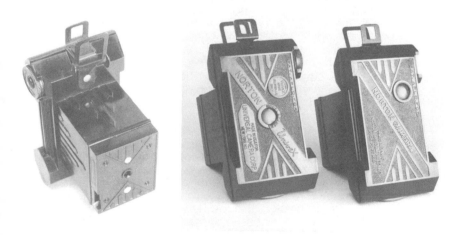

Fig. 1-11 The Norton-UniveX and Norton Cameras.

Fig. 1-12 The 1936 Norca "Rower" Camera, a french camera similar in design to the Norton and UniveX Model A Cameras.

Not long after, Universal converted all of the Norton cameras to accept UniveX #00 rollfilm instead of the original Kodak filmload, leading to the eventual introduction of a new Universal camera in 1936 — the Norton-UniveX Camera *(Fig. 1-11)*. Several changes were made to the Norton's film chambers to assure compatibility with the UniveX #00 filmroll. A UniveX film wind knob with the patented "V"-shaped flange was added to one film chamber, while the remaining opening in the opposite film chamber was filled in with plastic material. The rear covers were replaced with new covers, identifying the Norton-UniveX camera as a product of the Universal Camera Corporation. The new covers also indicated the required film load as Univex #00 rollfilm. To many in the photographic industry, this new Universal "by-product" was little more than a stark reminder of the difficulties that had come to pass between Norton and Universal.

About the same time, although somewhat unrelated, a French photographic manufacturer, Norca, began production of a camera called the "Rower" *(Fig. 1-12)*, a small bakelite model bearing an astonishing resemblance to the American Norton and UniveX Model A cameras. At first glance, the camera could easily be mistaken for either of its American counterparts. The "Rower" resembled the Norton and UniveX both in size and shape, although the ornamental design and the viewfinder system of the camera differed slightly. The Gevaert Company provided special six exposure filmrolls (3.5 x 4 cm negative size) for use with the little French camera. The film wind system of this UniveX look-alike was rather unique — unlike that of the UniveX or Norton, the film wind knob on the "Rower" was not permanently affixed in any way to the camera body or the filmspool. A thin metal screw,

½ inch in length, formed an integral part of the film wind knob. Once a new filmroll was dropped into the camera's film chamber, the screw was inserted into a small opening on the side of the camera body which led directly into a threaded hole found on the end of the patented metal filmspool. Once the screw was tightened completely, further rotation of the film wind knob would wind the film through the camera. About 10 years later, Norca decided to transform the "Rower" camera into a more sophisticated model. The camera was modified to accept a 12 exposure roll of perforated film, producing negatives that were 24x36 mm in size. An advanced film transport system involved the addition of larger metal film wind knobs, a system of locking cogwheels and an exposure counter. The front extension of the camera was reinforced with a chrome housing that served to support a 50mm f/3.5 lens. A multi-speed shutter with speeds ranging from ¹⁄₁₀ to ¹⁄₃₀₀ of a second was also added. This major overhaul resulted in the birth of a rare French camera known as the "Norca Pin-Up". It is estimated that less than 100 examples of this model were actually produced. Obtaining special filmloads for the camera appeared to be a problem for the company, forcing Norca to abandon a project that had already cost considerable time and expense.

A great deal of Universal's prosperity during the early 1930's was attributable to the overwhelming and extravagant advertising campaigns created by the company. In addition to the eye-catching multicolored ads commonly seen in metropolitan newspapers across the country, full-page advertisements for the Model A camera also appeared regularly in numerous magazines. Photo contests were occasionally used by Universal to promote the sale of its cameras. One example, a $5000 UniveX Photo Contest ran for a period of four months during the summer of 1935, with Universal awarding monthly cash prizes to the winners — all of whom were required to submit photographs taken with a UniveX camera. Announcements promoting the sale of UniveX products were frequently heard on the radio. Sales slogans such as: "Perfect photography at a new low cost", "UniveX pictures enlarge beautifully", and "Anyone can take good pictures with a UniveX" were commonly seen in stores, magazines and newspapers everywhere. Furthermore, Universal's dealer advertisements appeared regularly in trade papers and magazines relating to the jewelry, drug, stationery, photo, radio and department store retail businesses. These advertisements were generally more persuasive in nature than the consumer-oriented ads. Convincing signed testimonials from satisfied retailers substantiated unbelievable UniveX sales and Universal's assurance of "4-way profits on UniveX camera sales, UniveX film sales, UniveX developing and UniveX enlargements". Undoubtedly, Universal realized what an important part the retailer played in the successful marketing of its products. As Universal's only direct link with the customer, the retailer had to be well informed and familiar with each product, able to answer questions or expel doubts the customer might have concerning a probable purchase.

Universal got its start in the amateur photographic business with $1 million in financing from Philip Maslansky, the President of New York Merchandise Company, Inc., a business concern that began jobbing and importing notion and novelty merchandise back in 1906. The company distributed linens, clothes, shoes, dolls, costume jewelry, toys, common perfumes and countless other popular priced items to five and dime stores across the nation and in Canada. In the early 1920's, New York Merchandise Company established its main offices at 27-33 West 23rd Street and 8-18 West 24th Street, New York; in addition, branch offices were set up in many large cities across Europe and Asia. During Universal's early years, the New York Merchandise Company assisted heavily in certain areas of the new business, particularly with the provision of sales, credit and shipping facilities. The New York Merchandise Company was well-suited to assist in these operations involving mass marketing techniques and import/export activities. This arrangement proved instrumental in the successful sale and distribution of Universal's early products. Universal managed to organize its own sales department by 1934, but several more years passed before the company was able to formulate its own shipping and credit facilities. New York Merchandise Company was Universal's major stockholder and remained in affiliation with the firm as its parent company until 1952.

Over the years, millions of Model A cameras were either sold or otherwise distributed as premium giveaways. Occasionally, UniveX cameras were offered for sale in conjunction with other companies' products at a special discount price. One such example, offered by a large drug company in 1936, was the "Vacation Special", which included a $.50 UniveX Model A camera and a $.50 toothbrush for the special price of $.69. The Model A camera commonly appeared in many mail order catalogs across the nation. Johnson Smith and Company of Detroit, Michigan, a large supplier of novelty items, featured the UniveX Model A camera along with several other inexpensive amateur cameras in its large mail order catalog. One photographic collector claims to have a UniveX Model A camera marked, "Johnson Smith and Co., Detroit, Michigan, USA". Another collector has in his possession a UniveX Model A with a Lone Ranger decal affixed to it. The Model A camera was offered in many different premium offers over a span of about ten years.

In the midst of the Depression Era, Universal clearly demonstrated the existence of a substantial market in amateur photography, provided the

Fig. 1-13 The UniveX Model AF Camera.

24

cameras were easy to use, unique, and capable of producing good quality results at a low price. By 1935, other companies were also introducing inexpensive photographic products for the amateur photographer. The advent of low cost color photography was made possible by Eastman Kodak with the introduction of a new film called Kodachrome. Shortly thereafter, Eastman Kodak produced several inexpensive bakelite cameras in the $3 to $6 price range — the Jiffy Vest Pocket, the Bullet, and the Bantam. In addition, the 35mm bakelite Argus A, priced at just under $10, had become an overnight success, with sales surpassing the 38,000 mark less than eight months after its introduction. In April 1935 Universal announced the UniveX Model AF Camera *(Fig. 1-13)*, describing it as "the only Vest Pocket Camera that 'really' fits in a vest pocket and the only folding camera ever made to retail for just $1.00". In comparison, other amateur cameras seemed rather high priced. The UniveX Model AF resulted from the collaborative efforts of Githens, Universal's President, Jesse Norden, Universal's Production Manager, and Edward Mannerberg, a Universal engineer. Universal sought patent protection on the new camera and eventually the following two patents were granted — U.S. Des. Pat. #99,124 and U.S. Pat. #2,164,061. Constructed of cast aluminum with a baked enamel finish, the Model AF was capable of either snapshots or time exposures — the latter being accomplished with the camera freestanding by means of an extension leg on a firm, flat surface or mounted on a tripod in conjunction with a rather unusual UniveX accessory piece, the UniveX Tripod Clip. Decoratively packaged in a silver-trimmed black display box, the Model AF was an attractive miniature folding camera available to the customer in his choice of light green, light blue, grey, brown, or black *(Fig. 1-14)*. On today's collectibles market, blue and green Model AF cameras are rarely seen as opposed to the more common black, grey and brown models. It is quite reasonable to assume that most men would have displayed a definite preference for the black, grey, or brown models — this, in itself, suggesting that a lesser number of light green and light blue Model AF cameras were most likely produced. In 1940, it was reported that women

Fig. 1-14 The UniveX Model AF Cameras, the five color variations.

Fig. 1-15 The UniveX Model AF-2 Camera.

Fig. 1-16 The UniveX Model AF-3 Camera.

were responsible for 85% of all purchases in America, but less than 20% of amateur photo supply purchases could actually be traced to women. If given the choice, most women shopping for a camera would have preferred to purchase it in a light green or light blue color.

Within several months, two improved versions of the Model AF camera followed — the UniveX Model AF-2 Camera *(Fig. 1-15)* and the UniveX Model AF-3 Camera *(Fig. 1-16)*. Noteworthy improvements were a new hinged back cover and a quick-opening release lever. Packaged in a matching red, black and silver gift box and retailing for $1.00, the Model AF-2 was similarly finished in black with a red and silver art-deco design on the front plate. The Model AF-3 sold for $2.50, which was substantially higher in price than the previous AF models — it was, however, advertised as "the camera for the discriminating amateur". Manufactured with a color corrected Duo Achromatic Lens and a front plate distinctively finished in oxidized silver, the Model AF-3 was packaged in a black and silver hinged box. Both models included a slip-on "Karry Kase" to protect the camera and its finish. By 1937, one million UniveX Folding Cameras had been sold — meanwhile Universal was busy developing its two final versions of the Model AF camera, the UniveX Model AF-4 *(Fig. 1-17)* and the UniveX Minicam Model AF-5 Camera *(Fig. 1-18)*. With the exception that the front plate was no longer marked "Duo Achromatic Lens", the Model AF-4 seemed identical in every other way to the AF-3. The Model AF-4, priced at $1.95, was sold without a case. Five years into the business, Universal introduced the Minicam Model AF-5 -- its most expensive and sophisticated achievement to date. Priced at $3.50, the Minicam could be used to shoot either vertical or horizontal pictures, as both a vertical wire-frame viewfinder and a horizontal optical viewfinder were included in its construction. The Minicam, finished in antique bronze, was fitted with a factory adjusted 60 mm Ilex Achromar Lens and packaged in a matching red and gold gift box. Universal developed a special

Fig. 1-17 The UniveX Model AF-4 Camera.

27

Fig. 1-18 The UniveX Minicam Model AF-5 Camera.

eveready carrying case with a shoulder cord for use with the Model AF-5, selling separately for $1.00 *(Fig. 1-19)*. Universal produced two versions of the Model AF-5 camera — some models were stamped "Minicam" on the front plate and others were not.

Several exclusive renditions of the Model AF were created by Universal for certain organizations and special events. These cameras were often distributed as premium giveaways and souvenirs, or made available for sale through organizations such as the Girl Scouts. The UniveX Model AF Official

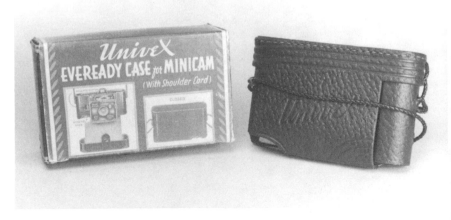

Fig. 1-19 The UniveX Minicam Model AF-5 Camera Carrying Case.

Girl Scout Camera *(Figs. 1-20, 1-21)*, first introduced in 1936, originally sold for $1.00 and could be purchased nationwide at Girl Scout distribution centers or through the Official Girl Scout Catalog. The 1936 Girl Scout Model AF was cast exactly like the first Model AF camera that Universal introduced in 1935. The camera housing was a grey-green color with a deep green front plate identified with the trefoil emblem and marked "Girl Scout Model AF UniveX". Two years later in 1938, Universal produced a second model AF camera for the Girl Scout organization. The previous Model AF housing, having an opening lever on the side of the camera, was replaced with a new housing currently being used by Universal on all of its new 1938 AF Model cameras. The 1938 Girl Scout Model AF had a new quick-opening release lever located at top center and was finished in black enamel with a green front plate stamped with the same Girl Scout markings as the original model. It is important to note here that these are two distinctly different Girl Scout Model AF cameras, each produced for a period of two years between 1936 and 1940. It is a little known fact that, from 1933 to 1936, the original "sunburst" UniveX Model A Camera and the variant "geometric" Model A were featured in Girl Scout catalogs as official Girl Scout equipment. It should be noted that catalogs did not indicate whether the Model A camera was marked in any way with the Girl Scout logo. The UniveX Model A was listed in the Official Girl Scout Catalog of 1933 as "A New Camera", priced at only $.35. Featured on the same page was the Girl Scout Kodak with its matching case, undeniably superior in quality, but priced at $6.00. For many a young girl whose family could not afford better, "A New Camera" would be the preferred choice. UniveX film for these cameras could also be ordered from the Girl Scout catalog at the usual cost of $.10 a roll.

Fig. 1-20 The earlier version of the UniveX Model AF Official Girl Scout Camera (left), marketed during 1936 and 1937, and the later version (right).

Fig. 1-21 The later model of the UniveX Model AF Official Girl Scout Camera. It was distributed from 1938 to 1940. (Courtesy: "The American Girl" magazine, July 1938, copyright Girl Scouts of the U.S.A., reproduced by permission.)

Fig. 1-22 The UniveX Model AF 1936 G. E. Topper's Club Convention Camera.

In addition to the Girl Scout Model AF, Universal manufactured the 1936 G.E. Toppers Club Convention Camera *(Fig. 1-22)*. This special model AF camera had a black camera housing and a black front plate bearing the General Electric symbol. A top hat and cane appeared on the camera's face plate in symbolism of the "Toppers Club". "Use UniveX No. 00 Film" also appeared in small letters on the lower left hand corner of the camera's front plate. Essentially, the Toppers Club was an organization comprised of General Electric's most outstanding salesmen. In 1936, the year of the Toppers Club Convention, the "top" salesman in the Toppers Club was Charles S. Witherspoon of Long Island, New York. His sales figures ranked highest among 10,000 General Electric refrigerator salesmen across the country. It was common practice years ago for General Electric to reward its hard working salesmen with various gifts — the UniveX folding camera was evidently one such token of corporate appreciation.

Universal manufactured one other special Model AF between 1936 and 1940 — The Hollywood Camera *(Fig. 1-23)*. Two versions of the Hollywood Camera are known to exist. The earlier version featured a lift-off rear body cover and a side release latch for extension of the bellows, while the later 1938 version featured a hinged rear body cover and front release latch for bellows extension. The body was finished in black enamel with a dark burgundy face plate. The face plate did not bear any Universal or UniveX markings whatsoever, however, the usual Universal marking could be found stamped on the inside of the camera's rear cover. No information was found regarding this particular UniveX model, although the Hollywood Camera is more commonly seen on the collector's market than either the Girl Scout or Toppers Club cameras.

Fig. 1-23 The UniveX Model AF Hollywood Cameras, two versions. The earlier version (left) had a lift-off rear cover and side release for bellows extension, while the later version (right) had a hinged rear cover with center release for bellows extension.

In 1936, Eastman Kodak began marketing its astounding new Kodaprinter to photographic dealers and photofinishing plants everywhere. Kodak claimed that this advanced automated printer had the ability to enlarge up to 700 prints per hour, though the general opinion of photofinishers using the automated printers was that the advertised speed of these machines was rather difficult to maintain. The extra expense to produce prints with the new machines was claimed to be a retail cost of only 3-5 cents per print. UniveX customers were offered the following choice of print sizes from UniveX #00 rollfilms: 1⅛x1⅞" contact print, 2x3" enlargement or 3x4" enlargement. Githens and Shapiro were quick to realize that UniveX film customers much preferred the 3x4" enlargement prints instead of tiny contact prints and decided to start a huge advertising campaign aimed at promoting enlarged 3x4" prints from Univex negatives.

One 1936 Universal advertisement in particular caused much dismay throughout the photofinishing industry. In an ad picturing a girl on a swing, Universal stated: "All good photofinishers can now take your UniveX Film (which costs you only ten cents per roll) and give you the most perfect, sharp, clear 3" x 4" prints at no extra enlargement charge. (You pay approximately the regular 3" x 4" contact-print price.)". After numerous complaints from leading photofinishers across the country, Universal was contacted by Master Photo Finishers of America, an organization dedicated to improving conditions within the American photofinishing trade. They

"UNIVEX PRINTS AT APPROXIMATE PRICE OF OTHER 3" x 4" QUALITY PRINTS"

A FEW photo-finishers have suggested that our consumer advertising may give amateurs the impression that they can get prints up to 3" x 4" in size from Univex Film at the same price as 1⅛" x 1⅞" contacts. This is not our intention . . . and we are revising our magazine and newspaper advertising as quickly as possible to make this point absolutely clear.

Leading photo-finishers are standardizing on three size prints from Univex Film . . . 1⅛" x 1⅞", 2" x 3" and 3" x 4" and charging approximately the same for the larger prints as for contact prints. They have tested this idea and find that it is the greatest opportunity for increasing developing business — not only for Univex, but for all miniature cameras and film.

With the new larger-print machines, it costs you little more to make the larger prints than contact prints of the same sizes. You can sell them at approximately contact print prices and make more money than you ever made before — because the volume is three times as great. Get on the band wagon and watch your business grow. Give the public what it wants. Remember . . . it's volume at a fair mark-up — not high prices—that MAKES FOR REAL PROFITS!

- **Univex consumer advertising states: "Now you can get sharp, clear photos up to 3" x 4" at the approximate price of other 3" x 4" quality prints." Remember, we are not telling the public what your contact print prices are. You're still running your own business!**

UNIVERSAL CAMERA CORPORATION

32-46 WEST 23rd STREET - - - NEW YORK CITY

Fig. 1-24 A Universal advertisement directed at photofinishers, taken from "Development Trade News", July 1936.

politely requested that Universal refrain from making statements in its advertisements that would "try to fix, in any way, the price at which UniveX prints are to be sold". Several days later, Universal's advertising agency responded to Master Photo Finishers of America. It was agreed that Universal would restate its advertisements to read, "UniveX prints at the approximate price of other 3" x 4" quality prints". In the same breath, Universal emphatically expressed to the photofinishing industry its firm conviction: "Give the public what it wants. Remember...it's volume at a fair mark-up — not high prices — that MAKES FOR REAL PROFITS!" *(Fig. 1-24).* This was not considered an unusual response from Universal — most often Universal demonstrated a somewhat unrestrained, pretentious attitude to other members of the photographic industry. It was no doubt quite difficult for Universal to be humble at a time when it claimed to be manufacturing "more cameras per year than any other company in the world".

CHAPTER TWO

1936-1938

"NOW MOVIES COST LESS THAN SNAPSHOTS"

The introduction of the UniveX Model A and AF cameras brought Universal a wealth of fortune and fame — however, Githens and Shapiro were well aware that Universal would have to introduce a new product sometime in the near future, something totally different from its original line of inexpensive still cameras, yet still "affordable". They began thinking in terms of a low cost 8mm home movie camera, priced under $10, and a companion 8mm projector, priced under $15, to complement Universal's line of low priced still cameras. For several months, Universal's Research Department had conducted an extensive survey among amateur photographers in the United States. The study indicated that there were approximately 17 million still cameras in use at the time compared to only about 500,000 amateur movie cameras. "Cost" was cited as the major drawback of home movie equipment. The results of this survey convinced Githens and Shapiro that a line of affordable and dependable amateur home movie equipment might very well become the next exciting chapter of the already extraordinary UniveX success story.

Githens and Shapiro were definitely on the right track — but there was one major drawback. Shapiro knew next to nothing about camera mechanics and construction. Githens, on the other hand, was a bit more mechanically inclined than his partner, though hardly capable of designing a movie camera and projector singlehandedly. Universal's last line, the UniveX Model AF Camera, was the combined effort of Githens, Jesse Norden, Universal's Production Manager, and Edward G. Mannerberg, a Universal designer who resigned from the company after the completion of the Model AF project to return to his hometown in Pennsylvania. This resignation left Universal in a somewhat precarious position. Githens and Shapiro knew they would have to acquire some qualified personnel if they were ever going to get their new low cost movie project off the ground, not to mention any other future projects. In October 1935, Universal placed an ad in the New York Times in search of a mechanical engineer or designer to handle the design and development of Universal's first low cost motion picture camera and projector.

In the next few weeks, Githens and Shapiro learned of Everett M. Porter. Porter had completed the design and construction of a relatively complex movie camera mechanism and this he showed to Githens and Shapiro. Porter had also started the design and construction of an 8mm movie projector. Seemingly an answer to their prayers, Githens and Shapiro were understandably elated. On October 17, 1935, Universal signed a contract

Fig. 2-1 George Kende, Universal Chief Design Engineer from 1935 through 1948.

with Porter, whereby Universal agreed to pay Porter a 2% royalty based on the sale of any Universal motion picture equipment relating all or in part to Porter's original camera and projector inventions. Universal also agreed to pay Porter a 1% royalty on the sale of all Universal motion picture equipment not related to Porter's original models. In exchange for this compensation, Porter agreed to assign all patent rights for his camera and projector models to Universal and to complete the construction of these models as quickly as possible. Porter was also required to provide Universal with whatever technical assistance was necessary to bring such motion picture products to market in a timely manner. Under the terms of this contract, the royalties paid to Porter during the period 1936 through 1944 totaled approximately $47,500. In 1937 alone, the year when Universal's home movie sales reached their peak, Porter received over $24,000 in royalty payments. Figures covering the period 1945 through 1947 could not be located, but it is presumed with relative certainty that Universal's immediate postwar sales yielded royalties equaling or possibly surpassing those royalties paid to Porter in 1937. Royalties collected by Porter for the years 1948 through 1952 totaled approximately $10,700.

About two weeks after Universal signed the contract with Porter, a 27 year old man named George Kende *(Fig. 2-1)* came to Universal's offices in response to the employment ad placed by Universal in the New York Times earlier that month. After a tour of the plant, Kende was introduced to Universal's President, Otto Githens; during their meeting, Githens listened intently as Kende offered a full account of his education and previous work experience. Kende had graduated in 1926 from the University of California - Berkeley with a Bachelor of Science Degree in Mechanical Engineering. His previous employment included work with such firms as Harrison W. Rogers, Inc. of New York City, General Talking Pictures Corp. (DeForest Phono Films) of New York City, African Consolidated Films, Ltd. of Capetown, Johannesburg and Durban in the Union of South Africa, Consolidated Film Industries, Inc. of Fort Lee, N.J., American District Telegraph Co. of New York City and United Research Corp. (Research Subsidiary of Warner Bros. Pictures) of Long Island City, N.Y. Kende's work with General Talking Pictures, Corp. involved the design of sound-on-disc and sound-on-film recording and reproducing devices and also a temporary assignment in South Africa with African Consolidated Films, Ltd., a company which owned and operated all of the motion picture theaters in South Africa. Kende spent two years in South Africa planning and managing the installation of sound equipment furnished by his previous employer, General Talking Pictures, Corp. Upon his return to the United States, Kende acquired additional experience working with motion pictures and film developing equipment at the New Jersey firm of Consolidated Film Industries, Inc. where he designed a line of automatic and continuous motion picture film processing machinery.

After learning of Kende's education and motion picture related work experience, it was obvious to Githens that Kende could easily be Universal's single, most valuable, asset. During the interview, Githens explained Universal's upcoming new project involving the design of a low cost home movie camera and projector. Enthusiastically, Githens showed Kende the camera model built by Everett Porter, explaining that a contract had just been signed with Porter and it was mutually agreed that all patent rights for the model would be assigned to Universal. After examining the camera model, Kende expelled extreme doubt as to whether Porter's camera invention could be manufactured at a cost low enough to allow a retail price tag under $10. It appeared that the camera model's weight, undesirable shape and the complexity of its mechanisms would all contribute to high production

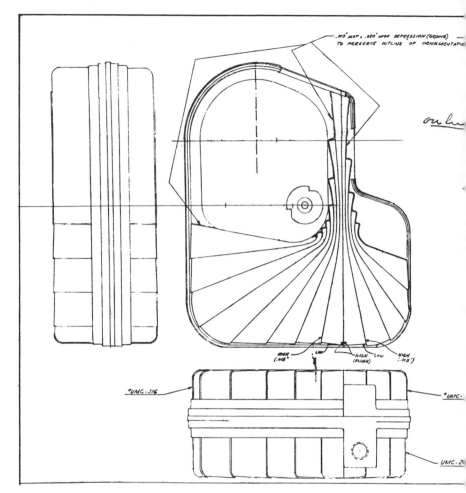

Fig. 2-2 Universal blueprint of the UniveX Cine-8 Camera, used to build an exact scale model from pear wood to determine how comfortable the camera would be to hold.

costs which, in turn, would push the retail price of the unit over the originally proposed $10 mark. Despite Kende's skepticism regarding the overall feasibility of Porter's model for low cost mass production, Githens managed to persuade Kende to accept a position with Universal as Chief Engineer.

During his first days on the job, Kende studied Porter's camera model carefully, considering any and all possible applications for low cost, high volume production. After much deliberation, Kende informed Githens he was completely certain that Porter's camera model would be of no value whatsoever to Universal as far as production of a low cost motion picture camera was concerned. Kende began his own design of an all new 8mm low cost movie camera that was more compact, lighter in weight and easier to assemble — far better suited for Universal's purposes than Porter's model. Before any pre-production tooling was done, an exact scale model of Kende's

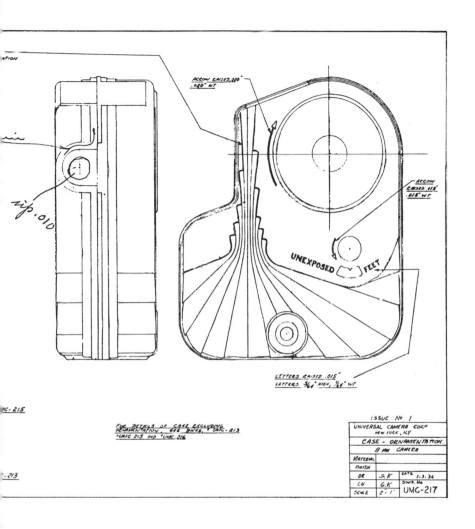

ATION

ACROW RAISED.020"
.020" WT

zip .010

ACROW
RAISED .015
.015" WT

UNEXPOSED FEET

LETTERS RAISED .015"
LETTERS 5/64" HIGH, 1/64" WT

IC-215

FOR DETAILS OF CASE EXCLUDING
ORNAMENTATION, SEE DWGS. # UMC-213
*UMC-215 AND *UMC-216

-213

ISSUE No. 1

UNIVERSAL CAMERA CORP
NEW YORK, N.Y.

CASE - ORNAMENTATION

8 MM CAMERA

MATERIAL			
FINISH			
DR	S.K.	DATE 1-3-36	
CH	G.K.	DWG. No	
SCALE	2:1	UMC-217	

camera was constructed from pear wood to determine whether the camera would feel comfortable in the user's hands *(Fig. 2-2)*. There was not one single feature of Kende's 8mm camera design, mechanical or constructional in nature, that even slightly resembled features found on Porter's camera model; nevertheless, Porter was compensated for his contribution as originally set up in the terms of the contract. Porter, who was never on the Universal payroll so to speak, was called in for a brief discussion and, after that meeting, there was reportedly no further contact between the two parties regarding present or future Universal motion picture equipment designs. After all was said and done, Githens and Shapiro had probably thought of having the Porter contract nullified through litigation, but realized such a decision would inevitably prove lengthy and costly for Universal. For this reason, Porter's name appeared next to Githens' and Kende's on all but

39

one of the U.S. patents relating to Universal's first 8mm camera and projector. The single exception to this was U.S. Design Pat. #99,544 relating to the exterior ornamental design of Kende's 8mm movie camera. Porter's name was not listed on this patent because the ornamental design shown in this particular patent illustration differed drastically from the somewhat "crude" casing used on Porter's model. Interestingly, on the faceplate of Universal's movie cameras, U.S. Design Pat. #99,544 was erroneously printed as U.S. Design Pat. #99,514, which incidentally relates to the design of a battery box.

With the introduction of the first UniveX 8mm camera and projector in September 1936, many of those in the industry wondered if Universal would continue to hold its newfound popularity with the amateur photographic populace and, at the same time, enjoy a significant profit from its new line of low priced cine products. Universal was relatively certain it would do just that! The first magazine advertisements for Universal's "Cine 8" home movie products were rather small and inconspicuous; nevertheless, orders for the new UniveX cine camera and projector literally poured into Universal's Sales Department. Late in 1936, production difficulties developed as orders for the new cine line flooded the department. This sudden overwhelming demand for UniveX low cost movie equipment forced Universal to postpone its $250,000 Fall/Christmas "Home Movie" advertising campaign until Spring 1937, when production of the UniveX cine camera and projector was finally back in full swing. Soon after, Universal's advertisements met the public's eye through some of the country's most prestigious national magazines — Collier's, Cosmopolitan, Liberty, Life, Look, National Geographic and Saturday Evening Post. Approximately 35 newspapers also carried advertisements for the UniveX "Cine 8" camera and projector. One other means of advertising for Universal resulted from its tie-in with a number of actors and actresses from the Hollywood movie industry. Such stars as Richard Arlen, Joan Bennett, Richard Bennett, Mary Carlisle, Ida Lupino and Douglas Montgomery appeared with a UniveX "Cine 8" camera in many of Universal's advertisements — an excellent advertising idea that proved quite successful with America's amateur photographers. In addition to this, Universal provided any interested photographic dealer with a series of standard theater screen slides for projection in local movie theaters. The dealer's name was added to each of the slides, making it an excellent advertising opportunity for both the local dealer and Universal.

The instant success of Universal was a bitter pill to swallow for many skeptics in the photographic industry, exasperated by the company's determination to manufacture and sell what was commonly referred to as "junk". During its history as a photographic manufacturer, Universal fell victim to frequent allegations of bad business practice. One such rumor developed in 1936, alleging that Universal's Cine 8 cameras and projectors were "assembled from cheap parts imported into this country from cheap labor countries". Universal's President, Otto Githens, publicly offered a reward of $5,000 in cash to any person or persons who could show proof that UniveX Cine 8 products were not manufactured entirely in the United States. Githens wrote in a 1936 bulletin, "The sensational new UNIVEX CINE 8 CAMERAS AND PROJECTORS are made entirely in the United States by AMERICAN CAPITAL AND LABOR. Each and every part thereof, including all lenses, is made in U.S.A.". The above statement specifies "all lenses", indicating there may have been a question regarding the manufacture of Universal's lenses. The standard lens used by Universal on its projectors had no markings whatsoever — the manufacturer of this lens remains as much of a mystery today as it was in 1936.

Universal was well aware that substantial capital had been regenerated into the company by the growing sale of its six exposure UniveX #00 rollfilm. Naturally the company assumed this pattern would continue in a similar manner for many years to come. For that reason, it was not at all surprising when Universal decided to design a movie camera that required a non-standard size film on a special patented film spool incompatible for use in any other manufacturers' cameras. Universal contracted with the Gevaert Company to manufacture its special 8mm film, which was commonly referred to as "Single-8" or "Straight-8". Unlike "Double-8" film, it was only necessary to run "Single-8" film through the camera once. Priced at $.60 and $.90 respectively, UniveX #100-S Standard (orange carton) and UniveX #100-UP Ultrapan (green carton) were produced in economical 30 ft. lengths providing about 2400 frames, or approximately 15 scenes at just pennies a scene. Compared to the popular 25 ft. lengths (50 ft. after processing) of "Double-8" film which sold for approximately $2.25, UniveX film was most certainly a good buy. Universal's "Film Insurance Policy" guaranteed replacement of any UniveX film if unsatisfactory results were obtained after correctly following all enclosed instructions. In 1938, Universal announced its first price increase on UniveX #100 films (Standard - $.69 and Ultrapan - $.95); in combination with this, the company offered film purchasers a 50% discount on processing, making the total film and processing expenditure less than it had been to start with. The colors on the new film cartons were changed so when the higher-priced film was sent to Universal for processing, a new red or blue carton would automatically entitle the customer to the new reduced processing charge. If an outdated orange or green film carton was sent in for processing, the customer was subject to the old $.30 processing charge. Universal explained that new high-speed automated machinery made the processing of Single-8 films less costly, resulting in a savings

Fig. 2-3 The UniveX Model A-8 Cine Camera with standard f/5.6 Ilex Univar Lens.

41

which Universal was pleased to pass on to its customers. In 1940, Universal introduced UniveX #100-UP Ultrapan Superspeed (rated twice as fast as regular Ultrapan) and thereafter production of the original Ultrapan film ceased. Processing of UniveX cine films was done at Universal's three photofinishing laboratories located in New York City, Chicago and Hollywood. For UniveX film processing abroad, Universal established approximately 50 additional processing stations (See Appendix B).

In previous years, other companies such as Pathé, with 9.5mm film, and Eastman Kodak and Victor Animatograph with 16mm film, made notable attempts to popularize cine photography for the amateur. In the midst of the Depression, 8mm cameras and film first began to appear in 1932 as a low cost alternative to 16mm, which had been the standard nonprofessional size in the movie industry since 1923. Universal attracted overwhelming attention in March 1936 with the introduction of its first 8mm cine camera — the UniveX Model A-8 Camera *(Fig. 2-3)*, priced remarkably low at only $9.95. More than 250,000 units were sold in 1937 alone. The body of the Model A-8 was constructed of die cast zinc alloy and the camera's internal mechanism constructed of rustproofed steel, brass and aluminum parts. Finished in black enamel, the Model A-8 featured a collapsible direct vision viewfinder, a lift-off film chamber cover, an exposure chart mounted on the camera's face plate, a footage indicator, a tripod socket and an interchangeable Ilex Univar f/5.6 lens. The Model A-8 was a single-speed camera, operating at 16 frames per second with a maximum run of six feet per wind. Compact in design and weighing only 16 ounces, the Model A-8 fit easily into a coat pocket and offered extreme ease of operation in comparison to other cine cameras on the market at the time.

At this point in time, Universal's production figures were unmatched by any other camera manufacturer in the world — thousands of cameras and projectors had been sold at prices never before dreamed possible — prices so low that persons with little or no interest in photography were often tempted to indulge! Universal was able to achieve this substantial reduction in the cost of 8mm home photography by manufacturing cameras in mass quantities and providing low cost film and processing. As the Model A-8 grew in popularity, other camera companies began taking immediate steps to establish a line of their own 8mm products or expand on an already existing line.

Between 1936 and 1939, Universal introduced a wide selection of 8mm accessory products, the most notable of which are described below.

--- **The UniveX Titler** *(Fig. 2-4)* was a collapsible unit consisting of three sections: a base plate, an easel frame and a shim mounting bracket. Constructed of pressed steel and finished in black enamel, the titler folded flat for easy storage. Sharp clear titles were possible with the camera's standard lens. In addition to the titler itself, the complete outfit included a silver pencil, one dozen title cards, a titling guide card and an instruction sheet. The UniveX Titler is commonly seen on the collectibles market, although an untouched, complete outfit is more difficult to find.

--- **The Universal Automatic Titler** *(Fig. 2-5)* consisted of a 4x5 black matte panel with 36 openings, divided equally into three horizontal rows. Each opening contained a black ribbon having 42 white characters (A-Z, 0-9, various punctuation marks and a blank space). On the rear of the titler were 36 cog-wheels. In selecting a specific character, the appropriate cog-wheel was turned until that particular character appeared in the opening. The process was repeated for each of the remaining openings until the title was completed. Universal recommended that the titler, which was self-standing by means of a rear extension leg, be positioned at a distance of 16 inches

Fig. 2-4 The UniveX Standard Titler with UniveX Model A-8 Camera.

Fig. 2-5 The Universal Automatic Titler.

43

Fig. 2-6 The UniveX Film Viewer and Editor Device in original display box (above) and Viewer/Editor device fitted on Model P-8 Projector (below).

from the camera. A metal lens shim was included for use with fixed focus lenses. Rarely seen today is the protective case Universal offered for use with this titler. The titler is almost always found still in the original box. The UniveX Automatic Titler is truly one of the more unusual UniveX accessory items. It is important to note here that although the Automatic Titler did carry the Universal name and trademark symbol, it was one of only a few Universal/ UniveX products manufactured and distributed, but not patented, by the Universal Camera Corporation — the actual patent for this device (U.S. Pat.#2,170,398) belonged to the Greist Manufacturing Company of Connecticut.

--- **The UniveX Film Viewer/Editor** *(Fig. 2-6)*, all metal in construction, was designed to work in connection with the projector's normal functions, making film viewing and editing a less costly and tedious process. Universal claimed that this device, originally priced at $1.95, could perform work previously requiring the use of three separate units. The viewer/editor unit comprised two film guide pulleys, an angled reflector, and a viewing screen (1⅝"x1¼"). The device fit snugly over the projector's gearbox, with the angled reflector and viewing screen extending several inches beyond the front of the projector in optical alignment with the projection beam. When the illuminated image was projected toward the angled reflector, it was reflected at a 90 degree angle onto the viewing screen. With the operator seated facing the reel-side

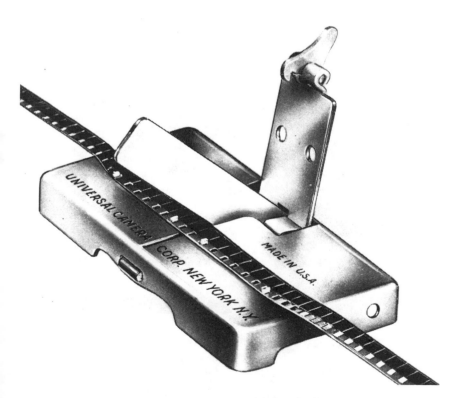

Fig. 2-7 The UniveX Splicer. The complete kit included a splicer with two screws for mounting, a knife, a water bottle and a cement bottle and instructions.

of the projector, the small screen could be easily viewed and, at the same time, all the necessary editing functions could be performed. Editing was done in one of the following ways: 1) the film was guided in the usual fashion over the projector's film sprockets, causing the image to appear as a moving picture on the small viewing screen; or 2) the film sprockets were by-passed completely by threading the film over two pulleys on the viewer/editor attachment, allowing the film to be projected more slowly by hand with the help of an accessory crank knob. A metal hook and stylus for marking sections of film were also included with the viewer/editor. The UniveX Viewer/Editor is a very rare collector's item. The device may be difficult to identify as a UniveX product unless it is found in the original unique fold-up display box. The UniveX Viewer/Editor carries the following marking: "GREIST Pat. Appl'd. For", which indicates that Universal was not the patent owner of this device. In 1939, a letters patent (U.S. Pat. #2,168,761) covering this viewer/editor was granted to the Greist Manufacturing Company of Connecticut. The Universal Automatic Titler and the UniveX Viewer/Editor were both designed by the same inventor, Samuel P. Caldwell. Without a doubt, these are two of the most ingenious accessory gadgets ever invented for the home movie enthusiast.

--- **The UniveX Splicer Kit** *(Fig. 2-7)* is commonly seen today. The complete kit included a knife/scraper tool, a pressure plate with two mounting screws, a ¾ oz bottle marked "Film Cement", a ¾ oz bottle marked "Water for Film Splicing" and an instruction sheet. The film cement has most likely hardened over the years, but brushes can still be found attached to the inside of the bottle covers.

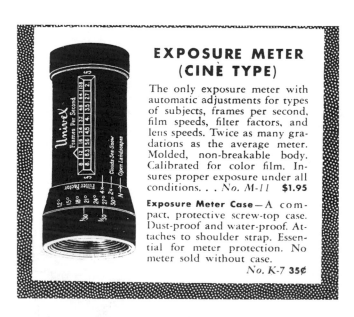

EXPOSURE METER (CINE TYPE)

The only exposure meter with automatic adjustments for types of subjects, frames per second, film speeds, filter factors, and lens speeds. Twice as many gradations as the average meter. Molded, non-breakable body. Calibrated for color film. Insures proper exposure under all conditions. . . *No. M-11* **$1.95**

Exposure Meter Case — A compact, protective screw-top case. Dust-proof and water-proof. Attaches to shoulder strap. Essential for meter protection. No meter sold without case.
No. K-7 **35¢**

Fig. 2-8 The UniveX Cine Exposure Meter.

--- **The UniveX Cine Exposure Meter** *(Fig. 2-8)* was a visual extinction-type meter, tubular in shape and constructed of GE Textolite plastic. A plastic carrying case, described as waterproof and dustproof, was mandatory with the purchase of each meter. By means of two rotatable rings, adjustments could be made to accommodate the particular film speed, shutter speed, filter factor and type of subject. The cine meter included an instruction booklet and a film value sheet that listed and compared film speed values for other manufacturers' films. The meter, calibrated for Weston film speed values, provided camera speed settings ranging from 8 frames per second to 128 frames per second and lens diaphragm settings ranging from f/2 to f/8. This meter could be used with almost any of the movie cameras on the market. As a collectible, the UniveX Cine Meter seems fairly common; quite often though, the meters are no longer functional. Many have started to warp, bulge and/or split open. Upon opening the plastic carrying case, more often than not there is evidence of a heavy chemical odor. In addition to this, the meter is usually covered with a liquid that appears to have oozed out from inside of the meter. It is advisable to discard these defective meters as serious injury to the eye or skin could possibly result if a person were to attempt to use a meter in such condition.

--- The **"How to Make Movies"** booklet contained 48 pages of illustrations and information for the amateur motion picture photographer. The pocket-sized booklet was offered by Universal to help photographers obtain satisfactory results with their UniveX movie cameras.

--- The **UniveX Crystalux and Silverlux Projection Screens** *(Fig. 2-9)*, priced between $1.49 and $15.95, were available in seven sizes, ranging from 18" x 24" to 30" x 40". The screen size is normally stamped on the back of each screen. The glass-beaded Crystalux screen was more reflective than the less costly Silverlux screen with its smooth silver surface. Each UniveX screen included two folding metal erecting easels which, when inserted into the four holes in the top and bottom wooden battens, allowed the screen to maintain a self-standing position. As an alternative, the easels could be dispensed with entirely and the screen hung on the wall with the attached eyelet. After many years of basement or attic storage, most of the screens show extreme signs of deterioration — rips and tears, discoloration and loss of beaded surface. For this reason, most screens are immediately discarded by their owners after being pulled from storage, making them somewhat difficult for the collector to obtain. In 1940, Universal offered one movie screen equipped with a collapsible floor stand for $19.95. Finished in black enamel, the all metal floor stand supported a retractable 30x40" Crystalux screen attached to a conventional spring wound roller.

--- The **UniveX Cine M-25 Optical Viewfinder** *(Fig. 2-10)*, priced at $1.95, and the UniveX Cine M-27 Auxiliary Optical Viewfinder, priced at $2.95, were two accessory viewfinders specifically designed for use with the Model A-8 camera. The UniveX Cine Optical Viewfinders provided the user with a more precise, clear view of the subject. Tubular in shape and finished in black enamel, the all metal optical viewfinders were partially die cast in construction. One of Universal's most popular cine accessory items, the M-25 optical viewfinder was designed for use with any of the following three ½" Univar lenses — the f/5.6, f/3.5, or f/2.7. There was, on the other hand, significantly less demand for the M-27 optical viewfinder designed to accommodate the larger lens mount diameter of the ½" Univar f/1.9 lens and the 1½" Univar telephoto lens. The M-27 viewfinder was merely a modified version of the original M-25 viewfinder — one of Universal's many afterthoughts — quite simply accomplished by drilling a larger opening in the original M-25 view-finder. This optical viewfinder is rarely seen today, owing to the fact that very few Model A-8 owners could actually afford to equip their $9.95 UniveX camera with expensive lenses such as the f/1.9 lens, priced at $39.75, or 1½" telephoto lens, priced at $37.50. The Model A-8 camera is rarely, if ever, found fitted with anything other than the standard f/5.6 lens. In a few instances, a camera can be found equipped with the faster, yet still affordable, f/3.5 lens.

LOWEST-PRICED QUALITY MOVIE SCREEN!

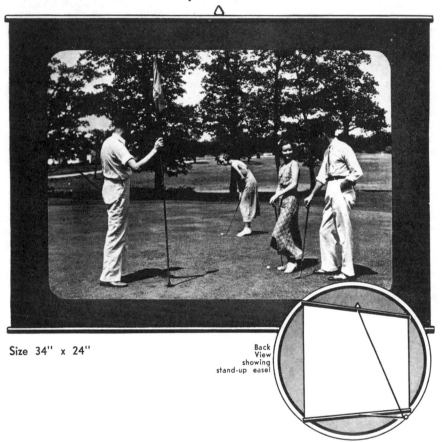

Size 34" x 24"

Back
View
showing
stand-up easel

This Silverlux Screen has a brilliant theatre-type surface. It is equipped with two sturdy wood battens to keep screen always smooth and rigid. A quick-erecting, folding easel enables screen to be set up on a table in a jiffy. A metal eyelet permits it to be hung on the wall. The screen allows any one to project movies 160% clearer than if they were projected on a white wall or a white fabric. Make sure you get the best results from your UniveX movie equipment by using this superior UniveX Silverlux Screen.

Price, $1.50

Fig. 2-9 The UniveX Projection Screen with erecting easels.

Fig. 2-10 The UniveX Cine Optical Viewfinder, available in two sizes — the more common was used with the Univar f/2.7, f/3.5, f/4.5, f/5.6 lenses (left) and the rarer version was used with the Univar f/1.9 lens (right).

*Fig. 2-11 The UniveX Model A-8 Cine Camera Standard (left)
and Deluxe (right) Carrying Cases.*

--- The **UniveX Standard and Deluxe Carrying Cases** *(Fig. 2-11)* were designed for use with the Model A-8 camera. Only one difference existed between the two cases — the deluxe version was equipped with a special accessory pocket, not found on the standard case. The standard and deluxe cases were both marked "Model A-8". These cases consisted of two basic parts — a flat metal base plate and a protective top cover. The metal base plate could be attached directly to the camera's tripod socket by means of a thumb screw. Once the base plate was attached to the camera in this manner, the top cover portion of the case could be slipped over the camera and fastened to the base plate by means of two metal snap-fasteners, one on each side of the case. The camera could be used without ever having to unscrew the metal baseplate from the camera. Due to the unique and functional design of this carrying case, Universal decided to apply for a patent on this important accessory item in December 1936 (U.S.Pat. #2,172,348). The Model A-8 carrying cases were originally termed "protector" cases, but the word "protector" was oftentimes mistaken for "projector", and confusion invariably resulted on many of Universal's merchandise orders. To remedy the situation, Universal eventually began using the term "eveready case", instead of "protector case", on all future carrying case packaging and related advertising material.

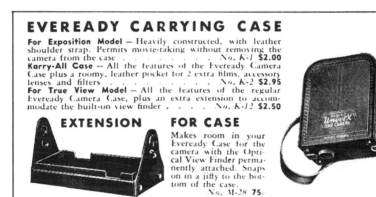

EVEREADY CARRYING CASE

For Exposition Model — Heavily constructed, with leather shoulder strap. Permits movie-taking without removing the camera from the case . . . . *No. K-1* **$2.00**
Karry-All Case — All the features of the Eveready Camera Case plus a roomy, leather pocket for 2 extra films, accessory lenses and filters . . . . *No. K-2* **$2.95**
For True View Model — All the features of the regular Eveready Camera Case, plus an extra extension to accommodate the built-on view finder . . . . *No. K-12* **$2.50**

EXTENSION   FOR CASE

Makes room in your Eveready Case for the camera with the Optical View Finder permanently attached. Snaps on in a jiffy to the bottom of the case.
No. M-28 **75c**

Fig. 2-12 The UniveX Cine Case Extension for use with the Model A-8 Carrying Case. This carrying case extension piece was necessary when using a Model A-8 camera with a tubular optical viewfinder attached or when using the Model B-8 camera with factory mounted tubular optical viewfinder in place.

--- The **UniveX Case Extension** *(Fig. 2-12)* was designed for use with the Model A-8 carrying case. When either one of the tubular optical viewfinders was attached to the Model A-8 camera, the height of the camera was increased by ½", rendering the Model A-8 carrying case obsolete as long as the accessory viewfinder was left in place. A clever idea indeed, the UniveX Case Extension was designed to increase the total height of the camera case just enough to accommodate the Model A-8 camera equipped with either of the accessory optical viewfinders. (The extension piece was also required when using the Model A-8 case with Universal's second cine camera, the UniveX Model B-8, which featured a factory mounted tubular optical viewfinder). The UniveX Case Extension was a rectangular open-framed piece of metal, approximately 2x4x¾" high, with two triangular pieces of

50

leather riveted to the two shorter sides of the rectangular frame. Each of the leather end-pieces had two snap fasteners which were used to connect the extension piece to the base plate of the Model A-8 case. The all black extension piece is unmarked, although any UniveX collector with a close eye should be able to spot the attachment mounted on a Model A-8 case or possibly mixed in with a box of photographic odds and ends.

In addition to the above 8mm accessories, Universal provided projector owners with UniveX 8mm feature films. Through an arrangement with the Educational Films Corporation, Universal began offering its home movie customers many low-priced UniveX feature films. Cartoons, comedies, westerns and other UniveX films were available in 25, 50, 100, and 200 ft. lengths, priced from $.60 to $3.75 (See Appendix F). Even though Universal did not manufacture a 16mm projector until years later, the company did offer a small number of 16mm feature films in 1938.

Fig. 2-13 The UniveX Model P-8 Projector with standard 1" f/3 Lens.

As a companion piece to the Model A-8 camera, Universal simultaneously introduced the UniveX Model P-8 Projector *(Fig. 2-13)*, originally priced at $12.50. Weighing approximately seven pounds, the Model P-8 projector was comprised of two main parts — a zinc alloy die cast base and a pressed sheet metal lamp housing, both finished in black enamel. The 100 watt 8mm projector operated on Alternating Current only, utilizing the following patented pre-focused projection lamps — the UniveX 40 watt Standard Projection Lamp or the UniveX 50 watt High-Intensity Projection Lamp. Later versions of the Model P-8 projector were upgraded to 150 watts and are marked as such. The design of the Model P-8 included a 200 ft. reel capacity providing 16 minutes of continuous projection, an automatic safety fire shutter for still picture projection with no damage to the film, lens interchangeability and forced draft cooling. Simple belt changes on the Model P-8 provided these additional features, one alternate (slower) projection speed and rapid film rewind. In addition to UniveX 8mm home movie films, the Model P-8 could project any standard 8mm film including all commercial 8mm library films. A slight, although somewhat annoying, flicker was apparent when projecting UniveX movies on other manufacturers' projectors. Universal advised its customers against using other manufacturers' projection equipment when showing UniveX films. This minor flicker was more or less an intentional flaw — one might say, a ploy to get UniveX camera owners to purchase a UniveX projector. In the first two years of production, Universal managed to sell over 175,000 Model P-8 projectors. Universal introduced two additional Model P-8 projectors which operated on Direct Current farm lighting units only. One model was designed and specifically marked for 6 volt Direct Current systems and the other model for 32 volt Direct Current systems. These two Direct Current Model P-8 projectors were produced in extremely small quantities and are to be considered extremely rare.

Fig. 2-14 The UniveX Model PU-8 Projector with ¾" f/1.65 Simpson Hi-Lux Lens.

Universal produced another similar type projector in 1936 — the UniveX Model PU-8 Projector *(Fig. 2-14)*, originally priced at $14.50. The Model PU-8 appeared much the same as the Model P-8, with the exception of a rheostat speed control knob mounted at the rear of the projector's base. The 200 watt Model PU-8 differed from the Model P-8 in the respect that it operated on Alternating or Direct Current, requiring the use of a pre-focused UniveX 125 watt Standard Projection Lamp or UniveX 150 watt High-Intensity Projection Lamp. For just $2.95, Universal offered a protective wood-framed case for storing and carrying the Model P-8 or PU-8 projector *(Fig. 2-15)*. The black leatherette-covered case provided additional space for a UniveX movie camera, reels and humidors, and an extra lamp.

Fig. 2-15 The UniveX Model P-8 Projector Carrying Case, also used with similar Universal projectors.

It was at the 1939-40 New York World's Fair and the San Francisco Golden Gate International Exposition that photographers from all over the world had the opportunity to examine Universal's products. In the two seasons of the New York World's Fair, an estimated 45 million people attended what was termed as a "Paradise for Photographers". Approximately 20% of the Fair's visitors brought cameras. Four million people reportedly visited the Eastman Kodak Exhibit — many of these same people undoubtedly stopped at the UniveX Exhibit located in the Communications Building. The UniveX Exhibit included a simulation of the company's production methods, a presentation demonstrating the internal operation of several UniveX cameras, along with techniques to test a camera's performance and also home movie projection demonstrations. Two of the new products featured at the Universal exhibit were the UniveX "Trueview" Model B-8 Camera *(Fig. 2-16)* and the UniveX Model C-8 Camera *(Fig. 2-17)*, both finished in bronze enamel and weighing approximately 26 ounces and 22 ounces respectively. The Model B-8 was really the Model A-8 camera with the collapsible open-frame viewfinder removed and replaced instead with the tubular optical viewfinder that had previously been sold as an accessory item for the Model A-8 camera. The Model B-8 should have been well received by the public, priced at only $9.95 with its factory mounted tubular viewfinder and f/5.6 Ilex Univar lens. As it turned out, it was not. Because of the minimal price increase and the addition of so many worthwhile features, the Model C-8 proved to be the better value when compared with the two earlier UniveX cine cameras. The "Trueview" Model B-8 camera is somewhat less common on the collector's market than either the Model A-8 or Model C-8 camera.

Fig. 2-16 The UniveX "Trueview" Model B-8 Cine Camera with f/5.6 Ilex Univar Lens.

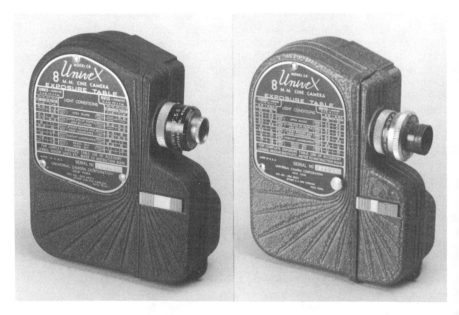

Fig. 2-17 UniveX Model C-8 Cine Cameras. The original model with f/5.6 Ilex Univar lens (left) had a die cast housing similar to the Model A-8. The later and more common model with f/4.5 Ilex Univar lens (right) showed a few minor changes in body design.

This stands much to reason — for only a few dollars more, the Model C-8, priced at $12.50 with an f/5.6 Ilex Univar lens, offered a built-in optical viewfinder, totally eliminating the inconvenience of an externally mounted viewfinder and the related problem of parallax correction. When the Model C-8 was first displayed and demonstrated at the International Camera Convention in Chicago in the Fall of 1938, it received so much attention that Universal decided to release the camera earlier than originally scheduled — just in time for the 1938 Christmas season. Several months later, the Model C-8 was heavily promoted as the "World's Fairs Cine 8 Camera" at both the World's Fair and the Exposition. The Model C-8 fared well as one of Universal's main exhibit items throughout the duration of the two fairs. The Model C-8 was commonly referred to in post 1939 Universal advertisements and dealer price guides as the "Exposition Model". New and improved features on the Model C-8 were a self-locking hinged cover, an improved governor for longer winds, and a shutter that would automatically close after each take, preventing annoying blank frames from appearing on the exposed film. The Model C-8 was a single-speed camera with an exposure time of $\frac{1}{30}$ second at 16 frames per second. The Model C-8, marked "Model C8 UniveX 8mm Cine Camera", can be found packaged in any one of the following colored boxes: an orange box marked "1939 World's Fairs Model", a blue box marked "Exposition Model" and a yellow box similarly marked "Exposition Model". All told, approximately 25,000 Model B-8 and 45,000 Model C-8 cameras were sold.

The following chart provides specific information regarding the complete line of uncoated cine lenses marketed by Universal from 1936 to 1942.

PREWAR UNCOATED CINE UNIVAR LENSES

LENS	CIRCA	1941 PRICE	CAT.#	COMMENTS
½" f/1.9 Wollensak	1936-42	$39.75	L-19	micrometer focusing mount
½" f/2.5 Universal	1941-42	$22.00	L-25	see note below
½" f/2.7 Wollensak	1937-42	$20.00	L-27	
½" f/3.5 Wollensak	1936-42	$12.45	L-35	
½" f/4.5 Ilex	1939-42	$ 5.00	L-45	built-in brown lens shade
½" f/5.6 Ilex	1936-42	$ 2.50	L-56	two types
½" f/6.3 Ilex? *	1941-42	*	*	
1" f/3.5 Wollensak or Ilex **	1939-42	$10.95	LT-135	micrometer focusing mount
1½" f/3.5 Wollensak	1936-42	$37.50	LT-35	micrometer focusing mount

* The ½" Univar f/6.3 lens should be regarded as very rare. There is no price or catalog number available on this lens, as it was never sold separately. The lens appeared briefly in 1941 on the Cinemaster Model D-8 Camera, Universal's least promoted model of the Cinemaster line. Relatively few orders were received for this particular camera. The manufacturer of the f/6.3 lens was most likely the Ilex Optical Company, although this has not been substantiated.

** The 1" Univar f/3.5 telephoto lens was produced for Universal by both Wollensak and Ilex.

Note: In 1940 and 1941, Universal began producing a limited quantity of lenses in its own optical shop. One of these Universal-made lenses was an uncoated ½" f/2.5 Univar lens, offered briefly in 1941 on the new Cinemaster line of 8mm cameras. After the war, Universal reintroduced the f2.5 Univar in a standard and deluxe chrome version, both coated.

Fig. 2-18 The UniveX "Turret" Model C-8 Cine Camera with f/3.5 Wollensak Univar Lens, f/1.9 Wollensak Univar Lens and 1" f/3.5 Ilex Univar Telephoto Lens.

Universal announced two additional cine products in 1939 — the UniveX "Turret" Model C-8 Camera *(Fig. 2-18)* and the UniveX Model P-500 Projector *(Fig. 2-19)*. Retailing for $25.00 with an f/4.5 Univar lens, the bronze-finished Model C-8 Turret was essentially the same as the Model C-8 camera except for the addition of a three lens turret frame screw-mounted to the top of the camera. Universal offered a 1" f/3.5 Univar Telephoto lens and a 1½" f/3.5 Univar Telephoto lens for use with the Model C-8 Turret camera. To compensate for these longer focus lenses, Universal incorporated into the design of the turret frame, a viewfinder masking plate with adjustable apertures. Rotation of the turret frame accomplished two things simultaneously — the telephoto lens assumed a functional position over the lens mount, while the viewfinder masking plate aligned itself with the camera's regular viewfinder window. The viewfinder masking plate constricted the viewfinder's normal field of vision, providing the photographer with a reduced view, similar to the actual portion of the scene being captured on film through the telephoto lens. The Turret camera could be purchased with a brown, all leather, eveready case, marked "UniveX Turret", that need not be removed while taking pictures. Compared to the Model A-8 case, the Turret case is considered quite scarce.

The bronze UniveX Model P-500 projector was constructed with a full die cast frame, the complete unit weighing approximately 10 pounds. Priced at $42.50, the 500 watt projector was powered by either Alternating or Direct Current. Characteristic features of the Model P-500 were a heavy duty Universal motor, forced draft cooling, 200 ft. reel capacity, adjustable speed control, pilot light outlet, removable condenser lens for maximum screen

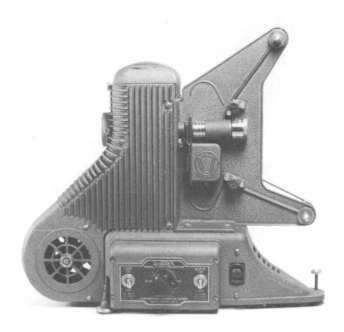

Fig. 2-19 The UniveX Model P-500 Projector with 1" f/1.6 Simpson Hi-Lux Lens.

illumination and interchangeable color-corrected lenses. As on previous UniveX projectors, film rewind was accomplished by belt change. Universal advertised the Model P-500 as the ideal projector for showing color films and underexposed films because of its ability to provide maximum illumination and a large screen image (up to 7x10 ft.). Approximately 15,000 of the Model P-500 projectors were sold between 1939 and 1941. The Model P-500 utilized the UniveX 500 watt Projection Lamp *(Fig. 2-20)* or any other T-10 projection lamp. A brown leatherette-covered case was available for the UniveX 500 watt projector at a cost of $5.50 *(Fig. 2-21)*. The wood-frame case has an unusual drop-down front panel, which revealed additional storage space for the camera, reels, humidors, and an extra 500 watt lamp.

With nearly three million dollars in net sales in 1937 alone, Universal was able to

Fig. 2-20 The UniveX 500 Watt Projection Lamp, in original box, made by Radiant Lamp Corporation.

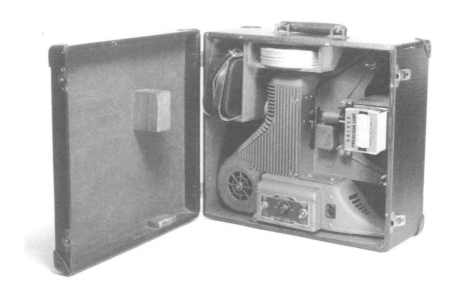

Fig. 2-21 The UniveX Model P-500 Projector Carrying Case, also used with similar Universal projectors.

continue expanding its photographic line with many new products for the amateur photographer. Universal tried everything imaginable to convince dealers and consumers of the many benefits that UniveX products had to offer. Universal offered its retailers free use of a 20 minute sales training film demonstrating various methods of selling UniveX Cine 8 products. The two reel "UniveX Sales Training Film" could be shown on UniveX projectors, making it quite convenient for the dealer with UniveX projectors in stock. For only $.75, retailers could purchase the UniveX Theatre and Demonstration Film *(Fig. 2-22)*, a combination counter display and demonstration item. With a UniveX projector in place on the counter, the retailer could project the UniveX Demonstration Film or any other film directly onto the UniveX Theatre's small silver viewing screen (later versions of the "theatre" were constructed with a translucent screen for rear projection) — a unique and novel means of presentation for the UniveX customer. Universal offered its retailers another unusual sales promotion item — the UniveX Continuous Projection Device *(Fig. 2-23)*, for use with the UniveX Theatre. Priced at $1.75, the device consisted of a baseboard, a vertical support arm, and three pulleys. A 68 inch film strip was threaded through the projector as usual and then channeled over the three pulleys. Two of the pulleys were located underneath the baseboard, the third was located at the top of the 18 inch vertical support mounted to the baseboard behind the projector. With this particular device, a film strip could run for hours without interruption on a store counter or in a window display. In June 1937, Universal began publication of its own monthly photographic trade paper providing detailed reports on UniveX products, information on future UniveX products and announcements of business affairs taking place within the company itself.

Fig. 2-22 The UniveX "Theatre" Demonstration Counter Display for use with a UniveX Projector.

Fig. 2-23 The UniveX Continuous Projection Device for continuous advertising demonstrations in photo stores.

One former Universal engineer described Universal's house organ, "Movie and Photo Merchandising" later renamed, "The UniveX Merchandiser", as "advertising blurb" and said copies were usually "discarded after superficial glancing" by those in his department. Testimonials from satisfied customers were oftentimes included in this trade paper. One specific example was the story of a San Diego man who cleverly mounted a UniveX Model A camera to his model airplane. The plane, powered by a miniature gas motor, incorporated a camera timer to actuate the camera's shutter release at a specific time during the plane's flight. This man's ingenuity seemed to fit the Universal image.

One thing was certain, Universal had steadily become the preferred choice among amateur photographers. Universal had seemingly accomplished what many others had unsuccessfully attempted in the past — to widely popularize various non-standard film sizes for use with its own products. In the years between 1936 and 1938, the Universal Camera Corporation was, for the most part, running smoothly without any serious problems. All of this would soon take a drastic turn — but for the moment, it was apparent to everyone that Universal was doing extremely well for a relatively new company. The following excerpt, taken from the New York Times on December 19, 1937 states, "Employees of the Universal Camera Corporation received yesterday a Christmas bonus of one week's extra pay for every six months in the employ of the company". Without question, business conditions were indeed favorable at that time. Universal had succeeded in making home movies affordable and accessible for everyone. *(Fig. 2-24)*

Fig. 2-24 National Sales Meeting of Universal District Managers at the Hotel Sherman in Chicago, Illinois on September 19-21, 1937.
Front Row, left to right: Chief Engineer George Kende, Director Milton Shaw, President Otto Githens, Vice President Jacob Shapiro, General Sales Manager F. G. Klock.
Back Row, left to right: District Managers John C. Dressler, Fred S. McDougall, Nate B. Glover, Advertising Agent Raymond L. Spector, District Managers Harry L. Shapiro, Richard B. Stollmack, Nate Rickles, Thomas LaPrelle.

CHAPTER THREE - PART ONE

1938-1941

"THE CAMERA OF TOMORROW"

Fig. 3-1 The UniveX Mercury Model CC Candid Camera with standard 35mm f/3.5 Wollensak Tricor Lens.

The existence of the "candid" camera was still at an early stage when in 1937 a well-known photographic publication sent out questionnaires to its subscribers. It was learned that 85% of those who responded considered themselves amateur photographers. A surprising 54% had already purchased a candid camera, in addition to 24% who indicated a preference for home movie equipment. One interesting aspect of the survey was that the average subscriber owned an estimated 2.8 cameras.

SPEEDS.

Aug. 2 -'37

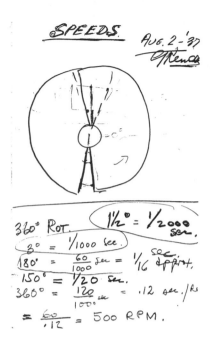

$360°$ Rot. $1\frac{1}{2}° = \frac{1}{2000}$ sec.

$3° = \frac{1}{1000}$ sec.

$180° = \frac{60}{1000}$ sec $= \frac{1}{16}$ sec. apprt.

$150° = \frac{1}{20}$ sec.

$360° = \frac{120}{1000}$ sec $= .12$ sec./Rev

$= \frac{60}{.12} = 500$ RPM.

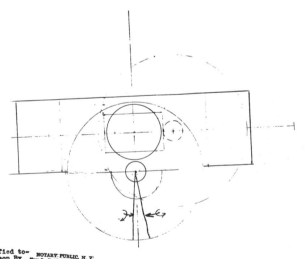

AUGUST 9-1937
George Kende

62

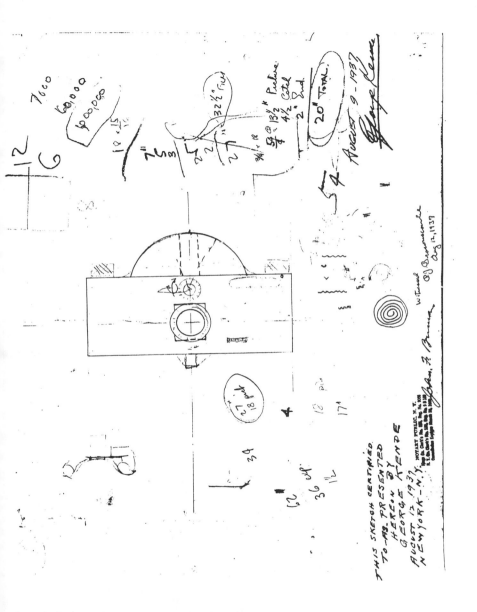

Fig 3-2. Three preliminary patent sketches of the Mercury camera and shutter rendered by George Kende in August 1937 and witnessed by secondary inventor, Universal Engineer Philip Brownscombe and John F. Bruns, New York Notary Public. (John F. Bruns became Universal's Treasurer from 1941 to 1943.)

After five years in the business, Universal finally gained a certain amount of attention and respect from its competitors in the photographic industry with the introduction, in October 1938, of the UniveX Mercury Model CC Camera *(Fig. 3-1)* — a notable contribution to the field of 35mm candid photography. (Author's Note: To eliminate any possible confusion, the Mercury Model CC Camera will henceforth be referred to as the Mercury I). It was readily apparent that the construction of the Mercury I camera was far superior to that of previous UniveX designs, by no means a camera of inferior quality. The unique design was nothing less than extraordinary and certain features on the Mercury I surpassed even those found on some of the more expensive foreign candid cameras of the day.

The first quality production model 35mm candid camera was the Leica, manufactured by E. Leitz, Inc. in Germany in 1925. During the decade that followed, Leitz introduced several improved versions of its original Leica, while another German manufacturer, Carl Zeiss Inc., produced the Contax line with unheard-of shutter speeds of up to $1/1250$ second. A camera trade paper estimated that approximately 25,000 Leica cameras had made their way into the country by 1936, with professional photographers eagerly awaiting their arrival. Amateur photographers were also developing a certain curiosity for the candid camera and soon became part of the growing trend toward "miniature" cameras, as they were sometimes called. Unfortunately, prices for the German-made candid cameras varied between $100-$400 in 1939 — presumably much higher than most amateur photographers could afford. Consequently, amateur photographers turned to the less expensive American-made candid cameras, such as one of the Argus C models ($25-$30), the Perfex 44 ($37.50), the Kodak 35 ($33.50) or the UniveX Mercury I ($25) — Universal's finest achievement to date.

Githens and Shapiro were firm in their belief that what America needed most was an "affordable" American-made candid camera incorporating many of the latest features found on the increasingly popular German-made candids. Universal's Chief Engineer, George Kende, was called upon to start the design work for the camera. Kende was quite confident about the project, assuring Githens and Shapiro that the idea of an "affordable" 35mm precision candid camera would soon become a reality for Universal. There was no reason why Githens and Shapiro should doubt his word. After only a few months with the company, Kende's sheer genius was apparent to everyone at Universal. His first assignment at Universal, the development of the company's low priced "Cine 8" camera and projector, had become an overnight success, winning wide acclaim for the young company and, at the same time, establishing a firm foundation from which Universal could expand and prosper in years to come. It was during this same period that Kende organized and set up many of Universal's departments and laboratories which, prior to his arrival, were either nonexistent or severely limited in their operations. When Kende first entered the doors at Universal, there was virtually no sign of any engineering and research facilities or operations. One simple drawing table stood alone in an otherwise empty room. Kende immediately began planning the set up of a small tool and model shop, later hiring the necessary draftsmen, model makers and tool makers to staff the new departments. Kende continued along these lines, expanding the company's existing engineering facilities and making future provisions for additional facilities, such as Universal's Optical Shop, Chemical Engineering, Photographic, Sensitometric and Electronics Labs, and three Film Processing Labs equipped with special automatic "continuous" film developing equipment designed by Universal especially for processing its UniveX Single-8 films. In addition to the establishment of these new facilities, Kende organized Universal's Test Engineering and Quality Control Department, Service Department, Purchasing Department and handled many other activities such as securing material supply sources and subcontractors for the company, factory planning and cost control, training the technical and production staff — the list is seemingly endless. By 1939, large shipments of finished cameras, projectors and accessory parts were arriving regularly at Universal's New York factory, providing enough work for some 350 workers. Essentially, George Kende was "the man" behind the company. When Kende joined the company in 1935, Universal's net sales for that year were approximately $450,000. Two years later, Kende's untiring efforts had definitely paid off for Githens and Shapiro — net sales for Universal had skyrocketed to approximately $2.8 million!

Kende and Philip J. Brownscombe, another Universal engineer, began work early in 1937 on Universal's lightweight candid camera design featuring

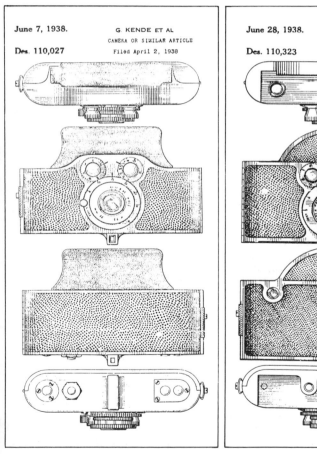
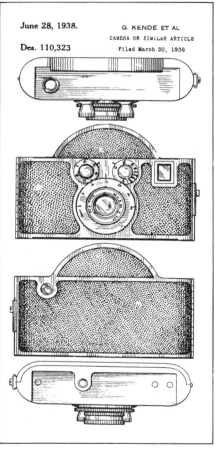

Fig. 3-3 Early conception of Mercury Camera Design, depicted in U.S. Des. Pat. #110,027, as compared to the final production design of Mercury Camera, depicted in U.S. Des. Pat. # 110,323.

the use of standard sprocketed 35mm film, interchangeable lenses, fast and accurate shutter speeds, and an automatic film transport enabling the user to advance the film and set the shutter all in one maneuver. Before the Mercury I reached the actual production stage, its various designs and test models *(Fig. 3-2)* had cost the company more than $100,000. Kende and Brownscombe decided to use die cast parts for the construction of the Mercury I, consisting mainly of aluminum alloy, with zinc alloy being used to a lesser degree. Aluminum alloy was chosen for the three-part housing, this attributing to the camera's light weight of only 16 ounces (without the lens). Kende and Brownscombe felt the expense of constructing dies for this particular camera would be significantly less than tooling for similar stamped or pressed parts. In addition to that, die casting significantly minimized the parts required to build the Mercury I, resulting in a reduction of assembly time — providing Universal with additional savings in manufacturing costs. Universal relied heavily on die casting in the manufacture of its photographic products. Approximately 15 million die cast parts were used by Universal during its first eight years in business. Add to that, the 30 million die cast UniveX film spools produced during that same time period!

Universal called the Mercury I "America's Challenge to the World's Finest Cameras". Packaged in a beige and brown felt-covered box, the Mercury I originally sold for $25.00 with the standard f/3.5 35mm Wollensak Tricor lens. The Mercury's weight and size made it extremely comfortable to hold, while centralization of the camera's controls around the lens mount made it relatively simple and convenient to operate. The Mercury, with its leather-covering and polished aluminum finish, was rather peculiar in appearance because of an unusual round protrusion on the top deck of the camera that served as a housing for the camera's rotary focal plane shutter. In an effort to divert attention from this, a depth of field scale was conveniently mounted to the exterior of the protrusion. The very first Mercury I models were produced with a depth of field scale mounted on the front of the protrusion only (the backside was leather-covered). In this particular case, the scale gave readings down to an f/3.5 aperture only. When faster lenses became available for the Mercury, the depth of field scale was continued to an f/2.0 aperture on the reverse side of the round protrusion. After 1939 this double-sided depth of field scale became standard on all Mercury models. The earliest Mercury I cameras lacked one feature that later became standard on all Mercury I cameras. This feature, called the "film movement indicator", appeared much like the head of a large screw and could be found on the bottom of the camera next to the cover release button. Its purpose was to alert the photographer in the event that the film was improperly loaded. A small free-turning brass gear, located inside the camera's film loading chamber, was connected to the "film movement indicator". This small brass gear moved simultaneously with the gear on the bottom of the film spool. If for some reason the film sprockets were not properly engaged with the film, the "film movement indicator" would not move while the shutter was being wound.

All things considered, the Mercury's unique design and impressive list of features made it an attractive buy for the amateur photographer. The Mercury I offered a top speed of 1/1000 second (special 1939 model, 1/1500 second), an automatic film transport with double exposure prevention, an optical viewfinder with parallax correction indicators, a depth of field scale, an exposure calculator, helical focusing down to 18 inches, and a 35mm single frame format (19x24mm) which yielded 18 or 36 exposures from a roll of UniveX #200 series film. The Mercury I pioneered the concept of internal photoflash synchronization, without the usual external wires between

Fig. 3-4 The UniveX Flash Units, the prewar version (left) with "ribbed" lamp socket housing and the postwar version (right) with bulb ejector button.

camera and flash. In January 1939, Universal applied for a patent (U.S.Pat. #2,277,233) on this unprecedented feature which eventually became known as the "hot shoe". The UniveX Mercury Flash Unit *(Fig. 3-4)*, priced at $3.95, could easily be slipped onto the hot shoe for night or low light picture-taking. Basically comprised of a bakelite battery compartment and a removable four inch reflector, the flash unit utilized screw-based flashbulbs. Universal offered a five inch Auxiliary Reflector for use with larger-sized flashbulbs. It is important to note here that three different versions of this flash unit were actually manufactured by Universal through the years: 1) the earliest prewar version had a "ribbed" lamp socket housing and required a standard flat two cell battery, 2) a later prewar version had the same "ribbed" design, but required two standard penlite batteries instead of the standard flat two cell battery previously used, 3) the last and only postwar version was slightly different in ornamental appearance, but is easily distinguished from the others by a special bulb ejector button on the front of the lamp socket housing. The UniveX Mercury Flash Unit was also sold under the following names: the UniveX Flash Unit and the Mercury Flash Unit. To avoid the problem of spoiled pictures and wasted flashbulbs, Universal offered the UniveX Photoflash Tester *(Fig. 3-5)*, which indicated whether or not the UniveX flash unit was operating properly. The tester was screwed directly into the flash lamp socket and if the flash unit and batteries were in good operating order, a tiny bulb at the top of the tester would light. Another

Fig. 3-5 The UniveX Photoflash Tester was used to check the condition of the batteries in the UniveX Photoflash Unit.

ingenious Mercury accessory was the UniveX Rapid Winder *(See Fig. 3-18 below, Mercury CC-1500 Camera is shown equipped with accessories)* priced at only $2.95. The UniveX Mercury I was probably the first camera to popularize the use of a rapid wind device at such a reasonable cost. The rapid winder came packaged with a special pinion film wind knob having small teeth around the entire shaft of the knob. After interchanging this knob with the original film wind knob, the rapid wind device was then mounted to the camera's cable release socket using a small screw. Upon stroking the rapid wind lever, the larger teeth on the rapid wind device would engage with the smaller teeth on the pinion knob, forcing the knob to rotate and in turn advance the film. After developing a natural feel for the device, multiple exposures were possible at an approximate rate of one picture per second. One other Mercury accessory item, a bit more common than the rapid wind device, is the extinction-type UniveX Mercury Exposure Meter *(Fig. 3-18)*, priced at $2.00. The exposure meter slipped onto the Mercury accessory clip located directly above the optical viewfinder and was used in conjunction with the 3-ring Mercury Exposure Calculator located on the camera's back. Internally, the exposure meter consisted of a circle divided into eight numbered sections, where each section was slightly darker than the section before. After looking through the exposure meter for approximately five seconds, the user would select the darkest (or highest-numbered) section that was clearly visible, and subsequently enter that number onto the 3-ring exposure calculator to get the correct exposure for that picture. The exposure calculator could be used with or without the help of a clip-on exposure meter, although calculations were significantly faster with a reading from the exposure meter. Without the Mercury Exposure Meter, compensation for such things as time of day, season of the year, lighting conditions and film speed had to be made — all of which made exposure calculation very time-consuming. An interesting feature of the Mercury Exposure Meter was the built-in accessory clip on top of the meter itself, allowing the user the option of stacking another Mercury accessory, such as the Mercury Rangefinder *(Fig. 3-18)*, on top of the exposure meter. The rangefinder was the super-imposed images type, whereby rotation of the footage dial made two images converge into one. The device featured a swing base for horizontal

68

or vertical positioning and 13 footage calibrations which conformed exactly to the calibrations found on the Mercury focusing mount. Universal recommended the rangefinder when using the f/2 Hexar lens on the Mercury because more precise distance readings were generally required with this particular lens.

Fig. 3-6 Original cartons of UniveX Ultrapan Superspeed #236 rollfilm and UniveX Dufaycolor #218 rollfilm for use in the Mercury I and Corsair I Cameras.

The Mercury I was designed to utilize a totally new UniveX film load available in three different emulsion speeds, with a choice of either 18 or 36 exposure lengths. Designated as UniveX #218 or #236 films *(Fig. 3-6)*, or generally referred to as UniveX #200 series films, Ultrachrome (an ortho-chromatic film), Ultrapan SS (a high speed panchromatic film), and Microtomic (a fine grain medium speed panchromatic film) were manufactured by Gevaert and originally priced between $.30 and $.50. For a short time, Universal offered 18 exposure rolls of Dufaycolor transparency color film for use in the Mercury I at a cost of $.90. This film was somewhat popular among amateurs because the film's additive color process made home developing quite feasible. During the late 1930's, a series of disruptions reportedly took place within the managerial staff at Dufaycolor. This, coupled with the rapidly growing popularity of Kodak's high quality Kodachrome film, contributed to the eventual disappearance of Dufaycolor from store shelves by 1941. Generally speaking, a UniveX #200 film load consisted of standard sprocketed 35mm film, cut into specified lengths fitted with either a protective paper (or film) leader and trailer to prevent fogging of the film. The film was wound onto a special UniveX patented spool incorporating a small brass gear on the base of the spool. This gear interacted with another small gear in the camera's film chamber, establishing the basis of the camera's film transport system.

Soon after the introduction of the Mercury camera, a large selection of accessory products followed. Some are considered extremely rare collector's items, such as the UniveX Micrographic Enlarger *(Fig. 3-7)* which originally

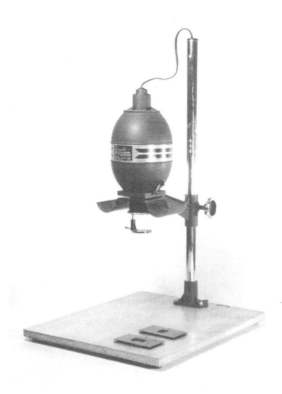

Fig. 3-7 The UniveX Micrographic Enlarger with two negative carriers.

sold for $27.50 without a lens. Included in the purchase price were two negative carriers — a single frame 35mm negative carrier and a double frame 35mm negative carrier. Negative carriers for UniveX #00 film and standard ½ Vest Pocket film were available at an extra charge. The enlarger head was suspended by a die cast support arm which was connected to a 28 inch high chromium plated steel column. The column was secured to a maple plywood baseboard (20x17 inches). The enlarger featured a double lens condenser system, special negative carriers which prevented unwanted scratches on the negatives, lens interchangeability and an adjustable ruby filter. An Ilex f/4.5 Univar 50mm enlarging lens *(Fig. 3-8)* was available for use on the enlarger, although any 35mm

Fig. 3-8 The 50mm f/4.5 Ilex Univar Enlarging Lens.

70

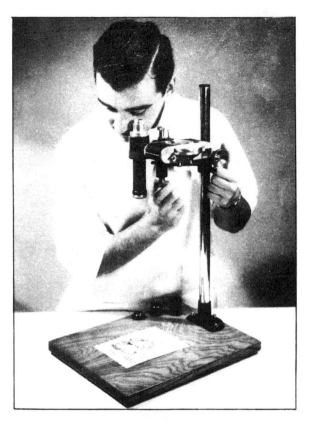

Fig. 3-9 The Mercury Copying Stand with Optical Focusing Device.

Mercury lens could be used in place of the f/4.5 enlarging lens if photographs were being made from the Mercury's 35mm single frame formatted negatives. Universal also offered special accessory lens adapters for utilizing Leica, Contax or Argus lenses on the UniveX enlarger. The UniveX Enlarger was guaranteed to produce results comparable to those obtained on enlargers two to three times the cost. Another extremely rare Universal product was the Mercury Copying Stand *(Fig. 3-9)*, a device used for photographing small objects and paperwork. Priced at $17.50, the copy stand consisted basically of a chrome-plated steel column mounted to a plywood baseboard (15⅜x12 inches). Attached to the steel column was a camera holding bracket and a micro-focusing device with a ground glass focusing screen. A Mercury Extension Tube Kit was included with the purchase of each copying stand. With a Mercury camera and the extension tube set it was possible to photograph objects smaller than 9x11½ inches, but larger than ⅜x½ inches. Each of the four tubes are marked with the object distance and size. The shim is unmarked: when used separately (without the other four extension tubes), the correct object distance would be 12 inches and the object size would be 5¾x7½ inches. If a customer was considering the purchase of both an enlarger and a copying stand, Universal provided that customer with a less expensive alternative. Priced at $12.50, the UniveX Copying Arm

71

was used together with the UniveX enlarger, allowing the enlarger to be converted whenever necessary into a copying stand — a viable option to consider. Aside from the savings in cost, this was also an excellent way of conserving important work space in a small darkroom. For the most part, Universal's copy stand was intended for use in professional fields, outside the realm of amateur photography. Doctors, librarians, teachers, scientists, police, and the like displayed an interest in this particular Universal equipment. In 1940, the UniveX Mercury I Camera and Mercury Copying Stand were selected by officials at the Yale University for use in various scientific research programs.

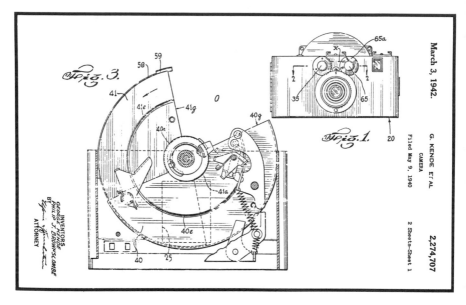

Fig. 3-10 The Mercury Shutter Design, depicted in U.S. Pat. #2,274,707.

Prior to the construction of the Mercury I, Universal studied the shutter accuracy on many popular American-made and foreign-made cameras. It was discovered that the "actual" speed of the shutters tested rarely matched the indicated speed. Universal decided to build an improved focal plane shutter that would give consistently accurate speeds through extreme variations in climate, thousands of times over. The Mercury Shutter *(Fig. 3-10)* is best explained in a Universal pamphlet entitled, "UniveX Mercury - Questions and Answers". The pamphlet states, "Because of the rugged, all-metal rotary design of the Mercury shutter, great accuracy of speeds is easily obtained. For all speed settings, from ½₀ to ½₀₀₀, the shutter mechanism revolves at a constant speed of ½₀ of a second. The 'width of the slot' in the revolving blade alone determines the speed of exposure; no variable springs are employed. For example, when the shutter speed knob is turned from ½₀₀ to ½₀, the slot is automatically opened up to 10 times the original arc, and the exposure is therefore 10 times as long." The Mercury shutter gained much recognition when Harvard University selected it in 1940 for use in its solar coronagraph, the only device of its type in the entire Western Hemisphere at the time. With this unique instrument, Harvard students were able to

HARVARD COLLEGE OBSERVATORY
FREMONT PASS STATION
CLIMAX, COLORADO

12 October 1945

Universal Camera Corporation
28 West 23rd Street
New York 10, New York

Gentlemen:

I thought you might like to have a report on the Mercury
Camera Shutter that your firm supplied to us in 1940 for use
in our automatic motion picture camera for study of phenomena
of the sun.

The shutter has performed amazingly and is still in operation after having exposed frame by frame, over 7000 feet of 16mm.
motion picture film at 16 frames per foot, or over 112,000 exposures.

The Mercury shutter has proved extremely satisfactory
under very trying conditions. We have been bothered considerably by extremely low temperatures at which the equipment must
operate, but the shutter has gone on taking thousands of pictures, one after the other, with clock-like precision and no
indication of change with age or temperature. The conditions
of use have been very severe with zero and sub-zero weather
common from October through April.

You may also be interested to know that the Mercury Shutter
was picked after careful comparative tests of a number of different shutters, including the Leica and Contax, and that we
found the comparative performance for our application to be very
much in favor of the Mercury.

It occurs to me that you might want to use the information
for advertising purposes. If you wish to contact me, I shall
be glad to supply any further details you may wish to have about
this application of the Mercury shutter.

Very sincerely yours,

Walter Orr Roberts

WOR/hcs

---

*Fig. 3-11 A letter from Harvard College Observatory, dated October 12, 1945, reporting
the continued accuracy and successful performance of the Mercury shutter since its
installation in the Observatory's solar coronagraph in 1940.*

photograph the sun's corona and study its related effects on worldwide radio communications. Construction and operational testing of the coronagraph was carried out at the university in 1940 by Dr. Donald H. Menzel, a Harvard astrophysics professor, and Walter Orr Roberts, a Harvard graduate student working toward a career in solar physics. Shortly after, the coronagraph was transported to Harvard's recently built astronomical research facility, the Harvard College Observatory, located at Fremont Pass Station in Climax, Colorado, approximately 11,520 feet above sea level. (In 1946, after a merger between Harvard University and the University of Colorado, the Harvard College Observatory became known as the High Altitude Observatory. Years later, in 1960, the High Altitude Observatory became a division of the National Center for Atmospheric Research, the principal research center for the University Corporation of Atmospheric Research located in Boulder Colorado.)

Interestingly, the Harvard Coronagraph was built using a 16mm motion picture camera from the silent film era. As a means of photographing the sun's corona, the camera was modified to produce an "artificial" eclipse that would remain present throughout periods of viewing and exposure. This phenomenon was accomplished by incorporating a circular-shaped object within the camera itself. In addition to this, certain factors, particularly intermittent exposure capability, necessitated the replacement of the camera's original shutter with a more suitable shutter. After receiving and testing several different shutters, including the Leica, Contax, and Mercury shutters, Harvard selected the Mercury shutter based on its operational simplicity, all metal construction, unique rotary design and its ability to perform dependably for extended periods in extremely low temperatures.

In October 1945, Universal received a letter from Walter Orr Roberts of the Harvard College Observatory *(Fig. 3-11)*. Apparently, the Mercury shutter had, without fail, performed hundreds of accurate exposures every day, despite months of sub-zero temperatures and intense heat directly from the sun. After personally selecting and installing the Mercury shutter, Roberts was pleased to report the shutter was "still in operation", having exposed over 112,000 frames with "clock-like precision". Shortly after, Harvard's letter appeared in Universal's postwar advertisements as a staunch testimonial to the shutter speed accuracy of the Mercury Camera *(Fig. 3-12)*.

Through advertising and promotional activities, Universal did its utmost to assure the public that the words "speed" and "accuracy" were indeed synonymous with the Mercury shutter. As an example, in 1939, Universal agreed to participate in a test conducted by the Electrical Testing Laboratories of New York City to determine the actual shutter speeds of different popular cameras currently on the market. The Mercury, Contax, Leica, and Argus cameras were randomly selected from dealers' stock. The results of the test appear below.

CAMERA	MARKED SPEED	MEASURED SPEED
Mercury	$\frac{1}{1000}$ sec.	$\frac{1}{1050}$ sec.
Contax	$\frac{1}{1250}$ sec.	$\frac{1}{700}$ sec.
Leica	$\frac{1}{1000}$ sec.	$\frac{1}{550}$ sec.
Argus	$\frac{1}{300}$ sec.	$\frac{1}{145}$ sec.

From this information, it appears that the accuracy of the Mercury I shutter far surpassed that of the other three models tested, indicating in fact that price or foreign manufacture had little to do with the accuracy of a camera's shutter. Not long after, these same test results appeared in Universal advertisements as a testimonial to the dependability of the Mercury I *(Fig. 3-13)*. Unlike the advertising practices used today, at that time

The Camera that went to Harvard

STILL IN OPERATION AFTER 112,000 EXPOSURES

PERFORMED AMAZINGLY

EXTREMELY SATISFACTORY UNDER VERY TRYING CONDITIONS

CLOCK-LIKE PRECISION

PICKED AFTER CAREFUL COMPARATIVE TESTS

COMPARATIVE PERFORMANCE VERY MUCH IN FAVOR OF THE MERCURY

*Cameras selling at 2½ and 4 times the price of the Mercury II.

its the MERCURY II
by UNIVERSAL

SUPER - SPEED! SUPER - PRECISION! ESPECIALLY DESIGNED FOR COLOR!

The 1/1000 second shutter combined with other advanced Universal features makes the Mercury II the camera that takes candid, action, portrait or still-life shots practically by itself. Film economy—Mercury II gives you 32 negatives on an 18 exposure standard 35 mm. color or black and white film cartridge.

UNIVERSAL CAMERA CORPORATION
NEW YORK   CHICAGO   HOLLYWOOD

Makers of Cinémaster Movie Equipment, Universal Photographic Equipment, plus Precision Optical and Electronic Instruments

Fig. 3-12 A postwar Universal advertisement for the Mercury shutter - "The Camera that went to Harvard".

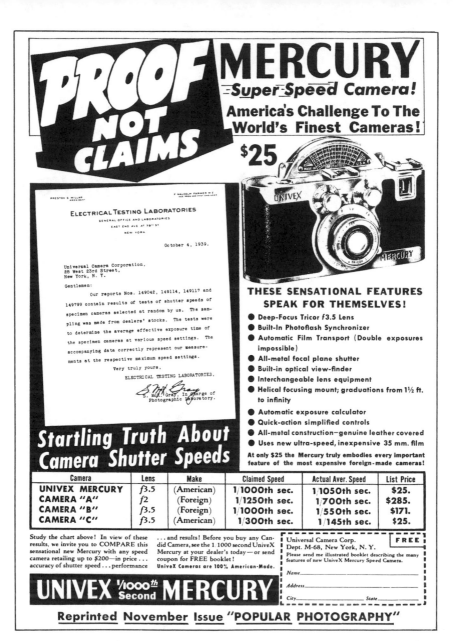

Fig. 3-13 A 1939 Universal advertisement comparing Mercury accuracy to the Contax, Leica and Argus cameras. At the time, the Contax, Leica and Argus cameras could not legally be named in this Universal advertisement, but results from comparison shutter speed tests, performed by the Electrical Testing Laboratories in 1939, clearly substantiated the fact that Mercury, Leica, Contax and Argus cameras were used in the performance of these shutter speed tests. The results of the test proved favorable for the Mercury Camera, prompting Universal to announce the results of the test to the public through this particular UniveX Mercury advertisement, taken from Popular Photography, November 1939.

it would have been illegal for Universal to identify the names of the other camera manufacturers in an advertisement of this type, which is why the cameras were anonymously labeled — foreign or domestic Camera "A", "B" or "C".

The following chart provides descriptions and other information relating specifically to the five uncoated lenses marketed by Universal for the Mercury I camera from 1938 to 1942.

PREWAR MERCURY I LENSES *(Figs. 3-14 through 3-18)*

APERTURE	f/2.0	f/2.7	f/3.5	f/3.5	f/4.5
MODEL NAME	HEXAR *[1]	TRICOR	TRICOR	TELECOR	---- *[2]
MANUFACTURER	Wollensak	Wollensak	Wollensak	Ilex	Wollensak
FOCAL LENGTH	35mm	35mm	35mm	75mm	125mm
UNIVEX FILTER	No.9	No.15 *[3]	No.11	----- *[4]	---- *[5]
FILTER DIAMETER	1.06"	.88"	.78"	1.28"	1.38"
CIRCA	1939-42	1940-42	1938-42	1939-42	1939-42
1940 PRICE	$45.00	$20.00	$12.00	$21.50	$65.00
LENS CATALOG #	L-62	L-67	L-63	LT-335	LT-545
COMMENTS				Use M-81 viewfinder. Leather case incl.	Use M-64 viewfinder.

* 1 - Two versions of the 35mm f/2.0 Wollensak Hexar lens are known to exist — the original version marked "Univex Hexar" and the later version marked "Hexar".

* 2 - The Mercury 125mm f/4.5 Wollensak telephoto lens did not have a special trade name, such as "Hexar", "Tricor", "Telecor" or "Univar" like other Universal lenses. Fortunately, the Mercury 125mm telephoto lens can still be identified by the following marking which appears around the end of the lens barrel; "WOLLENSAK-ROCHESTER U.S.A. 5 INCH f4.5 TELEPHOTO". The lens was advertised by Universal as a "125mm" lens, but this was not marked on the lens — only the marking "5 inch" appeared on the lens. The apertures of this lens ranged from f/4.5 through f/32 and the distance markings from 6 feet to infinity.

* 3 - This Univex slip-on filter could also be used on the Iris Standard, Zenith, Corsair I or II and AF-5 cameras.

* 4 & 5 - No evidence has been found indicating whether or not Universal ever manufactured larger-sized filters for use on the two Mercury telephotos.

Fig. 3-14 The Mercury 125mm f/4.5 Wollensak Telephoto Lens and screw-in lens shade, an extremely rare Mercury accessory.

Fig. 3-15 The 35mm f/2.0 Wollensak Hexar Lenses, two versions. The original version was marked "Univex Hexar" and the later, more common, version was marked only "Hexar".

Fig. 3-16 The UniveX Mercury Camera with rare 35mm f/2.7 Wollensak Tricor Lens.

Fig. 3-17 The UniveX Mercury Camera with rare 75mm f/3.5 Ilex Telecor Telephoto Lens and clip-on optical viewfinder. This particular telephoto lens came with its own special leather case.

Universal was rapidly becoming known the world over as the manufacturer of America's fastest candid camera — the UniveX Mercury I with a shutter speed of ¹⁄₁₀₀₀ second. The foreign market offered photographers an even higher shutter speed of ¹⁄₁₂₅₀ second on the German-made Contax II. Somewhat discontented by this fact, Universal decided to do something about it. In June 1939, Universal became known as the manufacturer of the World's fastest candid camera with the introduction of a special Mercury I model, the UniveX Mercury Model CC-1500 Camera *(Fig. 3-18)*. The Mercury Model CC-1500 is a true collector's rarity. Manufactured for only one year, this special model of the Mercury I featured an unheard-of shutter speed of ¹⁄₁₅₀₀ second. Almost all of the shutter speeds indicated on the special Mercury model (¹⁄₂₀, ¹⁄₄₀, ¹⁄₅₀, ¹⁄₈₀, ¹⁄₁₅₀, ¹⁄₃₀₀, ¹⁄₅₀₀, ¹⁄₁₅₀₀, T and B) were higher than the speed settings indicated on the original Mercury model (¹⁄₂₀, ¹⁄₃₀, ¹⁄₄₀, ¹⁄₆₀, ¹⁄₁₀₀, ¹⁄₂₀₀, ¹⁄₃₀₀, ¹⁄₁₀₀₀, T and B). To attain the shutter speed of ¹⁄₁₅₀₀ second on the special Mercury model, Universal's engineers simply overtensed the shutter spring, which also accounted for the differences noted in the other shutter speed settings. Unfortunately, this added tension posed a constant strain on the shutter spring, eventually causing it to fatigue prematurely, and affect the shutter's overall accuracy. Equipped with an f/2.0 Wollensak Hexar lens the Mercury Model CC-1500 sold for $65.00, but could be obtained at a considerably lower price if purchased with either the f/2.7 Wollensak Tricor or the f/3.5 Wollensak Tricor lens. It is estimated that Universal manufactured approximately 3000 Mercury Model CC-1500 cameras in comparison to some 45,000 of the standard Mercury cameras produced from 1938 through 1941.

Fig. 3-18 The UniveX Mercury Model CC-1500 Camera with 35mm f/2 Wollensak Hexar Lens and the following accessories: a Rapid Winder, an Exposure Meter and a Rangefinder. The Model C-1500 Mercury was manufactured during a short period in 1939 and featured a top shutter speed of $^1/_{1500}$ second.

Universal spared no expense advertising its products during the years 1938 and 1939. Many different forms of advertising were employed by the company in order to promote the more popular products. Universal's 1939 newspaper and magazine advertising campaign was considered the largest in the company's history. Ads for the Mercury I and the Exposition Model C-8 movie camera appeared in newspapers in some 45 cities nationwide and many leading magazines. Camera contests were another form of advertising used by Universal to promote the sale of a particular product. One such example was the $1000 Mercury Contest which began in August of 1940 and ran through July of 1941. The contest rules required amateur Mercury owners to submit any photo taken with their Mercury cameras. Out of 2432 entrants, 68 prizes were awarded in the form of U.S. War Bonds or Stamps. The first prize of $300 was awarded to F. Francis Jackson of Everett, Washington for a well-chosen photo entry entitled "War Worker". Universal also held a Mercury Photo Salon at its main office on West 23rd Street in December of 1939. Visitors to the UniveX Building were able to observe a large photo exhibit, in addition to ongoing demonstrations of a working darkroom and also the UniveX Shutter Speed Tester, previously demonstrated at the UniveX Exhibit *(Fig. 3-19)* at the World's Fair earlier that year. Universal urged camera owners to bring in their cameras, regardless of make, and

Fig. 3-19 Entrance to the UniveX Exhibit at 1939-1940 New York World's Fair. Photoflash bulb on large Mercury at left flashed continuously while the large camera lens was used for rear projection of color demonstration slides. (Courtesy: Photographic Dealer and Photo Finishers News, September 1939)

check the shutters for accuracy on the Mercury Shutter Speed Tester. Universal took the opportunity to demonstrate to these camera owners the accuracy of the Mercury shutter. Regardless of price, Universal's engineers claimed it was quite common to find significant shutter inaccuracies on most foreign and domestic camera models they had tested.

It was a stroke of good fortune indeed for Universal when Warner Bros. asked its permission to use the UniveX Mercury I camera and accessories as props in the upcoming comedy-drama entitled, "Everybody's Hobby" *(Fig. 3-20)*. Released by Warner Bros. on August 26, 1939 with a total running time of 56 minutes, the film starred Henry O'Neill and Irene Rich. Basically, the story went like this: O'Neill portrayed the father of a family in which each member, other than himself, had their own hobby. Father never cared much for the idea of having a hobby. Much to the family's surprise, he discovers photography after receiving a UniveX Mercury I camera and accessories as a gift. Second on a double bill. "Everybody's Hobby" opened on September 25, 1939 at the Fox Theater in Brooklyn, New York. Months prior to the film's opening, Universal had begun to make arrangements with dealers who were interested in demonstrating the UniveX Mercury with its

Fig. 3-20 "Everybody's Hobby", a 1939 Warner Bros. film with the UniveX Mercury Camera being used as a prop. (Courtesy: Minicam, November 1939)

accessories in the theater lobby during the showing of "Everybody's Hobby". Universal offered special displays to all dealers wishing to participate in the demonstration. A photograph of actor Henry O'Neill appeared in a 1939 issue of Minicam magazine promoting both the new Warner movie and also Universal's products. The picture appears to have been taken on the movie set, showing O'Neill seated in front of a UniveX Micrographic Enlarger. A Mercury I camera and UniveX Photoflash Unit can also be seen lying on the table to one side. Peculiarly, Warner Bros. did not use the UniveX enlarger in the actual movie: an unmarked enlarger appeared in its place. Similarly, when flash pictures were taken with the Mercury, O'Neill used a separate grip-type flash gun instead of the camera-mounted UniveX Photoflash Unit. Aside from the Mercury camera, the only other Universal product seen during the movie — though only for a moment — was the rare Mercury 125mm telephoto lens!

For quite some time, Universal boasted that its cameras and photographic equipment were widely used in various professional fields. UniveX camera instruction booklets and brochures stated, "They (UniveX Cameras) are official equipment of Metropolitan Police Forces, Explorers, Newspaper Reporters, Staff Reporters, Commercial Photographers and Youth Organizations throughout the world." To a degree, this statement was true. In 1939, Police Chief Charles Blair of the Beverly Hills Department of Police, equipped his entire force with UniveX Mercury I cameras. Described as an "innovative" man, Chief Blair was convinced that candid photographs taken at the scene of various crimes were invaluable evidence in prosecuting criminals.

Universal discontinued production of the Mercury I in 1941 after the company acquired military contracts from the United States and British Governments for production of binoculars.

CHAPTER THREE - PART TWO

1938-1941

THE UNIVERSAL 35MM
SINGLE LENS REFLEX PROTOTYPE

During the production years of the Mercury I camera, Universal began development of a remarkable new design — a fully automatic 35mm single lens reflex (SLR) camera with eye level viewing.

Single lens reflex cameras with eye level pentaprism viewing began to appear on the photographic market in the postwar 1940's, when the Italian-made Rectaflex and the German-made Contax S were introduced almost simultaneously. Despite the obvious benefits of the pentaprism for eye level viewing and focusing, these SLR cameras still lacked certain advanced features which had been employed previously on Universal's 35mm SLR prototype more than seven years earlier in 1941. In addition to eye level viewing, the 35mm prototype included such pioneering features as a front leaf-type shutter intercoupled with a preset automatic diaphragm, a depth of field preview button and a "fast action" film advance lever — each one virtually unheard-of in its time. Essentially, it would seem that this incredible camera design would have been a bright spark of prosperity for the financially troubled company. In all probability, a camera such as this, once on the market, would have been heralded the world over as an outstanding and unprecedented photographic achievement in its time.

The story surrounding Universal's 35mm SLR prototype began some years earlier, in 1937, in a small home workshop in the Bronx. It was there that Joseph Pignone, a young mechanical engineer, painstakingly devoted much of his spare time to the invention, development and hand construction of a small intricate camera which he appropriately called the "Microflex" *(Fig. 3-21)*. In an effort to facilitate construction at home, he scaled the working model down to the 16mm format. Upon completion of the "Microflex", Pignone applied for a patent in 1937, thereafter regarding his hand built working model as being the World's first eye level SLR camera.

Universal was totally unaware of this photographic breakthrough until 1939 when Pignone arrived at the company's New York office with the intention of demonstrating the "Microflex". Pignone proudly displayed the camera and its amazing capabilities. He also revealed his own detailed illustration of a full-sized 35mm SLR camera design, called the "Pignone Reflex" *(Fig. 3-22)*, exemplifying a more refined embodiment of his hand-made 16mm SLR camera. The design drawing and the hand built camera were visual evidence that Pignone was indeed a man of many talents. In

Fig. 3-21 The 16mm "Microflex" Camera. Characteristic features of the "Microflex" camera are shown here in a frontal view. Appearing clockwise in order, beginning at the lower left-hand corner are the following features:
Side: *1) Focusing Knob*
Top: *2) Shutter Release 3) Film Advance Knob 4) Viewfinder Eyepiece*
    5) Reflex Housing 6) Exposure Counter (barely visible at rear)
    7) Synchronized Photoflash Receptacle
Front: *8) Interchangeable Threaded Lens Mount 9) Aperture Selector Dial*
    10) Lens Mount Lock 11) Extension Bellows
Body front: *12) Shutter Speed Selector Dial*   *(Courtesy: Joseph Pignone)*

addition to earning a degree in Mechanical Engineering from Columbia University, Pignone also attended the Parsons Institute of Art — providing him with the advantageous ability to perfectly capture on paper every detail of an invention or design. For several years, Pignone had illustrated the front covers for various magazines such as Harper's Bazaar, Radio Craft, Mechanics and Handicraft, and other well-known publications. From 1934 to 1936, he was also the Associate Editor of Mechanics and Handicraft, where he wrote and illustrated hundreds of articles related to general mechanics.

U.S. PATENTS PENDING
JOSEPH PIGNONE, M.E.
NEW YORK

Fig. 3-22 The "Pignone Reflex" Camera Design. Characteristic features of the "Pignone Reflex" design are shown here in a frontal view. Appearing left to right, beginning at camera's top deck are the following features (* — front camera controls): 1) Shutter Release 2) Exposure Counter 3) Delayed Action Timer 4) Cable Release Socket 5) Timer Loading Lever 6) Film Minder 7) Extinction Exposure Meter 8) Shutter Speed Knob * 9) Focusing Mount * 10) Aperture Selector Ring *

Note: *When Pignone applied for a patent on this camera design in 1937, he was advised by his patent attorney not to reveal one particularly exciting aspect of his design to the public until the patent was actually granted. Pignone took this advised precaution and omitted the new feature entirely from his 1937 drawing. The complete absence of any conventional means of film advancement in this drawing definitely indicates that Pignone had indeed designed a means of film advancement that was new and radically different — that being, a "single stroke" film advance lever. (Courtesy: Joseph Pignone)*

Universal was sufficiently impressed with Pignone's 16mm "Microflex". Certain features, particularly unprecedented eye level reflex viewing and focal plane shutter speeds of up to ¹⁄₁₀₀₀ second, contributed greatly toward a distinctive and radically new camera design. A pentaprism small enough for the "Microflex" was not available in 1937; therefore, eye level reflex viewing was accomplished through the use of two periscopically aligned mirrors, in combination with an erecting prism, positioned directly in front of the eyepiece. The camera design also featured the use of threaded inter-changeable lenses. Because of the camera's 16mm format, Pignone was able to utilize cine lenses as supplementary telephoto and wide angle lenses. The metal focal plane shutter on the "Microflex" was not coupled to the camera's film advance system, but its shutter could be easily set by sliding a small knob along a slot on the backside of the camera body, creating the necessary amount of tension required to set the shutter spring. Upon actuation of the shutter release button, the shutter traversed the camera body lengthwise at a constant speed of $\frac{1}{20}$ second, carrying with it a reflexing mirror and an adjustable shutter capping plate. The position of the capping plate over the shutter determined the amount of light which would reach the film during an exposure. A body mounted rotatable shutter speed dial was used to adjust the position of the capping plate. An accurate speed of $\frac{1}{1000}$ second could be attained on the "Microflex" when, for example, the capping plate was positioned in such a way that the shutter aperture was reduced to little more than a narrow slit, allowing the least possible amount of light to pass. By varying the position of this shutter capping plate (with the shutter speed dial), a wide range of exposure speeds were possible.

During each exposure, the "cross-sliding" shutter of the "Microflex" would travel across the full length of the camera body. This type of shutter proved very effective for a small format such as 16mm. When Pignone envisioned his 16mm "Microflex" in a larger 35mm format, he realized that a full frame 35mm format would be impossible with the same type of shutter. Enlarging that particular shutter assembly to fit a full frame 35mm format would have necessitated construction of a camera body of questionable or unconventional length. Pignone explained to the managers at Universal that a larger full frame 35mm version of the "Microflex" as such, was not feasible. In its stead, he proposed a 35mm half frame format, to which management voiced no objection. Brief mention was made regarding the use of special UniveX film loads. Pignone adamantly expressed his disapproval of the idea, insisting that a standard film format was essential to the success of the design. Management was hardly in a position to argue — substantial financial damage had recently been sustained by Universal, resulting from the shortage of its foreign-made non standard film. Nearly 10 years would pass before Universal would attempt once again to use another non-standard film load in one of its cameras.

Initially, management wanted Pignone to concentrate on the development of a 35mm SLR design that would adapt suitably to the low cost volume production methods used at Universal. Management was somewhat

Fig. 3-23 Photographs taken with the "Microflex Camera". Shown above are four test photographs, taken in 1937, with the "Microflex" camera on 16mm film. Three of the prints have been enlarged to three times their original contact print size. One contact print has been included for sake of comparison. These photographs may well be the World's first from an eye level SLR camera. (Courtesy: Joseph Pignone)

concerned that production costs would be relatively high for the half frame 35mm "Pignone Reflex" design, resulting in a retail price that was out of range for the average UniveX customer. For this reason, Githens and Shapiro expressed interest in a 35mm SLR that was simpler and less complex than the 35mm "Pignone Reflex" design — something more consistent with the UniveX line of cameras. This, Pignone assured them, he could accomplish.

Upon joining the staff at Universal, Pignone was asked to assign his 1937 pending patent application to the company, the contents of which referred primarily to the "Pignone Reflex" design. Principal design features specified in the 1937 patent application were the following:

1) a combination cross-sliding focal plane shutter and reflex mirror;
2) the use of a shutter capping plate to regulate the amount of light exposure to the film;
3) a film advance lever which simultaneously advanced the film and cocked the shutter with a single stroke;
4) an optional operating mode for making quick successive exposures by repeatedly stroking the film advance lever. In this mode, the shutter release button need never be used.;
5) a depth of field preview button;
6) a body mounted synchronized flash plug receptacle;
7) the use of a pentaprism for eye level viewing and focusing;
8) control settings that were easily viewed and adjusted from above the camera.

Not long after Pignone was hired, a sudden change of plans occurred at Universal. Strange as it was, management asked Pignone to put aside all work on the 35mm SLR design and, at the same time, abandoned all interest in the patent application recently assigned to the company by Pignone — a very foolish and short-sighted decision it would seem! A 35mm SLR camera such as this would have astounded the photographic industry, putting Universal years ahead of its competitors. Nevertheless, Pignone was instructed to begin preparation of another design — a 2¼ inch square format SLR camera with waist level viewing. Management had already contacted Ilex regarding a standard front leaf shutter for use on the new camera. Pignone was perplexed. Managerial affairs had become somewhat closed-mouthed, almost secretive in some instances, presumably due to the company's critically poor financial state at the time. In the days and months that followed, management made little or no attempt to explain its reasons for aborting a project as significant and consequential in nature as that of an eye level reflex camera design.

After giving much forethought to the design of a 2¼ inch square format SLR camera, Pignone perceived that a waist level viewing SLR camera equipped with an uncoupled standard front leaf shutter as such, would be relatively inconvenient to operate. With this in mind, Pignone invented a leaf-blade shutter intercoupled with an automatic preset iris diaphragm (U.S. Pat.#2,380,610). Once the self-contained shutter model was completed and perfected, Pignone started design work on Universal's 2¼ inch square format waist level SLR model. Equipped with the recently completed diaphragm/shutter mechanism, the working camera model included a pioneering body mounted "cocking lever" which simultaneously set the shutter, auto diaphragm, reflex mirror and capping plate. A full stroke of the lever forced the reflex mirror and capping plate to swing down and back, preventing any light from reaching the film. The shutter and diaphragm leaves then automatically opened and remained at their maximum apertures, facilitating viewing and focusing. At this point, the camera was fully "loaded" or "cocked" and ready for preselection of the aperture setting and shutter speed. Because of the large film format of this design, the top speed of the low cost shutter was limited to ½₀₀ second, although Ilex indicated to Universal, with reasonable certainty, that a faster shutter speed of ¼₀₀ second could be attained. Upon actuation of the shutter release, the shutter leaves automatically closed; then in turn, the reflex mirror and capping plate swung upward — the mirror, sealing off all extraneous light from the ground glass, and the capping plate, unmasking the film in preparation for the upcoming exposure. The diaphragm leaves then shifted to the preselected aperture, after which time the shutter leaves opened for the preselected exposure time and then closed. The finished working model appeared very similar to the "Reflex Camera" illustration shown in Universal's patent, U.S. Pat.# 2,356,880 *(Fig. 3-24)*. The patent specified that film advancement was performed manually by means of a conventional winding knob, but further development work on the model eventually resulted in coupling the shutter and film transport systems. Initially, several short strokes of the cocking lever were required to move the paper-backed film along until the number "one" appeared in the red window on the camera's back cover. After the first exposure was made, each full stroke of the lever would cock the shutter/ diaphragm mechanism and also advance the film for subsequent exposures.

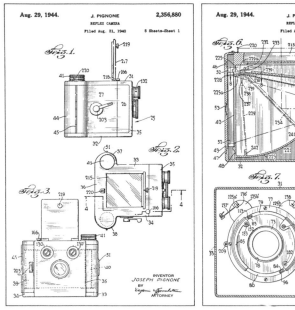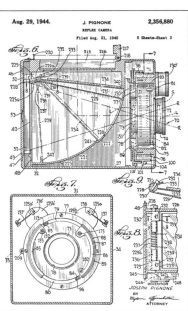

Fig. 3-24 The Universal 2¼ inch square SLR Camera Design. U.S. Patent #2,356,880 filed by Universal on August 21, 1940 depicting a waist level reflex camera invented by Joseph Pignone.

After months of work, the working model was finally complete and perfected. Management was exceptionally pleased with the camera's performance, although one aspect of the camera's operation appeared objectionable — the large reflexing mirror produced a loud "plop" each time an exposure was made. Management's conjecture was that such a noise would hamper public appeal for the camera. Despite widespread admiration from members of

Universal's Engineering and Sales Departments, management decided not to approve the working model for production.

Several weeks later, after giving much thought to the matter, management approached Pignone regarding a solution for the problem of excessive mirror noise. All agreed, logically speaking, that the noise resulting from the large reflex mirror mechanism would be significantly reduced in a smaller formatted camera equipped with a smaller reflex mirror. On this note, management decided Pignone should resume work on the 35mm SLR project, although this time around, their ideas for a 35mm SLR design were far more advanced in nature than previously characterized to Pignone when he first joined the company one year earlier. Management's interest in a more complex 35mm SLR model prompted Pignone to unveil, for the first time, a camera design drawing, self-rendered in 1938, depicting a sophisticated 35mm eye level SLR camera, called the "Pignone Speedflex" *(Fig. 3-25)*. Management took an immediate liking to the "Pignone Speedflex" design and asked that Pignone begin preparation of the design layout for Universal's 35mm eye level SLR prototype.

The design and construction of Universal's 35mm reflex prototype began late in 1940 and was completed several months later in 1941. Eye level viewing was accomplished through the unprecedented use of a pentaprism. The perfected automatic diaphragm/shutter model previously used in the 2¼ inch square format SLR working model was reduced to fit the 35mm full frame format. Because of the smaller shutter mechanism used in the 35mm SLR prototype, the top shutter speed attainable was ⅟₅₀₀ second, reasonably high for this particular type of shutter. In an effort to reduce the overall manufacturing cost, Universal located several available vendors who were willing to construct and preassemble the automatic diaphragm/shutter mechanism at a very reasonable cost. Many other internal parts previously used in the 2¼ inch square format SLR working model were similarly scaled down and incorporated into the 35mm SLR design. One pioneering feature of Universal's 35mm SLR prototype was a "single stroke" film advance lever, located on the camera's top right deck. A common sight on many 35mm cameras today, the film advance lever automatically advanced the film, cocked the shutter and its preset diaphragm, and activated the film exposure counter — all with a single stroke. Another unique feature included on this prototype was an optional operating mode, whereby a series of exposures were possible in rapid sequence of one another. (This feature was first conceived by Pignone in 1937 as part of the design for the "Pignone Reflex"). The problem of camera shake during rapid sequential shooting received much consideration. In this special operational mode, the shutter would not trip until the film advance lever was automatically on the return, a moment before it reached its starting, or resting, position. The shutter release button was rendered inoperative while in this special mode where repeated strokes of the film advance lever would automatically set and trip the shutter indefinitely.

Additional features incorporated into Universal's 35mm SLR prototype were a depth of field preview button, a synchronized flash clip, a built-in extinction exposure meter and an auxiliary telescopic viewfinder primarily intended as a "quick-sighting" device. The prototype was also designed to accommodate the use of several interchangeable lenses. The particular lens system used on this prototype consisted of a fixed lens group located directly behind the shutter blades and an interchangeable lens group in the front. The "normal" front lens group could be interchanged with either a "telephoto" or "wide angle" lens group. The "normal" lens group provided a focal length of 45mm, whereas the telephoto lens group provided a focal length of 90mm. As seen in the "Pignone Speedflex" drawing, all settings

Fig. 3-25 The "Pignone Speedflex" Camera Design. Features of the "Pignone Speedflex" design are shown here in a frontal view. Appearing from left to right, beginning at the camera's top deck are these characteristic features:
1) Shutter Release 2) Exposure Counter Dial 3) Delayed Timer Dial
4) Cable Release Socket 5) Loading Lever for Timer 6) Synchronized Flash Clip
7) Rewind Knob (not visible on far deck) 8) Film Reminder (not visible on far deck)

Appearing left to right, on the front of the camera are these additional features:
9) Shutter Speed Knob and Display Window
10) Lens Focusing Dial and Distance Display Window
11) Threaded Interchangeable Component Lens
12) Depth of Field Preview Button
13) Aperture Knob and Display Window
14) Auxiliary Telescopic Viewfinder Window
15) Extinction-type Light Meter Window

Note: *This drawing was rendered by Pignone in 1938 when his 1937 patent application was still pending. As in Pignone's earlier drawing of the "Pignone Reflex", the "single stroke" film advance lever was not included by request of Pignone's patent attorney. (Courtesy: Joseph Pignone)*

(distance, aperture, shutter speed) could be easily adjusted and viewed from atop the camera. In an effort to reduce production costs to a minimum, the delayed action timer dial, appearing in the "Pignone Speedflex" drawing, was not included in the construction of Universal's prototype. In every other respect, Universal's 35mm SLR prototype appeared nearly identical to the camera depicted in the "Pignone Speedflex" drawing.

Universal's 35mm prototype consisted of four main parts — an aluminum die cast body and rear cover, a lens housing and a deep drawn sheet metal top deck. Slight difficulties in die casting necessitated a few minor modifications from the "Pignone Speedflex" design, such as repositioning the neck strap lugs from the camera's top deck to the sides of the camera body. Cost projection for die casting the new 35mm model was figured only slightly higher than that of the Mercury. The camera was designed to provide many sophisticated features and still carry an "affordable" UniveX price. Universal predetermined that manufactured replicas of this prototype would retail for approximately $60-$70. At the time, other foreign or domestic waist level SLR cameras on the market were generally priced at $150-$300!

Incredible as it seems, Universal never filed a patent on its 35mm SLR prototype, thereby allowing its pioneering feature of unprecedented eye level pentaprism viewing to remain completely unprotected by patent law. The patent application filed by Universal on August 21, 1940, and issued in 1944 (U.S. Pat.#2,356,880), focused basically on the company's 2¼ inch square SLR working model. However, it is important to note here that the 21 claims specified in that patent were widely inclusive and adequate to have also covered some of the other features found on Universal's 35mm SLR prototype. Legally under this patent, Universal could have marketed exclusively, for 17 years after 1944, a reasonably priced camera so far advanced in concept that competition would have been restricted for years to come.

While following through on the finished 35mm prototype's development, Pignone learned that Universal would soon become entirely engaged in the manufacture of binoculars for the Armed Forces. As a result, further development of this prototype was discontinued. Specific and thorough testing was never completed, although preliminary tests conducted earlier indicated that the prototype was entirely functional, without any discernible complications. Universal was forced to shelve the entire project until such time that peacetime production of photographic products could be resumed once again.

As the prospect of WW II grew closer every day, Universal became deeply involved in the development of a method of mass producing binoculars. Pignone resigned from Universal in March 1941 and was henceforth employed as Chief Design Engineer of the Instrument Division at Thomas A. Edison, Inc. There he was predominantly involved in the invention and development of aircraft instruments, in addition to development of a fuse for anti-aircraft gun shells. During the latter half of World War II, Pignone was Supervisor of Design at Carl L. Norden, Inc., makers of the famous Norden Bombsight. He continued his career as a successful inventor and design engineer with several large corporations until his retirement in 1970 from the Charles Beseler Co., where he held the position of Senior Design Engineer for 10 years.

Githens and Shapiro failed to recognize the significance of the situation that was laid before them. After the war's end, work on the 35mm SLR prototype was never resumed. This was an irresponsible and costly blunder for Universal, one which Githens and Shapiro would certainly regret having made. Universal's managers demonstrated further imprudent behavior when they inexplicably and naively failed to acquire patent rights on such a photographic triumph, thereby permitting companies world-wide, to market reflex cameras in the United States, incorporating some of Universal's original features. If, in 1940, Universal had applied for and been granted a patent on the innovations in Pignone's 35mm SLR design, particularly eye level viewing, Universal's stature in the postwar photographic world would have been considerable indeed. Unfortunately though, Universal was never to regain the prosperity and success it had once known.

CHAPTER THREE - PART THREE

1938-1941

"NOW EVERYONE CAN AFFORD A CANDID CAMERA"

By this time, Universal was known the world over as a volume manufacturer of amateur photographic equipment. Most of Universal's cameras were very inexpensive indeed, generally considered inadequate for serious photographic purposes; nevertheless, they were extremely dependable cameras — providing millions of people with the opportunity to enjoy picture-taking for the very first time. It would not be unreasonable to speculate that a number of these photographic hobbyists eventually developed a serious attitude toward photography, directly attributable to their initial experiences with a simple UniveX camera.

Astounding sales of Universal's six exposure #00 rollfilm assuredly contributed to the company's prosperity in its first years of business. As the interest in candid cameras began to grow among amateur photographers, sales of the Model A and Model AF cameras began to falter. UniveX #00 rollfilm sales showed a similar decline because the Model A and the Model AF cameras were the only Universal cameras utilizing this particular filmload. In an effort to revitalize film sales, Universal designed a line of inexpensive candid cameras for use with the six exposure UniveX #00 rollfilm. Prior to the introduction of the Mercury I, in April 1938, Universal introduced the UniveX Iris Standard Candid Camera *(Fig. 3-26)*, first in a line of candids which the company would continue to produce for the next three years. One of Universal's 1938 advertisements encouraged people to "Get Out of the 'Snapshot Class'!" with the purchase of an Iris Standard Candid Camera for only $5.95. An eveready case was available for an additional $2.00. The camera housing was die-cast in a zinc-based alloy and then finished in black enamel — the result was a rather compact, weighty camera of approximately 19 ounces. The basic design of the camera included a single speed UniveX twin leaf shutter (I (⅒₅), plus T and B), a four stop iris diaphragm and an Ilex 50mm doublet lens set in a collapsible mount. The lens was of the fixed focus type. The Iris Standard sported these additional features: an optical eye level viewfinder, tripod and cable release sockets, and an inside storage compartment for one extra UniveX filmroll.

Immediately after the introduction of the Iris Standard, Universal followed with the UniveX Iris Deluxe Candid Camera *(Fig. 3-27)*, priced slightly higher at $7.50. The exterior appearance of the Iris Deluxe was far more appealing than that of its predecessor. Front and back, the camera body was covered

Fig. 3-26 The UniveX Iris Standard Candid Camera.

in black leatherette with the "Iris" trademark name stamped in white on the front of the camera: a satin-like chromium finish over the remainder made it a fairly attractive candid camera. Except for the exterior appearance, the Standard and Deluxe Iris models were alike, feature for feature. Early 1938 promotional ads for the Iris Deluxe clearly depicted and listed it as a "fixed focus" camera, as was the Iris Standard. Universal had second thoughts regarding this particular feature, because additional product information released by the company indicated that a new "focusing" Iris Deluxe would soon be available. Shortly thereafter, production of the "fixed focus" Iris Deluxe was discontinued and all "fixed focus" models remaining at the

Fig. 3-27 The UniveX Iris Deluxe Candid Cameras, two versions — the original fixed focus model (left) and the later more common focusing model (right).

Fig. 3-28 The UniveX Iris Standard Flash Candid Camera.

Fig. 3-29 The UniveX Iris Deluxe Flash Candid Camera.

factory were quickly converted to "focusing" models. Because of its extremely short period (one or two months) on the market, the original "fixed focus" Iris Deluxe model should be considered very scarce and difficult for the collector to obtain.

Universal pioneered the concept of internal photoflash synchronization, minus the external wiring typically found between camera and flash, with its incorporation of the hot shoe feature into the design of the Mercury I. By mid-1939, this important feature was also added to the Iris line, after which time the following two "flash" models appeared on the market — the UniveX Iris Standard Flash Candid Camera *(Fig. 3-28)* for $6.95 and the UniveX Iris Deluxe Flash Candid Camera *(Fig. 3-29)* for $8.50. Except for the addition of a factory-mounted hot shoe attachment, the Iris Flash Candids were nothing more than duplicates of the respective "non-flash" Iris models. The photoflash synchronizing attachment was constructed as a single die-cast part: fitted onto this was a flash clip and a convenient pushbutton mechanism to facilitate tripping the shutter. With this simple factory add-on, Universal was able to increase sales on an already popular line of candid cameras. A ½ inch "stop arm" was also added to the standard and deluxe flash models, preventing the user from tripping the shutter release while the collapsible lens tube was still in its innermost position. When the lens tube was fully extended to the picture-taking position, the shutter release lever was simultaneously moved clear of the stop arm, allowing the user to effectively actuate the shutter. Not only did this prevent pictures from being spoiled, it more importantly prevented expensive flashbulbs from being wasted on already ruined pictures. The stop arm projected from the lens mount plate immediately beneath the shutter release lever and, on most models, was die cast as an integral part of the lens mount plate. A small number of early flash models either lacked the stop arm altogether or were fitted with a screw-mounted stop arm instead: these models are rarely seen today.

In a little over one year's time, Universal had manufactured five different Iris Candid cameras — all derivatives of the original design invented in 1938 by George Kende. From the start, Universal had attempted to gain as much mileage as possible from its designs by producing more than one camera or projector model from each basic design. In most cases, it was simply a matter of adding one or two features to the design of a previous model or, at best, making a few minor improvements to a previous design. This trend in production design was distinctly demonstrated with Universal's introduction of five different Model AF Folding Cameras. All of these cameras evolved from just one basic design: this pattern was similarly manifested in the design of Universal's first movie cameras and projectors. Universal continued this practice throughout most of its years in business — it was, after all, one of the least costly methods of designing and manufacturing a steady stream of new products.

Universal introduced two final variations of the Iris design during the 1939 Christmas season — the UniveX Zenith Candid Camera *(Fig. 3-30)* and the UniveX Zenith Flash Candid Camera *(Fig. 3-31)*. The Zenith Candid was die-cast in lightweight aluminum and weighed approximately 13 ounces, 6 ounces less than the Iris Candid. (Some of the last Iris Deluxe cameras manufactured by Universal were also constructed of aluminum and, for this reason, weighed approximately the same as the Zenith Candid). Much like the Iris Deluxe, the Zenith camera body was covered, front and back, with black leatherette: the rest of the camera body had a polished chromium finish. The Zenith Candids included several advanced features not found on any of the Iris models. Included in the design of the Zenith was a non-collapsible f/4.5 UniveX 50mm lens with a micrometer focusing scale that focused to a

Fig. 3-30 The UniveX Zenith Standard Candid Camera.

Fig. 3-31 The UniveX Zenith Flash Candid Camera.

minimum of 3½ feet. The Zenith Candid also incorporated a UniveX Ilex Precise shutter, set between the lens, with four speeds up to ½₀₀ second, plus T and B. Priced at $12.50 and $15.00 respectively, the Zenith Candid and the Zenith Flash Candid became Universal's most advanced cameras designed for use with UniveX six exposure rollfilm. A marked eveready case was designed to fit either the flash or the non-flash Zenith model.

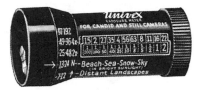

CANDID EXPOSURE METER

A candid-type exposure meter that adjusts automatically for film speeds, filter factors and types of subjects. Settings for shutter speeds up to 1/1250th of a second and for "*f*" stops from *f*1.5 to *f*22. General Electric Molded Construction, with official Weston film speed ratings. Calibrated for color film. Insures properly exposed pictures under all conditions. Compact, protective screw-tip case. Dust proof and water proof.

(Including case) . . . . . . *No. M-12* **$1.95**

Fig. 3-32 The UniveX Candid Exposure Meter.

Universal offered a number of accessory items for use with its new line of candid cameras. The UniveX Cable Release, priced at $.35, and the UniveX Table Tripod, priced rather high at $7.00, are two UniveX accessory items seldom to be met with. More than likely, these items were unmarked, making it extremely difficult to identify them as UniveX products. It is not unusual to find a dozen different cable releases that do not specify a manufacturer or distributor. The same holds true for small table top tripods from this period of which many are unmarked. The only possibility of verifying the manufacturer on an unmarked item such as this would be to obtain it directly from the original owner or be lucky enough to find the item still in its original factory box. For an example, Universal offered a gift box set that included an Iris Deluxe camera, an Iris eveready case and a UniveX cable release. Universal also offered a selection of slip-on UniveX Filters in a variety of sizes for its still and movie cameras. One example was the UniveX No.15 filter recommended for use on the Zenith or the fixed focus Iris, available in red, green, 2X yellow and 4X yellow. One of the more well-known UniveX accessory items was the UniveX Candid Exposure Meter *(Fig. 3-32)*, also termed the UniveX Photometer. Its tubular design and construction was identical to that of the UniveX Cine Exposure Meter. By rotating two end rings, adjustments could be made for subject type, film speed, filter factor and lens speed. The extinction-type candid meter featured diaphragm settings ranging from f/1.5 to f/22 and shutter speed settings ranging from ½ to ¹⁄₁₂₅₀ second. The meter was calibrated in accordance with the Weston Speed

Rating System, although a film speed conversion chart for other rating systems was included with the meter. (Note: If a strong odor is detected upon opening the meter's plastic case, prior to any further handling, please refer to the section in Chapter Two on the UniveX Cine Exposure Meter as it contains some important information relating to this problem.)

Fig. 3-33 The UniveX Corsair I Candid Camera.

After expanding the Iris line, Universal turned its attention to a completely new design that was also introduced in 1939 — the UniveX Corsair I Camera *(Fig. 3-33)*, a low-priced double frame 35mm candid camera, originally priced at $16.75. Less than 5,000 Corsair I cameras were produced by Universal between 1939 and 1941. The Corsair I utilized the same gear-based UniveX #218 or #236 filmloads originally used in the Mercury I. The UniveX #200 series filmloads, when used in the Corsair I, rendered 10 or 20 double frame exposures. A built-in shutter release button was incorporated into the design of this camera in addition to a factory-mounted combination extinction exposure meter/optical viewfinder attachment. A three-ring exposure calculator located on the rear of the camera body was designed for use in conjunction with the extinction exposure meter. The Corsair Exposure Calculator was far less complicated to use than the Mercury Exposure Calculator as it did not involve such specific settings as time of day, season of the year, etc. Other characteristic features included in the design of the Corsair I were a built-in flash synchronizer clip, an exposure counter and an f/4.5 UniveX 50mm lens set in an auto-retractable mount, with a minimum focusing capability of three feet. The automatic film transport system was intercoupled with a four speed rim-set leaf shutter with speeds up to ½₀₀ second, plus T and B. Constructed of lightweight General Electric

Textolite and weighing only 19 ounces, the Corsair I was essentially a very reliable camera for the amateur unable to afford more costly features such as lens interchangeability, faster shutter speeds and add-on accessory equipment (i.e. exposure meters, rangefinders, etc.). The larger double frame 35mm negative format, the built-in exposure meter and built-in synchronized photoflash clip all contributed to a camera that was well worth the price.

Late in 1939, after the onset of the war in Europe, Universal met with sudden financial difficulties. Gevaert's film shipments from Antwerp, Belgium ceased abruptly and Universal was immediately faced with the problem of locating a film manufacturer in the United States for the production of its special UniveX films. It was during the first six months of 1940 that all sizes of UniveX film were virtually unobtainable in stores across the country. Complaints regarding the unavailability of UniveX film were still being voiced months, even years later. Between 1940 and 1942, Universal assured its customers that two of the largest film manufacturers in America were busy producing substantial quantities of UniveX #100 Standard and Ultrapan movie film, in addition to the six exposure UniveX #00 Ultrachrome still film. By mid-1940 Gevaert had finished construction of its American factory located at 182 Cole Avenue in Williamstown, Massachusetts *(Fig. 3-34)* and Universal once again contracted with the company. This time though, Universal promised its customers that all UniveX films would be 100% "made in America". Universal also began purchasing film in bulk at a much cheaper price, after which time the company began spooling a certain portion of its own film. It was estimated that approximately 45,000 Mercury I and 5,000 Corsair I cameras were sold between 1938 and 1941, indicating the existence of a substantial demand for the UniveX #200 series filmloads. A shortage of raw materials in 1942 forced the company to offer its customers

Fig. 3-34 The Gevaert Company of America, Inc., Manufacturing Division Head Offices, 182 Cole Avenue, Williamstown, Massachusetts, 1940-1953.

only one of the three emulsion types (Ultrachrome, Microtomic, Ultrapan SS) previously offered for use in the Mercury I and Corsair I cameras — that being, UniveX #236 Ultrapan SS in 36 exposure lengths only. Universal continued to provide this UniveX #236 filmload well into the late 1940's.

UniveX film production and distribution remained in a state of turmoil for some time after 1939. In the midst of this precarious situation, Mercury I and Corsair I cameras were being thrown aside by confused and frustrated camera owners unable to purchase the required UniveX films. Further adding to Universal's problem was the growing popularity of Eastman Kodak's 35mm Kodachrome film. Dufaycolor film for Mercury and Corsair cameras had been discontinued by its manufacturer shortly after it reached the market, leaving UniveX camera owners without any possible means of photographing their subjects with color film. In an attempt to prevent the Mercury I and Corsair I cameras from becoming obsolete, Universal introduced the UniveX Daylight Loading Cartridge *(Fig. 3-35)* as a replacement for the UniveX #200 series filmload, and the UniveX Daylight Bulk Film Winder *(Fig. 3-35)*. Constructed of black and red bakelite material, the bulk film winder could be loaded with up to 100 feet of standard 35mm bulk film, either color or black & white. The gear-based metal film loading cartridge, with its swing gate lock, sold for $.60. Loading film into the cartridge was relatively easy with the UniveX bulk winder. Depending on which camera was being used (the single frame Mercury or the double frame Corsair), the bulk film winder would measure out the exact amount of film necessary for 18, 24 or 36 single frame exposures or, 10 or 20 double frame exposures. Sales of the Mercury I had shown a decline in 1940, so Universal decided to offer the camera at its regular price with the bulk film winder and two daylight cartridges

Fig. 3-35 UniveX Daylight Bulk Film Winder and UniveX Daylight Loading Cartridge.

included free of charge — a $4.65 savings. The UniveX Loading Cartridge and the UniveX Bulk Film Winder are today considered quite rare and difficult to obtain: seemingly more uncommon is the latter of the two items.

Universal realized it could no longer rely quite so heavily, as it had in the past, on the sale of UniveX film. As a "last ditch" attempt to keep the company solvent, Universal began manufacturing still and movie cameras that could be used with standard filmloads. The first still camera produced by Universal for use with a standard filmload was the UniveX Corsair II Camera *(Fig. 3-36)*. Manufactured in 1940, the camera was designed to use any standard 35mm black & white or color film cartridge. The Corsair II was identical to its forerunner, the Corsair I, except for certain changes that were necessary to accommodate the standard 35mm film cartridge instead of the UniveX #200 series filmload previously used in the Corsair I. Basically, a permanent take-up spool, rewind release knob and rewind key were added to the Corsair II, along with a different exposure counter and calculator to correspond correctly with the standard 35mm cartridges in use at the time. Introduced less than a year after the Corsair I, the Corsair II was priced at $19.75, only three dollars more than the Corsair I. The same eveready case, marked "UniveX Corsair", was used for both Corsair models. Universal ceased production of the Corsair II late in 1941, having produced approximately 2,700 cameras in two years.

Above:
Fig. 3-36 The UniveX Corsair II Candid Camera.

Left:
Fig. 3-37 The UniveX Uniflash Camera and Flash Unit.

After the introduction of the successful Mercury and Iris candid camera lines, Universal anticipated a growing interest in night time photography, or indoor flash photography, as it was more commonly referred to by camera enthusiasts. In February of 1940, Universal launched one of its largest advertising campaigns to promote a new synchronized flash candid camera outfit — the UniveX Uniflash Camera and Flash Unit *(Fig. 3-37)*. Packaged in a divided carton, the Uniflash camera and flash sold together as a set for $4.95 and could not be purchased separately. Full page ads promoting the "sensational" Uniflash appeared in many well-known publications like Popular Mechanics, Life and the New York Mirror. The Uniflash camera was advertised by Universal as the first low-priced "positively synchronized" flash camera. Furthermore, Universal emphasized that the Uniflash camera and flash unit were actually priced lower than many other non-flash amateur cameras. Eastman Kodak had reportedly shown great interest when Universal introduced the patented "hot shoe" feature on its Mercury and Iris candid cameras, not to mention the inexpensive synchronized Uniflash camera priced under the $5 mark. Apparently, Kodak met several times with Universal in an attempt to persuade the company to sell its patent rights to the Uniflash camera, special flash and synchronized shutter. As the story goes, Githens and Shapiro were firmly convinced the Uniflash would be a huge success for Universal and, for this reason, they declined Kodak's proposal.

Design work on the Uniflash outfit was completed in record time. Otto Githens and George Kende, Universal's President and Chief Engineer, were together responsible for the invention and ornamental design of the Uniflash camera. Meanwhile, Philip Brownscombe, the engineer who had worked closely with Kende on the Mercury, was primarily involved in the design of the synchronized flash unit for the Uniflash camera. Another Universal engineer, Richard Lotz, was responsible for inventing the shutter used in the Uniflash camera. The basic design of the Uniflash incorporated an optical viewfinder, a 60mm Vitar fixed focus lens, and a single speed UniveX behind-the-lens shutter (I ($\frac{1}{40}$), plus B). A special flash unit was provided with the Uniflash camera and, when used properly, the outfit was guaranteed to produce positive flash timing with perfect results or Universal would replace the spoiled film with a new filmroll. The flash unit had a threadless socket and an automatic bulb ejector button that eliminated the problem of handling hot flashbulbs. To operate the flash unit, two penlight batteries had to be inserted into a battery compartment inside the camera body. Unlike the Mercury flash unit, the Uniflash unit did not have a self-contained battery compartment. For this reason, the Uniflash flash unit could not be substituted for the Mercury flash unit on any of Universal's other flash model cameras. When the Uniflash flash unit was not being used, the battery compartment served as a storage compartment for two spare filmrolls. Designed for use with UniveX #00 rollfilm, the Uniflash had a sleek look to it, different from that of previous UniveX models. The Uniflash camera and flash unit were constructed of General Electric Textolite plastic and weighed only 10 ounces. Universal produced the Uniflash camera and flash unit in extremely large quantities, thus contributing to the outfit's unbelievably low price. Prewar sales figures indicated that the Uniflash was one of Universal's most popular cameras; therefore, the company decided to continue production of the Uniflash after World War II, making it the only prewar UniveX camera model reproduced for the retail market after the war. (The original Model A camera was manufactured again after the war, but distribution was limited strictly to premium offers). In 1947, the Uniflash sold for $8.75 — a far cry from the $3.98 price tag it held in 1942 when Universal was forced to clear its inventory in an effort to acquire desperately needed floor space for wartime production activities. Prewar and postwar Uniflash models differ in one respect only: all postwar models featured a "coated" lens for reduction of glare. In 1948, Universal discontinued production of the Uniflash — it was the only remaining Universal camera on the market utilizing the original six exposure UniveX rollfilm which had been introduced, along with the UniveX Model A camera, some 15 years earlier in 1933.

Fig. 3-38 The UniveX Flashing Display used in 1940 and 1941 to promote the Mercury, Iris Flash, Uniflash and Zenith Flash cameras.

Through the years Universal designed many unique window and counter displays — any of which would make interesting additions to a collection of Universal photographica. Most of these displays were offered to dealers for a token amount or free for the asking. One particular display originally offered to retailers in 1940 was so unique that it deserves special mention. The UniveX Flashing Display *(Fig. 3-38)* was used by retailers to display either the Mercury, Iris, Uniflash or Zenith flash models. The display depicted a life-sized man holding one of the UniveX flash cameras in front of his face, as though he were ready to snap a picture. Any one of Universal's four flash camera models could be secured directly onto the display. Interchangeable name panels for the Mercury, Iris, Uniflash and Zenith cameras were included for attachment to the lower portion of the display. The display's flashgun was specially wired to use an ordinary 120 volt bulb, flashing intermittently to emphasize the fact that UniveX cameras were equipped with built-in synchronized photoflash capabilities. Alternating illumination from the flashgun and the lower name panel created a rather eye-catching advertising form. "Motion" was another technique later incorporated into Universal's displays in an effort to attract the attention of people passing by store windows.

A few months after the introduction of the Uniflash, Universal announced yet another new camera. It was, in fact, the last still camera manufactured and distributed by Universal prior to the United States' entry into war in December of 1941. Priced at $4.95, the UniveX Twinflex Camera *(Fig. 3-39)* was radically different in design, as opposed to being just another by-product of another UniveX camera model. Universal described the Twinflex as the first "genuine" American-made reflex camera ever offered for under $35. "You Get The Picture You See!" was the sales slogan most often associated with the Twinflex. The camera utilized UniveX #00 rollfilm and featured a f/4.5 viewing lens, ground glass focusing to a minimum of three feet and a pair of matched lenses (viewing and taking), making it possible to view the focused picture before taking it. Parallax was reduced to a minimum because of the short distance between the viewing and picture-taking lenses. The Twinflex was a relatively small reflex camera constructed of General Electric Textolite plastic, with a folding metal hood to cover the ground glass viewing area. Universal produced two different versions of the Twinflex. One version of the Twinflex appeared frequently in Universal's brochures and advertisements and was boldly marked "UNIVERSAL CAMERA CORP." on the metal folding hood. The words "TWINFLEX, A UniveX Product" appeared on the front of the camera, between the upper lens and the hood, permanently formed into the plastic as part of the original design mold. On the more common version, the metal folding hood was marked only "UniveX" and a small metal plate, marked "Twinflex", was screw-mounted onto the face of the camera between the metal folding hood and the upper lens. The Twinflex case was constructed of an imitation leather material and sold for $1.50. The design of this front-opening case

Fig. 3-39 The UniveX Twinflex Camera.

Fig. 3-40 Cinemaster "Standard" Model D-8 Cine Camera with f/4.5 Ilex Univar lens.

was unique — it allowed for easy viewing and focusing of the camera without necessitating removal of the case and it provided special pockets on the inside of the case for storage of two UniveX filmrolls.

Universal was hard-pressed to repair the damages caused by Gevaert's unexpected termination of UniveX film shipments. For the most part, people were quite disturbed to learn that Universal was entirely dependent on a foreign supplier for its non-standard films. To appease both customers and retailers alike, Universal publicly gave its assurance that all UniveX films would thereafter be produced in the United States. With a serious dilemma hopefully in the past, Universal set out, determined to convince amateur photographers to rely on the company once again for all of their photographic needs. Universal attempted to accomplish this by developing a new array of products which were appealing, practical and, most importantly, unheard-of at such low prices — products that were certain to recapture the public's eye! Universal felt especially optimistic about the all new Uniflash and Twinflex cameras and with their timely introduction Universal hoped to eventually regain its foothold in the amateur photographic industry. Unit sales of the Uniflash and Twinflex cameras totaled approximately 200,000 by the end of 1941. Unfortunately, this in itself was not enough to put the ailing camera company back on its feet again.

Despite the fact that Universal had been operating under a huge deficit during the years of 1940 and 1941, the company was by no means ready to admit defeat. In the summer of 1941, Universal introduced a totally new line of 8mm movie cameras with interchangeable lenses known as the Cinemaster "Standard" Model D-8 Camera *(Fig. 3-40)*, the Cinemaster "Special" Model E-8 Camera *(Fig. 3-41)*, and the Cinemaster "Jewel" Model F-8 Camera *(Fig. 3-42)*. With the popularity of Kodachrome growing more and more each day, Universal was forced into the harsh realization that its cameras would almost certainly suffer a quick death unless they were built to accept a standard filmload. After giving the matter deep thought, Universal designed the three Cinemaster models with a Dual-8mm film system that would provide the photographer with a choice of filmloads — economical UniveX Single-8 film for black & white movies or standard Kodachrome Double-8 for color movies. The versatility of this Dual-8 system seemed to satisfy the customer and, at the same time, Universal was able to bolster its UniveX Single-8 film sales. In the first few months following the introduction of the Cinemaster line, Universal acquired over 30,000 orders for the Cinemaster

Fig. 3-41 The Cinemaster "Special" Model E-8 Cine Camera with f/3.5 Wollensak Univar Lens.

cameras. Unfortunately, a potential success was thwarted — before the first 15,000 cameras had passed through the production line, the United States became involved in war, forcing Universal to shut down almost all of its peacetime operations to begin tooling up for binocular design and production.

Depending on the particular model and lens combination chosen, the Cinemaster line of cameras was priced between $15.95 and $62.50. The least expensive model was the Cinemaster "Standard" Model D-8 Camera with a ½" Ilex Univar f/6.3 lens. Incidentally, this particular lens was the slowest lens ever offered by Universal on any one of its cine cameras. It was available only on the Model D-8 and was never sold separately. For a few dollars more, the Model D-8 could be purchased with a faster ½" Ilex Univar f/4.5 lens, previously used on the Exposition Model C-8 camera. Universal wanted to keep the cost of the Model D-8 near the

Fig. 3-42 The Cinemaster "Jewel" Model F-8 Cine Camera with f/3.5 Wollensak Univar Lens.

$20.00 mark for the people with "limited budgets"; for this reason, it was sold only in combination with one of the two above mentioned lenses. Universal did little to promote the Model D-8 in its media advertisements and announcements, primarily because it lacked many of the attractive features found on the other two Cinemaster models. Customers and retailers alike displayed little interest in the Model D-8; consequently, few were sold, making the Model D-8 Cinemaster one of the most difficult Universal cameras for the collector to obtain. The major factor supporting the rarity of the Model D-8 was Universal's sudden shutdown of peacetime production activities in December of 1941 to prepare for war contract work. This shutdown took place just a few short months after the prewar Cinemaster line was first announced to the public. Production was never resumed on any of the three prewar Cinemaster models. Evidence suggests less than 2000 Model D-8 cameras, 3000 Model E-8 cameras and 10,000 Model F-8 cameras were produced in 1941 by Universal. In its postwar years, Universal produced approximately 65,000 Cinemaster II Model G-8 cameras. In comparing the production figures of these four models, it is easy to see the relative scarcity of the prewar Cinemaster models.

Constructed of die cast metal and weighing approximately 32 ounces, the Model D-8 incorporated a built-in optical viewfinder, featuring two etched rectangular masks for use with the 1" and 1½" telephoto lenses. Because of the short distance between the viewfinder and the lens, parallax correction was necessary only in extreme close-up situations. Finished in a dark green enamel, the Model D-8 was designed as a single speed camera (16 frames per second) having an exposure time of $\frac{1}{30}$ second. The camera's spring motor provided six feet of film per wind, while an improved governor assured uniform film speed throughout the entire film run. The camera was additionally equipped with a tripod socket, a self-locking hinged film chamber cover, a focal plane reciprocating shutter, a footage counter calibrated for both Single-8 and Double-8 films, and a two-ring exposure calculator that allowed for various weather conditions, time of day, season of the year, type of subject and film rating. A Cinemaster eveready case with an accessory pocket could be purchased for only $4.95. The case, marked "Cinemaster", was all black and similar in construction to the Model A-8 deluxe eveready case, but larger in size. Universal redesigned the Cinemaster eveready case after the war. The new postwar case was front-opening and brown in color. The sides of the case had cut-outs to facilitate use of the camera's controls without having to remove the case.

The Cinemaster "Special" Model E-8 Camera was finished in an antique bronze enamel and included certain features not found on the Model D-8, particularly an extinction exposure meter which was built into the optical viewfinder. The Cinemaster Exposure Meter was similar to the Mercury Exposure Meter, consisting of a disc divided into eight numbered wedge segments of gradual, decreasing translucency. The brightest section was number "one" and the darkest section was numbered "eight". The meter was easily brought into position within the viewfinder frame by rotating a small knob on the outside of the camera body. After looking into the meter for a period of five seconds, the user selected the highest number that was clearly visible. The knob was then released, allowing the meter to spring back to its original position outside of the viewfinder area. The number selected from the meter was then transferred to the two-ring exposure calculator on the film chamber cover to produce the correct exposure setting for that particular scene.

The Model E-8 was designed for the more discriminating amateur photographer wishing to experiment with various special effects. The Model E-8 offered three speeds of 16, 24, and 32 frames per second and a special continuous run lock lever enabling the user to photograph himself. Universal offered the following selection of ½" lenses in combination with the Model E-8 camera: the f/1.9 Wollensak Univar, the f/2.5 Universal Univar, the f/2.7 Wollensak Univar and the f/3.5 Wollensak Univar. Telephoto lenses and filters could be purchased separately. Considering the features, the Model E-8 camera with the standard ½" f/3.5 Wollensak Univar lens was reasonably priced at $27.50.

The Cinemaster "Jewel" Model F-8 Camera was the top of the Cinemaster line, originally selling for $32.50 with the ½" f/3.5 Wollensak Univar lens. The Model F-8 was available in combination with the same lenses previously mentioned for the Model E-8 camera. Feature for feature, the Model F-8 was identical to the Model E-8 except for the gray enamel finish and the chromium panels on the front and back of the Model F-8. The front chromium panel carried a monogram shield: advertisements for the Model F-8 indicated that the camera could be "personalized" with engraved initials.

In connection with the new Cinemaster line, Universal introduced two "new" projectors in 1941 — the 100 watt UniveX P-300 Projector *(Fig. 3-43)* and the 200 watt UniveX PU-300 Projector. These projectors were almost identical to the Model P-8 and PU-8 projectors manufactured by Universal since 1936. In fact, small red nameplates, marked "Model P-300" and "Model PU-300", were placed over the marking "Model P-8" and "Model PU-8"

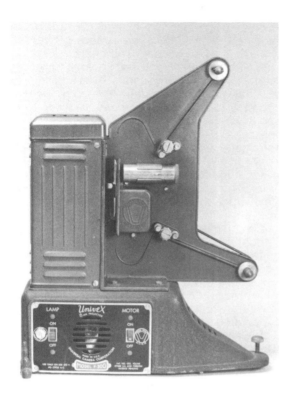

Fig. 3-43 The UniveX Model P-300 Projector with standard 1" f/2.7 lens.

on the original projector nameplates. The only other discernible difference was the color of the enamel finish. The Model P-300 and Model PU-300 projectors had a dark charcoal gray crinkle finish instead of the black finish originally found on the Model P-8 projector. With the standard unmarked 1" f/2.7 lens, the Model P-300 sold for $18.50, and the Model PU-300 for $21.00. Promotional ads for the Cinemaster line quite often included the 500 watt Model P-500 projector, at almost twice the cost of the Model PU-300. Due to the onset of war, the actual time that the Model P-300 and PU-300 projectors were produced and available on the market was extremely short, making them two of the rarest and most difficult Universal projectors for collectors to obtain. Once again, after the war's end, Universal decided to make use of these same projector dies to manufacture a number of other "new" projector models for the postwar photographic marketplace.

From 1936 through 1941, the following uncoated projection lenses were sold by Universal:

| 1" | f/3 | (unmarked) * | 1" | f/1.6 | Simpson Hi-Lux |
| 1" | f/2 | Ilex Hi-Lux | ¾" | f/1.65 | Simpson Hi-Lux |

* The unmarked standard 1" f/3 projection lens was replaced in 1941 by an unmarked lens of similar appearance advertised by Universal as the standard 1" f/2.7 lens. The manufacturer of either unmarked lens is not known.

After the war, the prewar projection lenses listed above were no longer available. In postwar years, Universal began selling the following line of coated lenses manufactured in the Universal optical shops.

| 1" | f/2 | Universal Hi-Lux | 1" | f/1.6 | Universal Superlux |
| 1" | f/2 | Universal Superlux | 2" | f/1.6 | Universal Superlux |

Fig. 3-44 One experimental modification of the UniveX Model A-8 Cine Camera — a permanently fixed viewfinder was substituted for the camera's original collapsible direct vision viewfinder.

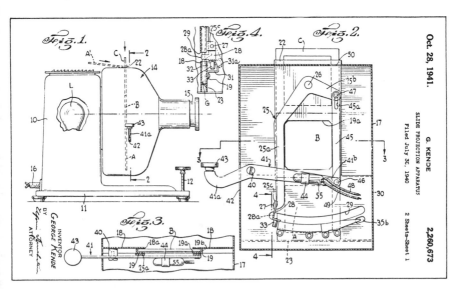

Fig. 3-45 An electric 2x2 slide projector design, depicted in U.S. Pat. #2,260,673, invented by George Kende.

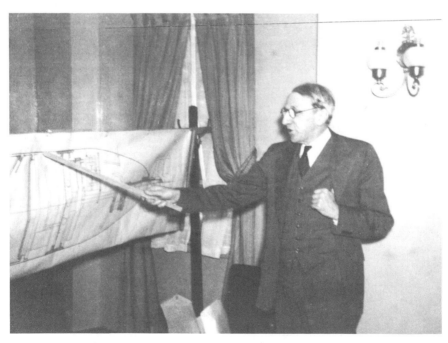

Many ideas for the design of new Universal products originated at monthly meetings of the Universal Engineering Staff, held informally at the Gramercy Park Hotel in New York City *(Fig. 3-46)*. In addition, staff members used this time to discuss possible modifications to improve existing products *(Fig. 3-44)*.

Universal designed and patented several photographic products which, for various reasons, never reached the production stage. One example was an electric 2x2 slide projector *(Fig. 3-45)* designed by George Kende in 1939. The design incorporated the use of an incandescent lamp in optical alignment with a conventional projection lens. Several slides could be inserted at once into the vertical guideway located at the top of the projector. After actuating a lever on the projector's right side, the slides would travel in a downward path until the first slide reached the bottom of the guideway. At that point, the slide was in the correct position for projection. After viewing the first slide, the manual lever was actuated once again, causing the slide to be channeled off to the left and automatically ejected out through a slot on that side of the projector. The remaining slides in the vertical guideway would automatically fall into their successive positions for sequential slide viewing. As this occurred, additional slides could be inserted into the top opening of the vertical guideway. If Universal had considered manufacturing a

Fig. 3-46 Informal photos taken at a monthly luncheon meeting held at the Gramercy Park Hotel in New York City in 1940. Photo #1 - Left to right: Universal Chief Engineer George Kende and guest speaker from General Electric. Photo #2 - Universal Engineer Otto Cazin, inventor of Corsair Camera and formerly of the Whitehead Corp., makers of torpedos, giving a lecture on the torpedo. Photo #3 - Left to right in center, Universal Engineers Philip Brownscombe, secondary inventor of the Mercury, and Joseph Pignone, inventor of Universal's 35mm eye level SLR prototype.

111

slide projector such as this, it would have been much to the company's benefit to simultaneously establish additional facilities specially equipped for slide processing and mounting. At the time, most photofinishers would not concern themselves with mounting 35mm single frame slides from cameras such as the Mercury, usually returning the processed strip of transparencies to the owner unmounted. Mounting an entire strip of single frame slides proved to be a very tedious home project for the Mercury camera owner. After giving it much thought, Universal felt there was little profit to be gained in manufacturing and marketing a slide projector such as this — it hardly seemed worth the extra expense and burden of establishing and operating film labs additionally suited for this specific purpose.

Universal's financial state had been weakened severely by the unexpected cut-off of UniveX film shipments. As a result, Universal was no longer bustling with enthusiasm and activity as it had in past years — instead, all peacetime operations were drastically curtailed. In 1940, Universal's net sales fell 42% from the previous year and the company's net profits took a similar plunge, leaving Universal with a year-end deficit in excess of $125,000. Eight years had passed since Universal first opened its doors: in that time the company had managed to surmount many obstacles to achieve undeniable success as a volume manufacturer of amateur photographic products. Success was short-lived and seemingly at an end for Universal. The large camera concern stood ruined and near bankruptcy.

CHAPTER FOUR - PART ONE

1941-1946

THE UNIVERSAL OPTICAL SHOP

Universal gained significant recognition during the war years for its timely development and implementation of efficient grinding and polishing methods in the mass production of precision lenses and prisms. These methods incorporated the use of several new automatically operated machines designed to regulate and speed the processes used to manufacture large quantities of precision optics. Moreover, this automated optical machinery made it possible for Universal to staff its entire optical plant with unskilled workers. All things considered, the mass production operation devised by Universal was a radical departure from the industry's tried and true methods of optical glassworking, methods which had remained essentially unchanged since the turn of the century. Every piece of Universal's optical machinery, including thousands of optical tools and lens blocks, was distinctly different in design from other optical grinding and polishing tools and machinery found elsewhere in the United States or Europe. With the exception of certain component parts, all of the lens and prism manufacturing equipment in Universal's optical shop was constructed in Universal's own toolroom by the company's own engineers and toolmakers.

Initially in 1936, while the UniveX Cine 8 line was still in the early stages of planning, Universal sought the services of a suitable American lens supplier. Previous to this, Universal's cameras had been fitted with lenses of German import. For the company's low-priced photographic products to gain mass appeal among the working class people of America, Universal knew it would have to rely almost totally on American manufacturers for labor and parts. Based on solid reputations of dependability and quality workmanship, Wollensak Optical Company and Ilex Optical Company were chosen to produce the lenses for Universal's cameras and projectors. In the next year, sales of the UniveX Cine 8 Camera skyrocketed, prompting Universal to increase what was already considered an extremely high production schedule. For all practical purposes, mass production of precision lenses was unheard-of at the time and, for this reason, it was not at all surprising that Wollensak and Ilex experienced difficulty meeting Universal's high volume demand. Aside from this, neither optical firm was equipped with the instruments necessary to accurately test lenses of the "interchangeable" type, such as those which were to become standard equipment on all of Universal's cine cameras. In light of these and other significant factors, it was clear that Universal needed an optical workshop of its own where more efficient mass lens production methods could be employed to produce precision lenses at great speed in quantities theretofore unheard-of in the optical industry. In October 1937, Universal allocated funds for the development of a research program to investigate the various methods used to grind and polish lenses, with particular emphasis on the formulation of more effective mass production methods. The knowledge acquired during this research program was fundamental in establishing a pilot optical plant put into operation at Universal's West 23rd Street factory, in January 1939, under the direction and supervision of George Kende, Universal's Chief Engineer. Initially, Universal employed approximately 100 unskilled workers to staff the new optical plant, but that number was significantly increased in December 1941 when Universal began conversion from peacetime activities to war production. During the war years, production of optical parts for Universal's binoculars was an around the clock operation necessitating approximately 400 workers in Universal's optical plant alone. Hundreds more were employed for the fabrication of metal binocular parts and the final assembly and testing of each binocular. During the 1940's, articles appeared in magazines such as Fortune, Popular Science and Sales Talk, explaining and outlining the quality controlled methods and machinery used at Universal for the mass production of lenses and prisms.

For many years, optical companies here and abroad conducted independent studies into the problems of mass lens and prism production. Typically, there was little or no exchange of ideas between firms, resulting in the employment of a wide variety of methods and machinery, none of which seemed to approach the concept of mass lens and prism production as a whole, from beginning to end. While most optical companies thought only to increase the number of grinding or polishing spindles per operator, Universal carried things a bit further. Multiple spindle machines designed at Universal were equipped with automatic timers to signal the end of each grinding or polishing cycle and directional nozzles to automatically apply a steady flow of lubricating fluid or polishing compound. The machinery typically used in most other optical production plants was not as well subordinated, much due to the fact that optical production in mass volume was generally an unaccepted theory by the optical industry. The common belief was that high quality optical elements could only be produced through slow and careful workmanship. This type of thinking allowed Universal to pioneer the development of optical manufacturing equipment and assembly line methods specifically geared for mass production. As far as efficiency and cost were concerned, Universal's operations far surpassed any other attempt at mass optical production known to the industry at the time.

With the conventional method of lens manufacture, lens blanks were put through four basic steps — roughing, trueing, smoothing and polishing; or, more simply stated — rough grinding, medium grinding, fine grinding and polishing. Before performing these steps, lens blanks were mounted in a group on a special metal base most commonly known as a lens block. Lens blocks came in any number of sizes and curvatures and were either dome-shaped for making convex lens surfaces, cup-shaped for making concave lens surfaces, or flat for making flat lens surfaces. The number of lens blanks that could be mounted on a particular size lens block ranged anywhere between 1 and 220, the exact number depending on the amount of space between each lens blank and the size of the lenses being produced. Most often, the lens blanks were secured to a lens block using molten wax or pitch compound and, in doing so, the utmost care had to be taken so that each and every lens blank was mounted on the lens block at precisely the same elevation to avoid varying thicknesses in the finished lenses. After mounting the lens blanks, or "blocking" as it was called, the lens block was placed on a spindle and then rotated at medium to high speed while a metal grinding tool, having a curvature exactly opposite that of the lens block, was placed on top and oscillated over the lens surfaces. A course grade of wet abrasive, such as emery, carborundum or synthetic aluminum oxide, was applied by hand to the grinding tool. After rough grinding the first side, the lens blanks were removed from the block, reversed and remounted so the same process could be repeated on the opposite side. In trueing, or medium grinding, a medium grade of abrasive was used; but, before progressing to this stage of grinding, it was extremely important that all of the courser abrasive particles left behind from the previous rough grinding operation were washed away to avoid any possibility of scratching or pitting the lens surfaces. After thoroughly rinsing the block of lenses, the lenses were then ground to a medium smoothness on one side and then removed from the block, reversed and remounted for medium grinding on the opposite side. Smooth grinding was carried out in exactly the same manner as the previous two grinding operations except an abrasive finer than the most expensive face powders was used. In polishing a block of lenses, a wet red oxide of iron paste, or rouge compound as it was commonly called, was carefully applied by hand to the polishing tool and then the tool was slowly oscillated over a slowly rotating lens block. Needless to say, in 1940, the conventional method of lens manufacture was not only time-consuming and tedious, but it was a job requiring great skill.

With Universal's new method of lens manufacture, the entire process was speeded considerably and the need for skilled workers was almost entirely eliminated. To accomplish this, Universal designed and built all new metal lens blocks which would retain a perfectly spherical shape indefinitely. Universal's lens blocks were also designed with machined recesses intended to simplify the otherwise time-consuming process of mounting lens blanks. With these new recesses, only a thin layer of pitch or wax was needed to mount the lens blanks onto the lens block and this, in turn, eliminated the problem of varying thicknesses in the finished lenses. Using these specially designed lens blocks, it was possible for the unskilled worker to perform what had previously been considered a skilled task. In another aspect of lens manufacture, it had always been conventional practice to remove all the lenses from a lens block, reverse them and remount them back on the lens block between each different stage of grinding and final polishing. At Universal, innovative thinking eliminated these repetitious steps — a block of lenses was put through every stage of grinding and polishing before removing the lenses and reversing them to grind and polish the opposite sides. According to an account provided by George Kende, Universal's Chief Engineer and Optical Shop Manager, it seems that Universal may have been the first optical shop to develop and utilize a "curve generating machine" with diamond-impregnated grinding tools for manufacturing precision optical lenses. Curve generators were originally used before the war by optical firms to grind spectacle lenses. As early as 1939 or 1940, Kende developed several automatic curve generating machines with hydraulic control for use in precision optical work. Operating at an extremely high speed, these curve generators were capable of rapidly removing excess glass from a lens and then producing an accurate curvature of medium smoothness in an approximate time of ten seconds to one minute without requiring the loose abrasives formerly applied during conventional rough grinding and medium grinding operations. The conventional rough grinding method took from ten minutes to one hour or more, depending on the size and curvature of the lens block being used. It wasn't until 1943 that

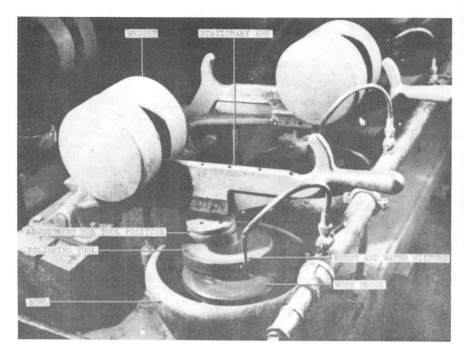

Fig. 4-1 Weighted stationary arm polishing tool machine designed by George Kende. Conventional polishing machines used oscillating arms.

other optical shops such as the American Optical Company and the Frankford Arsenal were reportedly using curve generating machines adapted from Delta drill presses — one for rotating the lens block and one for rotating the grinding tool. The polishing method employed by Universal involved extremely rapid rotation of the lens block under a weighted stationary arm polishing tool *(Fig. 4-1).* The stationary arm polishing tool did not impart the usual slow oscillating motion which was customarily seen on most conventional polishing machines. A continuous flow of re-circulated liquid rouge was directed at the rotating lens block until automatic timers signaled the end of the polishing cycle. A polishing cycle at Universal took approximately one hour and twenty minutes, as opposed to the conventional polishing method which averaged about three hours. In a conventional plant, one skilled operator attended to approximately one to six spindles, applying rouge by hand with a brush and making frequent inspections of the work; in Universal's optical shop, one unskilled worker operated approximately six to twenty spindles at a time. To say the least, the optical quality of the lenses and prisms manufactured at Universal was more than satisfactory during the war years and this can be substantiated by the following facts. Optics in second-rate binoculars were normally measured in tolerances of $\frac{1}{10,000}$ inch. At Universal, lenses were ground and polished to a tolerance of $\frac{1}{100,000}$ inch. Only the world's finest optical firms were able to manufacture optics within more precise tolerances such as $\frac{1}{1,000,000}$ inch or less.

Although production operations at Universal's optical plant had been conducted on a preliminary basis during 1939, the company managed to produce enough lenses to satisfy approximately 30% of its peacetime requirement. Universal's draftsmen, tool and die makers, and engineers had spent many months designing and building optical production machinery capable of mass producing lenses with little or no skilled labor. By mid 1940, Universal's optical shop was well established, having progressed to the point where production was more than double that of the average conventional optical plant. About this time, the British Government Purchasing Commission and U.S. Government began displaying interest in Universal's high volume lens production machinery, questioning whether similar principles could be applied to the formation of optical prisms for binoculars. Universal's engineers were certain that something could be done and began working on a design for an automatic prism grinding machine capable of forming 10-20 optical prisms at once without assistance from skilled opticians *(Fig. 4-2).* In meeting this challenge, Universal had one very distinct advantage over the other photographic and optical manufacturers — from its very first day in business, Universal's main concern had always been high volume production. Successful application of mass production concepts learned in previous years made it possible for Universal's engineers to approach the design and construction of an automatic prism grinding machine with great confidence. An automatic prism grinding machine was completed and fully operational by late 1941 and it was, without a doubt, radically different from anything in use at the time. News of the automatic prism grinding machine spread quickly throughout the optical industry — after all, the idea of mass producing optical prisms was considered entirely preposterous at the time. Despite an abundance of skepticism, Universal's automatic prism grinding machine proved to be an effective and functional piece of equipment that set the precedent for more advanced prism grinding and polishing machines that followed in years to come. Sophisticated prism grinding machines in use by some of the larger American optical companies today appear to be direct descendants of the automatic prism grinding machine designed and built by Universal in 1941. Almost all of the procedures, tools and machinery used in Universal's optical shop were original and drastically different from the other methods and equipment used in conventional optical plants. During the war, Universal provided the U.S. Government with designs for optical production tools and machinery such as lens cementing fixtures, lens centering and edging machines, prism end trimmers, pressure bombs, multiple spindle adjustably weighted lens polishing tables and diamond wheel automatic prism grinding machines. These and other Universal designed machines were immediately built according to the company's specifications and used for defense contract work in war production plants around the country. Government-owned optical production machines designed by Universal were said to carry the inscription, "built from designs donated by Universal Camera Corporation to the United States Government".

On March 2, 1942, Universal applied for a patent (U.S. Pat.# 2,352,551) on the automatic prism grinding machine, listing its inventors as George Kende, Universal's Chief Engineer, Eli Elison, a Universal designer, and Sten Johanson, Universal's Chief Designer. The Universal prism grinding machine was designed to perform three different operations — simultaneously grinding both sides of a prism, simultaneously grinding both corners and the top of the apex of a prism, and grinding both ends of the base of a prism. Although each of these grinding operations could be performed successively on one prism grinding machine, it was more cost effective to have three prism grinding machines operating simultaneously, each machine set up to perform one of the three grinding operations. With this latter method, prisms could be put through all three grinding operations without having to make mechanical readjustments before the start of each new

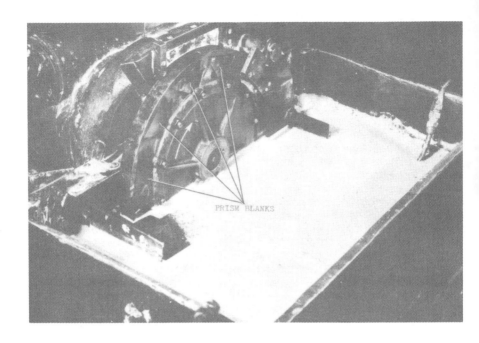

PRISM BLANKS

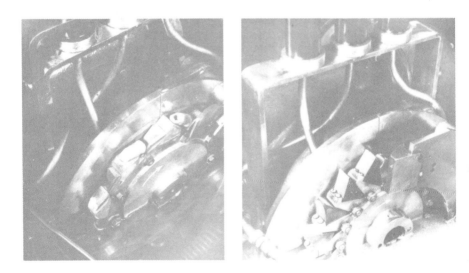

Fig. 4-2 Automatic prism grinding machine, designed by Universal Engineers George Kende, Eli Elison and Sten Johanson. Photo #1 - Grinding simultaneously both sides of the prism. Photo #2 - Grinding simultaneously two 45 degree corners and the top of the prism's apex. Photo #3 - Rounding one end of the prism's base.

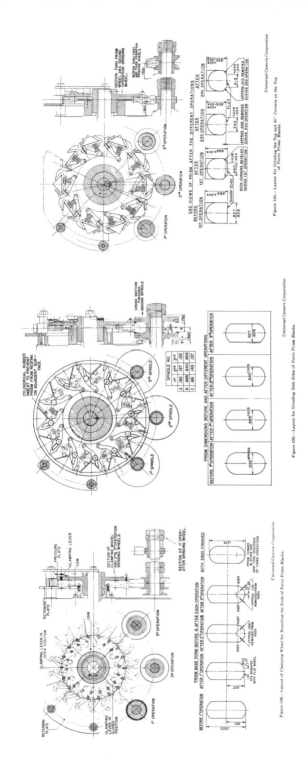

Fig. 4-3 Three diagrams of the Automatic Prism Grinding Machine showing its different clamping wheels, or work carriers, as they were also called.

grinding operation. It became a simple matter of removing the prisms from one machine after the first grinding operation was completed, then transferring them to another machine already set-up to perform the second grinding operation and so on. If only one machine was used, manual set-up adjustments for each different grinding operation required skilled attendance, but when three machines were used and set-up in advance, unskilled workers had only to insert the prisms into the machine and then remove them for insertion in the next grinding machine after an alarm signaled the end of each cycle. According to U.S. Army ordnance records, at least three automatic prism grinding machines were built by Universal for government contract work at an initial cost of $3000 each. After the war, approximately $550,000 worth of other government-owned tools, gauges, jigs, machinery and equipment were removed from Universal's plants. Universal retained only one automatic prism grinding machine in its optical shop for production of prisms used in a 6x30 commercial prismatic binocular sold by the company in the immediate postwar years.

The automatic prism grinding machine can best be described in the following manner. A metal wheel, known as a "work carrier", was constructed with a number of recesses spaced equally around its periphery. A single prism was inserted into each of the recesses, or "work seats" as they were called, and a clamping lever, extending out over each work seat, secured the prisms during the grinding process and automatically released them after grinding was completed. The work carrier revolved in a vertical plane at a very slow speed, approximately 8-10 times a minute, permitting the removal of completed prisms from the work seats and subsequent replacement with new prism blanks — all without ever having to stop the machine. One unskilled worker could easily perform this maneuver on several machines of this type at one time.

Three different work carriers were designed for use with the automatic prism grinding machine, each one having a completely different set of work seats designed to expose a different portion of the prism to the grinding elements. The first work carrier was designed for simultaneous grinding of both sides of a prism. Fully loaded, this specific work carrier held a quantity of twelve prisms. A second work carrier held a total of ten prisms and was designed for grinding the apex, or top, of a prism. A third work carrier held a group of eighteen prisms and was designed to round the ends of a prism, one end at a time in two successive operations.

A series of three grinding elements, operating at extremely high speeds in the same plane as the work carrier, were positioned at equal distances from each other just under the lower half of the work carrier. The grinding elements were set up to grind in a progressive manner. As a prism passed through the first set of grinding elements, a significant reduction of the prism's surface occurred, the second set of grinding elements reduced the surface a bit further and the third set of grinding elements completed the reduction process. The diamond grinding elements were comprised of single grinding elements and also mated, or paired, elements capable of grinding, for example, both sides of a prism or rounding both sides of a prism's base in a single operation. All three sets of grinding elements and the lower half of the work carrier were submerged in a basin of water attached to the front of the machine. Cool water was constantly recirculated through the basin to reduce temperatures during the grinding process. Interestingly, the slowly revolving work carrier and the high speed grinding elements of the automatic prism grinding machine were powered by a single motor unit — the shafts for the three grinding elements had direct pulley drives to the motor and the shaft for the work carrier was controlled by a speed reducer which also had a direct drive to the motor.

Fig. 4-4 The Universal Optical Shop. In postwar years, conventional multiple spindle oscillating arm polishing tables were also used by Universal.

Postwar photographs taken In Universal's Optical Shop and accounts from two former Universal managers employed with the company between the years 1946 and 1949 indicate that Universal either replaced or supplemented existing optical production machinery with more conventional optical production machinery *(Fig. 4-4)*. Reportedly, multiple spindle oscillating arm polishers were used instead of Universal's weighted stationary arm polishers and Delta drill presses were adapted for use with almost all of Universal's postwar lens grinding machinery. In addition to Universal's patented automatic prism grinding machine, the company adapted a Blanchard rotary grinder, originally employed for precision metal work, for use in polishing the faces of prisms. The Blanchard grinder used by Universal had a rather large rotary table charged with polishing rouge, approximately six feet in diameter. A quantity of prisms were inserted into a special brass carrier developed by Universal and then the carrier was placed between the rotating table charged with rouge and an upper non-rotating element. Unfortunately, after financial difficulties began to develop in 1948, the tools and machinery in Universal's Optical Shop saw very little use and, from that point on, there were almost no manufacturing activities carried out in this area of the factory.

To fully recognize the significance of Universal's wartime contributions, the circumstances confronting the U.S. Government and the American optical industry, just prior to the United States' involvement in the war, must first be understood. In many optical workshops in the United States and Europe, lens making in 1940 was still an operation being performed by expert optical craftsmen. Lens and prism makers were highly regarded workers of the optical industry, many having spent years and years developing their expertise in the trade. Many of America's finest optical workers had acquired their initial skills and training in Europe. With little knowledge of the English language, it was difficult for these workers to convey their skills to apprentice workers. It was even more unfortunate to discover a certain reluctance on the part of some of these workers to share the knowledge and skill they had acquired in Europe with other optical workers new to the trade. There were no optical trade schools to speak of where one could go to become trained in lens and prism making, only apprenticeships offered by some of the larger optical firms. In 1940, for instance, an apprentice worker at the Bausch & Lomb Optical Company would need to devote approximately one year to developing the skills of lens grinding. A period of at least four years could be spent learning the skills associated with hand polishing certain rangefinder lenses and an even longer span of five years developing expertise in the painstaking and meticulous art of hand polishing optical prisms.

At the time of the United States' entry into war, the U.S. Armed Forces required approximately 350,000 binoculars. This was an extremely large quantity, considering the fact that, in the entire peacetime year of 1940, a large firm like Bausch & Lomb had only produced about 10,000 binoculars. Bausch & Lomb was, however, the only company in America at the time producing binoculars in accordance with U.S. Navy standards. In 1941, Bausch & Lomb signed a government contract for the production of 20,000 6x30 binoculars. Unfortunately, this was not nearly enough — hundreds of thousands of binoculars were still urgently needed by the military and it was quite clear that Bausch & Lomb, regardless of its past experience in optical manufacturing and the vast expanse of its facilities, would not be able to single-handedly produce all of the nation's binoculars. As it was, the U.S. Government had other plans for Bausch & Lomb — the expertise of the well-established and highly respected firm would be required for the production of large quantities of optical glass and the design and construction of many sophisticated wartime optical instruments such as rangefinders, aircraft heightfinders, telescopic gunsights and periscopes. By order of the U.S. Army and U.S. Navy, binocular production at Bausch & Lomb was eventually curtailed, much to the point of becoming only a secondary operation at the plant. Several other private companies were later selected by the military to help supply the country with binoculars.

About the same time, in an effort to meet the nation's increased defense needs, the U.S. Government put out a nation-wide request for 350 qualified lens and prism grinders for employment in federal arsenals and navy yards; unfortunately, the Employment and Civil Services were unable to locate any available optical workers. It was evident that the vast majority of the nation's skilled lens and prism makers were already employed with private optical firms across the country. The U.S. Government immediately instituted a training program whereby a handful of supervisors and skilled optical workers were used to train hundreds of unskilled workers. Technical assistance was requested from Bausch & Lomb Company and Eastman Kodak Company. These two private optical companies worked closely with supervisors from the optical facility at the Frankford Arsenal in Philadelphia to assure the successfulness of the government optical training program. Three years later, by December 1943, a total of 750 workers staffed the Frankford Arsenal optical shops, with approximately 75 per cent having developed an extremely high degree of proficiency in their work. This, coupled with the industry's most modern machinery and equipment, made the Frankford Arsenal optical facility one of the most outstanding shops in the world, well-known during World War II for the strictest of standards in optical glassworking and for the production of some of the world's finest precision optics. Lenses and prisms produced at the Frankford Arsenal were said to equal German-made optics which were, for many years, considered second to none in precision and quality. Within three years of the institution of the optical training program, some 1300 individuals had received intensive training in optical work. After completion of the training program, the newly skilled workers either remained as paid employees of the Frankford Arsenal or were employed doing defense contract work at one of the private optical shops across the country.

The Frankford Arsenal supervised production at several plants selected by the government to assist the nation's larger optical firms with production of military binoculars. Bausch & Lomb offered to lend experienced personnel to help supervise initial operations in these newly selected plants, providing whatever assistance was necessary to get production running smoothly, as quickly as possible. Most of the companies knew little or nothing about manufacturing binoculars or optical glassworking. Initially, these companies were assisted with tooling and setup operations, general production activities and final testing of binoculars. In less than one year's time, with the assistance of Bausch & Lomb and the Frankford Arsenal, good quality military binoculars were being produced by Anchor Optical Company, the Kollsman Instrument Division of Square D Company, Nash-Kelvinator, Westinghouse Electric & Manufacturing Company, Research Enterprises Limited and Universal Camera Corporation. Other firms involved in the manufacture of binoculars were Hayward Manufacturing Company, National Instrument Corporation and Optical Film & Supply Company. Larger well-established firms such as Eastman Kodak, Wollensak Optical Company and Spencer Optical Company expanded their defense contract work to help circumvent the nation's critical shortage of precision optical instruments. Nash-Kelvinator and Westinghouse Electric & Manufacturing Company were chosen primarily because of the overall adaptability of their existing machinery for use in the production of binoculars. Operations at these two plants were limited strictly to the fabrication and assembly of metal binocular parts, with neither firm being involved in the manufacture of lenses and prisms. Optical elements were supplied to these firms by one or more of the 50 different companies under government contract at the time for production of lenses and prisms. Universal Camera Corporation, on the other hand, machined metal binocular parts and also produced optical elements for its binoculars.

On Saturday, March 13, 1943, nearly 3000 employees and guests of the Universal Camera Corporation gathered enthusiastically inside the Grand Ballroom of New York City's Waldorf-Astoria Hotel eagerly anticipating an exciting and memorable evening *(Fig. 4-5, 4-6)*. For many of these people, the

Fig. 4-5 Photograph of the 3000 Universal employees and guests attending the Award Ceremony in the Grand Ballroom of the Waldorf Astoria.

123

PRESENTATION PROGRAM

Musical Selections   LESTER LANIN and his Orchestra

Posting of the Colors   U.S. Army Color Guard

Master of Ceremonies   PERCIVAL H. CASE
General Manager, Universal Camera Corporation

Address of Welcome   J. J. SHAPIRO
Vice President, Universal Camera Corporation

Presentation of Army-Navy "E" Pins
COMMANDER E. B. OLIVER, U.S.N.

Acceptance of Army-Navy "E" Pins
RAY COOPER, GEORGE KENDE, *Chief Engineer*
JESSE NORDEN, *Prod. Mgr.*, JEANNE SCHRAGER,
MARY WALSH

MUSIC   DINNER

Address on Behalf of Employees   RAY COOPER

Presentation of Army-Navy "E" Award
COLONEL GORDON B. WELCH, U.S.A.

Raising of Army-Navy "E" Flag
U.S. Army Color Guard

Acceptance of Army-Navy "E" Award
O. W. GITHENS
President, Universal Camera Corporation

"The Star-Spangled Banner"
LESTER LANIN and his Orchestra

DANCING

Fig. 4-6 Pages from the original program passed out to those attending the Universal Army-Navy "E" Award Ceremony on March 13, 1943.

ensuing events would remain vividly clear in their memory for many years to come. On this date in time, Universal was bestowed the highly coveted Army-Navy "E" Production Award, an award presented by the U.S. Government to companies for exceptional performance in war production work *(Fig. 4-7)*. By the end of World War II, the Army-Navy "E" Flag had been presented to a total of 4283 companies. This represented only five per cent of all the companies involved in war production work. Synonymous with the words pride, ingenuity and excellence, the Army-Navy "E" Flag was awarded to Universal in recognition of its achievements in conquering countless obstacles previously associated with the mass production of prismatic binoculars. Particular attention was paid to the company's development of assembly line methods and automatically controlled machinery used in the mass production of lenses and prisms. Astonishingly, in 1943 Universal manufactured enough lenses, prisms and metal binocular parts to complete the assembly of an average of 11,000 binoculars per month. George Kende, Universal's Optical Plant Manager, recalled that production of binoculars at Universal climbed to 15,000 units per month by the end of 1944. Other optical companies were reluctant to divulge the exact number of binoculars produced at their plants during the war years, but the figures were believed to be only a "few thousand" per optical firm. If these figures were indeed correct, Universal had produced nearly six times the number of binoculars each month as opposed to other wartime optical plants. In postwar years, Universal boasted wartime production of binoculars in excess of "25 times the combined average monthly output of all American manufacturers in

WAR DEPARTMENT

OFFICE OF THE UNDER SECRETARY

WASHINGTON, D. C.

February 13, 1943

To the Men and Women
of the Universal Camera Corporation
28 West 23 Street
New York, New York

This is to inform you that the Army and Navy are
conferring upon you the Army-Navy Production Award for your
fine achievement in the production of war equipment.

This award consists of a flag to be flown above
your plant and a lapel pin, significant of major contribution to victory, for every individual in your plant.

The high and practical patriotism of you men and
women of the Universal Camera Corporation is inspiring.
Your record will be difficult to surpass, yet the Army and
Navy have every confidence that it was made only to be
broken.

Sincerely yours,

Robert P. Patterson
Under Secretary of War

*Fig. 4-7 Letter from U.S. War Department, dated February 13, 1943, informing
Universal that it had earned the highly coveted Army-Navy "E" Flag.*

prewar years". Whatever the exact figures in this case, it was an astounding feat for a company that had never even ground a lens or prism before 1939. By the end of the war, Universal had produced a total of approximately 250,000 binoculars for the American, British and Canadian Armed Forces.

The award ceremony began with an introduction from the master of ceremonies, Percival H. Case, General Manager of Universal. Jacob Shapiro, Vice President of Universal, gave the first speech of the evening, welcoming everyone present by stating —

"We here at Universal work with the firm resolve that every
binocular we make shall do full justice to commemorate the valor
of the soldiers and sailors and marines and all men and women
of the United Nations engaged in this total war effort."

On behalf of Under Secretary of War Robert Patterson and Under Secretary of the Navy, James V. Forestal, Col. Gordon B. Welch, U.S. Army, Chief of the Frankford Arsenal Instrument Division, presented Otto Githens, President of Universal, with the Army-Navy "E" Award *(Fig. 4-8)*. During his speech, Welch commended the employees of Universal for their fine work with the following remarks —

"You seized upon the new and ingenious in the manufacture of
lenses ... foresaw and forestalled the difficulty in the manufacture of
prisms to such an extent as to influence the development of the
entire optical industry of the country. When the machine tool
industry of the Nation was occupied in what appeared to be the
larger makings of tooling for guns and tanks, you circumvented
the shortage by adaption and original thinking. When tires for
armored cars and motor transports called for every ounce of the
Nation's rubber, you met the challenge by research into the very
corners of industrial chemistry so that today your binoculars are
covered in a manner to rival the best of Malaya's Latex ... You
have solved technical difficulties of great magnitude, problems
as knotty as any that have challenged the brilliant minds of
American industry ...

"Your citation is high. The Universal Camera Corporation and all
the people connected therewith, with high courage and devotion
to duty, and with products built for safety, has produced and is
producing those products of warfare required by the armed
forces in such quantities and of such quality as to enable the
armed forces to meet the enemy with every assurance of Victory."

Upon accepting the Army-Navy "E" Flag for Universal, Githens remarked —

"In the presence of such a great honor, it would be impossible to
stand here without a sense of overwhelming emotion, without a
feeling of deepest humility, and without a consciousness of the
enormous responsibility which this great honor imposes."

Fig. 4-8 The Army-Navy "E" Flag Presentation. Col. Gordon B. Welch, U.S. Army (left) presenting the Army-Navy "E" Flag to Universal President Otto Githens (right).

At the same time, Githens offered his sincere praise to the employees of Universal for a job well done. Silver "E" insignia pins were presented to representatives of the company by Commdr. E. B. Oliver, U.S. Navy in recognition of their individual contributions to the war effort. The award ceremony was attended by representatives from various photographic outfits such as Willoughby's, the Gevaert Company and the Wabash Photoflash Corp., along with officials from the U.S. Army, U.S. Navy, U.S. Marine Corps, British Ministry of Supplies and British Purchasing Commission. Reporters from the Brooklyn Daily Eagle and other area newspapers were also present to witness the ceremony. Technicians from WINS radio station were on hand with equipment to broadcast the entire event over the airwaves to the area's radio listeners. The award ceremony was immediately followed by a dinner-dance celebrating Universal's receipt of the Army-Navy "E" Flag and also the company's 10th anniversary as a peacetime photographic manufacturer.

In January and February of 1943, Universal and the U.S. Navy collaborated regarding the formation of a management group capable of supervising optical production at a number of other production plants. Since the start of the war, Universal had contributed a great deal of time and effort toward developing better mass production methods and machinery for use in the manufacture of binoculars and other optical instruments. The U.S. Navy was extremely pleased with Universal's progress in war production and relatively confident of the company's ability to handle the additional work of coordinating the new management group. In March 1943, the "Universal Management Group" was formed by Universal Camera Corporation for the initial purpose of directing operations at the National Instrument Corporation in Houston, Texas. Universal immediately assigned key personnel to the Houston plant to advise and direct the production of the 7x50 U.S. Navy Mark 32 Mod.1 binocular which National Instrument Corporation was already under contract to produce. Meanwhile, the demand for binoculars remained overwhelming as the war approached its peak. Having supervised all aspects of production on the 7x50 U.S. Navy Mark 32 Mod.1 binocular at the National Instrument Corporation, Universal was more than qualified to handle production of this particular binocular at its own plant in New York City. Later that year, Universal agreed to sign a contract with the U.S. Navy to produce 20,000 binoculars of this type. The Universal Management Group was coordinated from Universal Camera Corporation's main offices in New York City under the direction of George Kende, Universal's Chief Engineer. The Universal Management Group continued operating by order of the U.S. Navy until September 1945, when the war's end signaled an abrupt cessation to the production of military optical instruments. Naval records seem to indicate that Universal also supervised activities in 1944 at a Chicago plant, the Ajax Optical Company. A number of Universal employees were apparently sent to work at the Chicago plant where they became part of the Ajax payroll until the war's end.

From January 1942 to July 1944, Universal's activities focused primarily on the design and production of service binoculars and also the design and construction of specialized mass production optical tools and machinery used in the manufacture of binocular lenses and prisms (Fig. 4-9). In July 1944, another project, totally unrelated to binoculars, was undertaken at Universal. Although production of binoculars at Universal continued through the war's end, the new project assigned by the U.S. Navy consumed a good share of Universal's time and effort. At the request of the U.S. Navy, Universal assisted in the refinement and production of an electrically powered optical scanning instrument or "sun telescope", code-named Icaroscope (Fig. 4-10).

127

Fig. 4-9 A Universal advertisement concerning defense work at the plant, taken from "Popular Photography", June 1943.

Fig. 4-10 The U.S. Navy BuShips Icaroscope, Mark 1 Mod.0 (Type 1), a top-secret wartime instrument engineered and manufactured by Universal in 1945. Rear view, front view and view showing swivel bracket for shipboard mounting.

The name Icaroscope was taken from the mythical story of Icarus, a Greek lad having wings of wax. In the story, Icarus flew too close to the sun, letting the heat from the sun melt his wax wings. Consequently, Icarus fell to the sea and drowned. Initially, the Icaroscope was developed as a tool for observing and studying the solar disk itself — the U.S. Navy soon realized there were other, more important, uses for this instrument. Like many other wartime instruments, the Icaroscope was manufactured with a very specific purpose in mind. It had always been extremely difficult, if not impossible to sight enemy airplanes approaching from the direction of the sun. The Icaroscope eliminated this problem entirely by allowing one to see without difficulty aircraft approaching from the sun's direction at distances of 25,000 feet or more. Viewed through the Icaroscope, at a distance of 25,000 feet, the cross section of an airplane, approximately 10 feet in diameter, appeared as an image having an approximate diameter of 0.005 inches. Small images such as this were easily seen on the Icaroscope viewing screen due to its excellent power of resolution. The optical system of the Icaroscope consisted of a 1.3 inch aspheric doublet ocular lens with a focal length of 2 inches, an erecting roof prism providing a 75 degree angle of deviation, a 1.6 inch focal plane plate lens, and a 4.3 inch doublet objective lens with a 12 inch focal length. The Icaroscope provided a seven degree angle of view and six power magnification *(Fig. 4-11)*.

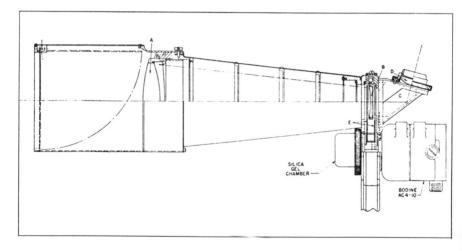

Fig. 4-11 Sectional view of the Type 1 U.S. Navy Icaroscope, Mark 1 Mod.0. Diagram shows (A) objective lens, (B) phosphor screen, (C) prism, (D) eyepiece lens and (E) rotating shutter blades.

The ability with which one was able to view the sun and surrounding sky clearly through the Icaroscope was accomplished through the use of a special afterglow phosphor developed at the University of Rochester in 1943 by Dr. Brian O'Brien, Professor of Optics and Physics, and Dr. Gordon G. Milne, also on staff at the university. Once exposed to light, phosphor had the ability of producing an afterglow that remained visible for some time, the exact time being dependent on the type of phosphor used. A layer of fine phosphor particles, 25 microns thick, was applied to a slightly concave glass disk, producing what was known as a phosphor screen. This phosphor screen was then incorporated into the construction of the Icaroscope. Extra fine particles of phosphor powder were used to achieve excellent resolution of small images. The phosphor material used in the Icaroscope, a "zinc sulfide-cadmium sulfide 'base' with a silver 'activator' and a sodium iodide 'flux'", was one that produced an afterglow of extremely short duration. A phosphor such as this was necessary to allow continuous movement of the Icaroscope during viewing without the formation of image trails on the phosphor screen from scenes previously viewed moments before. The phosphor used in the Icaroscope also exhibited what was technically known as an "upper-limit brightness response". In other words, when the phosphor screen was exposed to the sun and surrounding blue sky, the afterglow image of the sun appeared only 20 to 50 times brighter than the surrounding sky area. Viewed with the naked eye, the difference was obviously greater, the sun being 10,000 to 100,000 times brighter than the surrounding sky. The phosphor used in the Icaroscope had the ability to reduce the brightness of the sun without reducing the brightness of the surrounding sky, making it possible for the observer to view details in either area without the problem of glare.

The phosphor screen, yellowish-green in color, was positioned on the instrument's optical axis, in the focal plane of the objective lens, between two rotating metal disks. The relatively large size of the disks, approximately seven inches in diameter, contributed to the peculiar shape of the telescope-like instrument. Each disk had a sector opening, or aperture, which allowed it to act as a rotating shutter. The disk nearest the objective lens was rigidly fixed to a second disk positioned approximately ½ inch behind the first. The disks were coupled together in such a way that the sector openings were always in direct opposition of each other. This entire disk assembly was mounted on a shaft powered by a Bodino AC 4-10 motor operating on 115 volt 60 cycle alternating current. The motor's 10 watt input requirement also permitted the use of dry batteries or portable storage batteries as an alternative source of power. The disk assembly revolved at a speed of 2000 r.p.m., each single revolution or cycle allowing approximately ¹⁄₁₀₀ second for exposure and viewing of the phosphor screen. To the observer, viewing appeared continuous much like a high speed motion picture camera. The period in which the phosphor screen was exposed to light occurred during the first half of each cycle and the period for viewing the resultant afterglow image occurred during the second half of each cycle. More specifically, when light passed through the aperture of the front disk, the phosphor screen was excited and an image of the sun and surrounding sky formed on the phosphor screen. As the disk assembly continued through its cycle, the opaque portion of the front disk momentarily blocked all outside light from reaching the phosphor screen. It was during this period that the aperture of the rear disk allowed the observer to view the phosphor screen and the image formed there. Under no circumstance did the Icaroscope permit direct viewing of scenes — the image observed in the Icaroscope was merely a phosphorescent afterglow. Extraneous light was never allowed to meet the eye of the observer directly.

Two production prototypes of the Icaroscope were engineered and constructed by Universal. The model described above, known as the Type 1 Icaroscope, was assigned the military nomenclature "U.S. Navy BuShips Icaroscope Mark 1 Mod. 0, 1945". Overall dimensions for the Type 1 Icaroscope were 17.75 inches length, 10.75 inches height and a total weight of 9 pounds. The Type 1 Icaroscope was supplied with an altitude-azimuth swivel bracket for shipboard mounting. Several hundred models of the Type 1

Icaroscope were produced by Universal during 1945. Meanwhile, design work was started in January 1945 on a second type of Icaroscope, known as the Type 2 Icaroscope. Universal presented the completed production prototype of the Type 2 Icaroscope to the U.S. Navy in July 1945. More compact in size, the Type 2 Icaroscope was designed exclusively for handheld use, featuring a pistol grip handle and a total weight of only 4.3 pounds. The optical system of the Type 2 Icaroscope provided four power magnification and included a 2.67 inch objective lens with a focal length of eight inches. This particular Icaroscope was equipped with a 28 volt DC Eastern Air Devices motor which operated at 4000 r.p.m., twice the speed of the Type 1 Icaroscope motor. This particular motor made it possible to operate the Icaroscope from an airplane rather than a ship. The military nomenclature of the Type 2 Icaroscope remains uncertain, however this author believes the unit to be marked "U.S. Navy BuShips Icaroscope Mark 2 Mod.0", 1945.

From the time of its development, the U.S. Navy mandated the Icaroscope "top secret", making it one of America's many wartime secrets. News of the instrument was finally released to the public during the atom bomb tests at Bikini, Marshall Islands in July 1946. Another important use for the instrument had been discovered — the Icaroscope was the only instrument that could allow a person to view the atom bomb blast and its devastating effects. Universal was asked by the U.S. Navy to speed production of additional units in preparation for the atom bomb tests. Universal was the only manufacturer of the Icaroscope. More than a half century after its development, the Icaroscope has not been forgotten — its potential uses are still the subject of periodic discussion by the Atomic Energy Commission and other government agencies.

Having gained extensive wartime experience in optical manufacturing, Universal's postwar outlook as a commercial photographic and optical instrument manufacturer seemed indeed favorable. Although the war years had proven profitable for the company, additional working capital was still needed if Universal was serious in its intentions to meet or beat postwar competitors. On November 20, 1944, Universal filed a registration statement with the Securities and Exchange Commission for the sale of 50,000 shares of 80 cent Cumulative Dividend Preferred Stock with a par value $5.00 per share *(Fig. 4-12)*. Of this stock offering, 25,000 shares were sold to the public at $10.00 per share, while the other 25,000 shares were sold to the New York Merchandise Company at $8.75 per share, with estimated proceeds of the sale totaling $410,928. Universal acquired additional working capital in November 1945 through a stock offering of 498,500 shares of one cent par Class A Common Stock at a cost of $5.00 per share. In this particular stock offering, 298,500 shares represented partial holdings of various Universal executives and directors. The remaining 200,000 shares were offered for sale to the public at $4.125 per share, providing Universal with additional funds of nearly $825,000. Approximately $275,000 of the cash acquired from these transactions was to be used for building and/or purchasing new tools and machinery for the production of new peacetime photographic products and a possible line of optical instrument products. Additional funds were used by Universal to establish an unbelievably huge inventory of new peacetime products in a very short time. Company ownership and voting power were determined through the sale of 500,000 shares of one cent par Class B Common Stock, divided and purchased as follows: 50% by the New York Merchandise Company, 25% by Universal's President, Otto Githens, and 25% by Universal's Vice-President, Jacob Shapiro. This particular stock provided Universal's three major stockholders with a voting power equal to one vote per share. All things considered, valuable wartime

D3266

Fig. 4-12 Two specimens of Universal Stock Certificates - 80 cent Cumulative Dividend Preferred Stock Certificate (above) and a reproduction of an actual Universal Class A Stock Certificate (below).

experience, substantial net earnings during the war years, 1543 experienced and dedicated wartime employees (as of May 1945) and substantial proceeds from the sale of stocks provided Universal with an excellent chance to succeed again in the upcoming postwar years *(Fig. 4-13)*.

Fig. 4-13 A Universal advertisement reporting that 1543 employees were still involved with war production work, taken from "Popular Photography", May 1945.

CHAPTER FOUR - PART TWO

1941-1946

THE UNIVERSAL BINOCULARS

In times of war, it was common for individual companies to show their cooperation to the war effort by allowing the government full use of any designs of possible value to the services. As far as binocular designs were concerned, most originated from the larger optical manufacturing firms in America — most often, the designs were not, as many people mistakenly believe, conceived and developed by the U.S. Army or U.S. Navy. The military did, however, conduct extensive studies and testing on binocular designs

Fig. 4-14 A 6x30 binocular produced by Universal for Canada.

donated by private companies to determine each instrument's overall suitability for military use. Many times, the results of these tests established the need for various modifications; after these changes were made, the designs were considered acceptable for service use.

Universal commenced production of military binoculars on January 1, 1942. The company's first binocular contract was acquired from Great Britain in 1941 and called for the immediate production of $1 million worth of 6x30 binoculars. Later that year, Universal agreed to produce an additional quantity of 6x30 binoculars for the Canadian government, examples of which bear the legend, "REL-CANADA Prismatic-2S" *(Fig. 4-14)*. Binoculars produced for the British or Canadian governments are considerably rare, in comparison to the binoculars manufactured by Universal under U.S. government contracts. The British and Canadian marked binoculars were produced by Universal until mid-1943. After that time, Universal produced binoculars exclusively for the U.S. Army, Navy and Marine Corps. All of the binoculars produced in mass quantity by Universal were built according to one of three designs — the first design belonging to the Bausch & Lomb Company, the second to the Universal Camera Corporation and the third to the Anchor Optical Company.

The 6x30 "Bausch & Lomb" Design Binocular

The first type of binocular produced by Universal was originally developed for commercial sale in the 1930's by Bausch & Lomb *(Fig. 4-15)*. The Bausch & Lomb design was selected in 1940 by the U.S. Army and U.S. Navy for use in the production of a standard issue service binocular. Various aspects of the Bausch & Lomb design — a two lens ocular system, also known as a "Kellner" ocular system, two porroprisms in an erecting system, an optical system containing a total of ten light dispersing surfaces, adjustable inter-pupillary distance and individual eyepiece focusing — combined to make a binocular

Fig. 4-15 A 1938 Bausch & Lomb advertisement showing the basic 6x30 binocular adopted for military use in 1940. Model shown here has central focusing, not individual eyepiece focusing which was required for military use. Taken from "American Rifleman", September 1938.

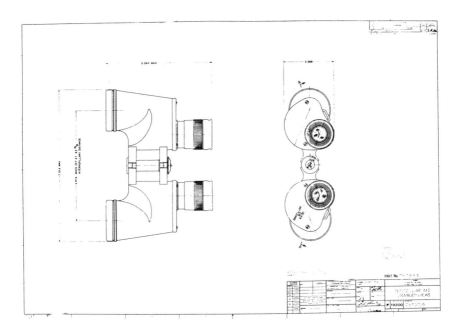

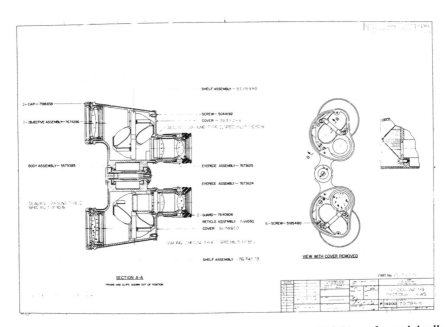

Fig. 4-16 Assembled and Sectional views of the U.S. Army M3 binocular, originally designed by Bausch & Lomb Company.

Fig. 4-17 U.S. Army M6, U.S. Navy Mark XXIX and U.S. Marine Corps binoculars, originally designed by Bausch & Lomb Company.

that was well-suited and readily adaptable for military use. Few, if any, design modifications were necessary before production was started, this in itself facilitating the timely manufacture and distribution of binoculars to needy servicemen. The specific military models that eventually evolved from this particular Bausch & Lomb design were the U.S. Army M3 *(Fig. 4-16)*, M6, M8, M9, the U.S. Navy Mark XXIX binocular and an undesignated 6x30 binocular produced for the U.S. Marine Corps. Each of these military models was under production at Universal during 1942 and early 1943 *(Fig. 4-17)*. In classifying binoculars, the U.S. Army assigned a specific model number to each different size or type of binocular. The model number always appeared on the prism coverplate preceded by the capital letter "M". In some instances, the marking "A1" followed indicating an improvement had been made to the original design of that particular binocular. The U.S. Navy, on the other hand, classified its binoculars using an entirely different system of nomenclature consisting of "Mark" and "Mod" numbers. The "Mark" number was used to differentiate between certain types and sizes of binoculars. A specific "Mark" number was also assigned when a binocular was designed and produced by only one manufacturer. The "Mod" number appeared immediately after the "Mark" number to indicate specific improvements or modifications that had been made to the original design of the binocular.

The most important difference between the commercial Bausch & Lomb binocular and the military version of this binocular was in the addition of a military reticle, a small disc made of flint or spectacle crown glass having various types of grids or scales permanently etched onto one side. Although many different reticles were employed during the war, the reticle most frequently used in binoculars had a small horizontal scale calibrated in increments of 10 mils (1 mil = $\frac{1}{6400}$ of the circumference of a circle) and a vertical scale, or range scale as it was sometimes called, calibrated in increments of 500 yards *(Fig. 4-18)*. The horizontal scale was marked in the

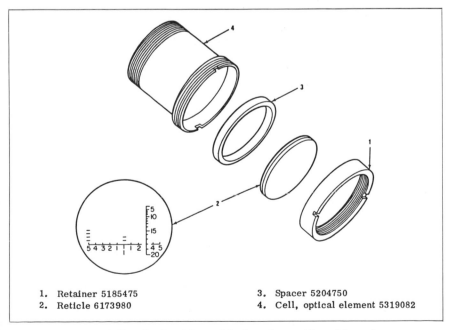

1. Retainer 5185475
2. Reticle 6173980
3. Spacer 5204750
4. Cell, optical element 5319082

Fig. 4-18 Standard reticle used in American military binoculars.

following manner — "5, 4, 3, 2, 1" and "1, 2, 3, 4, 5" — each series of numbers representing a total of 50 mils on either side of the vertical center point. The vertical scale was marked with the following series of numbers — "5, 10, 15 and 20", representing a range from zero to 2000 yards. "Mil scales", as they were frequently called, were commonplace on many World War I & II binoculars. The British referred to these etched scales as "graticules" and, more often than not, "degrees" were used as calibration on British reticles instead of "mils". Through the use of a reticle, small horizontal or vertical angles and distance ranges in the field of view could be calculated. Most U.S. Army binoculars were equipped with reticles, whereas most U.S. Navy binoculars were not. The 6x30 U.S. Army M3, M8, M9 *(Fig. 4-19)*, M13 and M13A1 binoculars and the 7x50 U.S. Army M16, M17 and MI7A1 binoculars were equipped with reticles in their left telescopes. The 6x30 U.S. Army M6 binocular was the only model equipped with a reticle in the right telescope. Reticles were not included in the 8x50 U.S. Army M2 binocular or the 7x50 U.S. Army M7, M15 and M15A1 binoculars. In many instances, reticles can no longer be found in the military binoculars that once contained them. During the post-World War II years, hundreds of thousands of binoculars were reconditioned for surplus sale — during the process, reticles were deliberately removed as they served no practical purpose for the typical civilian user.

Fig. 4-19 The 6x30 U.S. Army M9 binocular.

In the months immediately following the attack on Pearl Harbor, production of all types of military equipment was stepped up and, as a result, shortages of various raw materials developed. One material in extremely short supply at the time was rubber. In addition to its use in the production of tires for military vehicles, rubber was used as a covering for binoculars. To help circumvent this shortage, the U.S. Army and U.S. Navy set up a program for the development of a suitable replacement material for covering binoculars. Thirty-five plastics companies assisted the U.S. Naval Observatory and the Bureau of Standards in the development and testing of different binocular covering materials. A heavily embossed vinyl resin material was finally chosen by the U.S. Army and U.S. Navy in August 1942. Prior to 1942, military binoculars were covered with either a thin coat of crinkle finish paint or, more frequently, leather or rubber. A small number of Universal binoculars

Fig. 4-20 A 1942 U.S. Army M6 binocular, showing the initials of one U.S. Government Inspector, "J.K.C.", referring to Lt. Col. John K. Christmas, U.S. Army.

were produced early in 1942 with a hard rubber covering. As soon as sufficient vinyl material was produced and distributed to the nation's binocular manufacturers, the use of leather and rubber was discontinued.

Aside from the usual military nomenclature, binoculars frequently carried a stamped marking consisting of a group of two or three capital letters. The letters comprising such a marking were not always the same, oftentimes varying from one group of binoculars to another. The reason for this was that the letters were actually initials for various U.S. Government Ordnance Inspectors. For example, the initials "J.K.C." appeared on many U.S. Army binoculars produced by Universal Camera Corporation *(Fig. 4-20)*. These initials referred to Ordnance Inspector Lt. Col. John K. Christmas, U.S. Army. Another set of inspectors' initials appearing on many World War II binoculars was "F.J.A." — these initials were traced to Ordnance Inspector Lt. Col. Frank J. Atwood, U.S. Army. In-plant offices for these and other government inspectors were maintained in many production plants during the war to facilitate frequent and thorough inspection of a company's production activities. Initials of U.S. Government Inspectors began appearing on military equipment many years prior to World War II, in some instances as far back as the late 1700's on certain military guns and rifles.

The 6x30 "Universal" Design Binocular

During the summer of 1942, Universal directed its efforts at redesigning and improving the Bausch & Lomb design 6x30 binocular that had been in production at the plant since January 1942. Universal's primary concern was to improve the waterproofing protection of the 6x30 standard service binocular. This special project was undertaken by Percival H. Case, Universal's General Manager, and Sten Johanson, Universal's Chief Designer. Percival Case *(Fig. 4-21)* was a familiar name to many

Fig. 4-21 Percival H. Case, General Manager, 1937-1945.

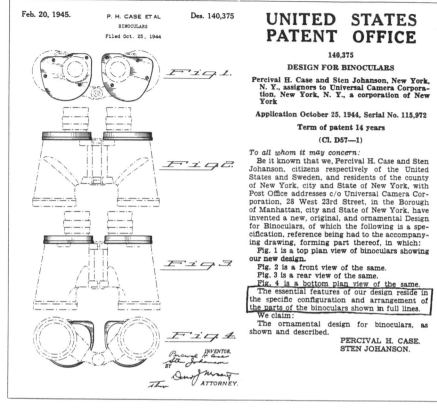

Feb. 20, 1945.   P. H. CASE ET AL   Des. 140,375

BINOCULARS

Filed Oct. 25, 1944

Fig. 1.

Fig. 2.

Fig. 3.

Fig. 4.

INVENTOR.

BY

ATTORNEY.

UNITED STATES PATENT OFFICE

140,375

DESIGN FOR BINOCULARS

Percival H. Case and Sten Johanson, New York, N. Y., assignors to Universal Camera Corporation, New York, N. Y., a corporation of New York

Application October 25, 1944, Serial No. 115,972

Term of patent 14 years

(Cl. D57—1)

To all whom it may concern:

Be it known that we, Percival H. Case and Sten Johanson, citizens respectively of the United States and Sweden, and residents of the county of New York, city and State of New York, with Post Office addresses c/o Universal Camera Corporation, 28 West 23rd Street, in the Borough of Manhattan, city and State of New York, have invented a new, original, and ornamental Design for Binoculars, of which the following is a specification, reference being had to the accompanying drawing, forming part thereof, in which:

Fig. 1 is a top plan view of binoculars showing our new design.

Fig. 2 is a front view of the same.

Fig. 3 is a rear view of the same.

Fig. 4 is a bottom plan view of the same.

The essential features of our design reside in the specific configuration and arrangement of the parts of the binoculars shown in full lines.

We claim:

The ornamental design for binoculars, as shown and described.

PERCIVAL H. CASE.
STEN JOHANSON.

Fig. 4-22 Exterior design of Universal's 6x30 binocular invented by Percival H. Case, Universal's General Manager, and Sten Johanson, Universal's Chief Designer, as depicted in U.S. Des. Pat. # 140,375.

in the photographic industry, having started his career in 1916 as an industrial engineer for Eastman Kodak. After spending four years with Kodak, Case resigned to handle outside engineering and sales jobs. In 1928, he accepted a position with Gevaert and remained there until November 1937, when he joined the staff at Universal. Due to illness, Case retired from Universal in 1945. Sten Johanson was responsible, in part, for the designs of a number of patented Universal peacetime products, particularly the UniveX Micrographic Enlarger and a combination exposure meter/viewfinder incorporated into the construction of the Universal Cinemaster Camera. Johanson also assisted in the design and construction of Universal's automatic prism grinding machine.

The basic styling of Universal's improved 6x30 binocular design *(Fig. 4-22)* was adapted from the Bausch & Lomb 6x30 commercial binocular design under production at the time by Universal and several other companies. After distribution to thousands of servicemen, the Bausch & Lomb design binocular had reportedly begun to accumulate moisture inside the telescopes, thereby affecting the instrument's optical performance. Frequent exposure to extreme climatic changes and conditions was generally blamed for this problem. It was also reported that many of the Bausch & Lomb design binoculars were unable to withstand the shock and vibration to which they

Fig. 4-23 Comparison photographs of the prism coverplate and corresponding body flange design on the U.S. Army M3 (above) and M13 (below) binoculars.

were subjected during the initial transportation period and, in some cases, the impact and stress of actual combat situations.

The improved binocular included a number of significant modifications over the original binocular designed by Bausch & Lomb. In redesigning the 6x30 Bausch & Lomb binocular, Universal concentrated on improving the instrument's ability to withstand excessive moisture through the development of heavier prism coverplates, each cast with a deep ¼ inch rim, and specially designed gaskets capable of creating an effective seal between the prism coverplates and the binocular body. Another important change involved the addition of an "auxiliary shoulder", or flange, integrally cast as part of each telescope *(Fig. 4-23)*. This flange provided a solid support for the deep-rimmed coverplates and, at the same time, helped to provide further waterproofing protection. In addition to this, the inside face of each prism coverplate was die cast with raised surfaces encircling each of the coverplate screw holes *(Fig. 4-24)*. Once the specially designed gaskets were placed between the coverplates and the binocular body, and the coverplate screws tightened, compression of the gaskets occurred between the raised surfaces of the

Fig. 4-24 Comparison photographs showing external and internal prism coverplate design of the U.S. Army M3 and the U.S. Navy Mark 33 (equivalent to the U.S. Army M13) binoculars.

inside face of the coverplates and the corresponding lug surfaces inside each of the telescopes. This particular feature rendered a tortuous seal which significantly reduced the possibility of moisture penetration in the area of the coverplate fastening screws. To further safeguard against water and moisture problems, a thin groove along the outer edge of each prism chamber was integrally cast as part of the binocular's die cast design. Before fastening the prism coverplates to the binocular body, sealing compound was applied along the entire length of this groove. Once the prism coverplates were properly seated and the coverplate screws tightened, the sealing compound dispersed itself to form an effective long-lasting seal that was impervious to both air and water. By this time, a number of other companies had also incorporated various types of coverplate gaskets into the design of their binoculars, but none provided the same degree of waterproof protection as the gasket and coverplate designed by Universal *(Fig. 4-25)*. Initially, the

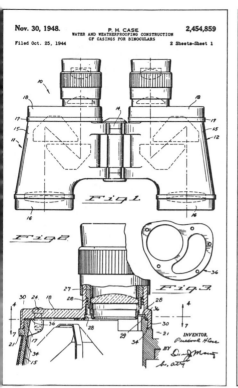

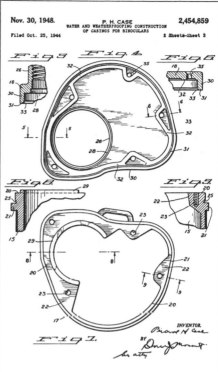

Fig. 4-25 Waterproofing features of Universal's 6x30 binocular invented by Percival H. Case, as depicted in U.S. Pat. # 2,454,859.

Universal prism coverplate was designed with openings for four fastening screws, as opposed to the original Bausch & Lomb design binocular which employed only two screws for this same purpose. A fifth fastening screw was later added to the binocular coverplate design. One final die casting modification relating to the prism coverplates remains to be mentioned — a tubular housing, designed to carry the eyepiece assembly, was integrally die cast with each coverplate to eliminate the possibility of moisture entering the instrument at that critical point. This important feature was developed and patented by Bausch & Lomb during the war and was quickly adopted by the Government for use on all standard 6x30 and 7x50 military binoculars. As a whole, all of these improvements greatly increased the standard 6x30 service binocular's ability to withstand frequent exposure to water and moisture.

Blueprints *(Fig. 4-26)* and completed models of Universal's improved 6x30 binocular, consisting of 114 separate parts, were submitted for military approval late in 1942. After a thorough study at the Frankford Arsenal, some additional modifications were necessary before the binocular could be considered suitable for World War II usage — the placement of a silica gel cartridge inside the binocular to prevent the formation of internal moisture and the use of an improved sealant wax better suited to extreme changes in temperature. Universal began full scale retooling for the new binocular in mid 1943 and production commenced shortly thereafter. Universal's improved 6x30 binocular was the second style of binocular manufactured by the company in mass quantity for the military. By the fall of 1943, Nash-Kelvinator,

145

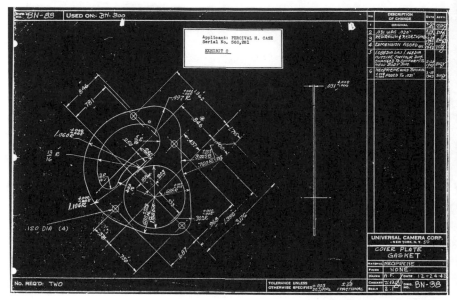

Fig. 4-26 This Universal blueprint, dated December 24, 1942, depicting a "Coverplate Gasket", was submitted to the U.S. Patent Office for the purpose of antedating three rather significant patent applications pertaining to binoculars filed by Bausch & Lomb in February, April and October of 1943. Although the patents filed by Bausch & Lomb involved several different features considered novel in a binocular at the time, all claimed the use of a prism coverplate gasket. In conjunction with other related Universal blueprints and signed affidavits from Percival H. Case, Universal's General Manager, and Sten Johanson, Universal's Chief Designer, this particular Universal blueprint, the original of which was rendered by Sten Johanson on July 20, 1942

No.	DESCRIPTION OF CHANGE	Date	Appv.
1	ORIGINAL	7-20-42	
2	.031 WAS .020"	4-14-1943	
3	REDRAWN & REDESIGNED	12-24-1942	
4	DIMENSION ADDED RK	1-27-1942	
5	1.088 DIA WAS 1.068 DIA OUTSIDE CONTOUR DIM. CHANGED TO CONFORM TO NEW BODY DIM.	2-28-1943	
6	NEOPRENE WAS THIOKOL ±.008/.000 ADDED TO .031"	3-18-1943	

(see detail photo), helped establish the fact that Universal had indeed conceived the design of a unique prism coverplate gasket long before Bausch & Lomb had filed its three binocular-related patent applications in 1943. After considering the evidence submitted, the Patent Office decided to issue a patent (U.S. Pat. # 2,454,859) to Universal for the design of its prism coverplate, corresponding body flange and gasket.

Westinghouse and a number of other companies were also producing the same binocular.

The Universal design binocular was designated the "U.S. Navy Mark XXXIII Mod.0 binocular" *(Fig. 4-27)* by the U.S. Navy and the "U.S. Army M13 binocular" *(Fig. 4-27)* by the U.S. Army. Universal also produced this binocular for the U.S. Marine Corps, examples of which bear the following marking, "6x30 U.S.M.C." *(Fig. 4-27)*. Several months later the U.S. Navy changed the designation for this binocular to U.S. Navy Mark 33 Mod.0 *(Fig. 4-28)*. During WWII, U.S. Navy binoculars were marked in one of two ways — for example,

Fig. 4-27 U.S. Army M13, U.S. Navy Mark *XXXIII* and U.S. Marine Corps binoculars with improved prism coverplates, coverplate gaskets and corresponding body flange design invented by Universal. (M13 - from the collection of Larry Tieger. Photo Courtesy: Larry Tieger).

Fig. 4-28 U.S. Navy Mark 33 Mod.0 binocular.

using Roman Numerals, as in Mark XXXIII, or more commonly using Arabic Numerals, as in Mark 33. There was no noticeable difference in the design or construction of the Mark XXXIII and Mark 33 U.S. Navy binoculars produced at Universal, although serial numbers indicate that the Mark XXXIII binocular was produced prior to the Mark 33 binocular. According to naval records, the U.S. Navy discontinued use of Roman Numerals in mid-1943, after which time all U.S. Navy binoculars produced by Universal and other companies were marked using Arabic Numerals only. Oddly enough, some Universal binoculars were designated "U.S. Navy Mark 33" *(Fig. 4-29)* with no "Mod" number, serial number or year. Binoculars fitting this description appear to be relatively scarce in comparison to the conventional U.S. Navy Mark XXXIII or U.S. Navy Mark 33 binoculars having the additional "Mod.0" or "Mod.1" marking.

Long after Universal's improved 6x30 binocular was accepted by the U.S. Government as standard issue military equipment, Universal continued working to further improve certain aspects of its design and construction. Universal assisted in developing a method of discharging all the air contained inside the binocular and then recharging it with dry nitrogen, a process which virtually destroyed the possibility of internal fogging or moisture accumulation.

This process was eventually adopted as standard government practice, after which time the internal placement of silica desiccant cartridges was discontinued. In addition to this, in late 1942, Universal developed a new and effective method of positioning and mounting optical prisms inside a binocular which would provide better protection against occurrences of optical misalignment caused by severe impact and shock. This new method of mounting prisms was easily performed by the unskilled worker, as opposed to the method in practice in the optical industry at the time which required the expertise of a skilled worker. Universal brought its new and simplified method of mounting prisms to the attention of the military, after which time it was adopted by the Government and applied to the production of military binoculars. With the conventional method, skilled workers were needed to correctly position and secure the prisms on a "prism shelf", as it was commonly referred to — one prism being positioned in a special recess on the top side of the prism shelf and the other being positioned in a recess on

Fig. 4-29 U.S. Navy Mark 33 binocular. Bottom photo shows the disassembled prism shelf assembly showing the thermoplastic vinyl resin washer developed by Universal engineer Adin Daniel Falkoff.

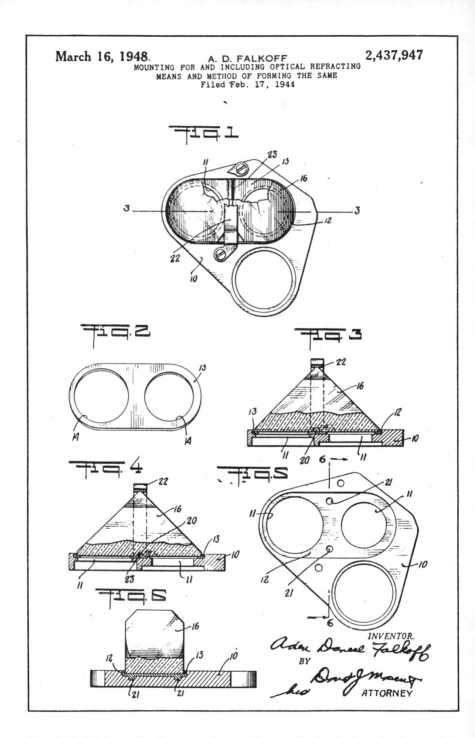

Fig. 4-30 Method of prism assembly in Universal's 6x30 binocular invented by Universal engineer Adin Daniel Falkoff, as depicted in U.S. Pat. # 2,437,947.

150

the bottom side of the prism shelf. On some manufacturers' binoculars, prism shelves were completely flat, with no recesses whatsoever, making the proper placement of prisms even more tedious and time-consuming. Cracking, shifting or loosening of prisms oftentimes occurred with this method because the prisms were mounted directly to the metal prism shelf itself, with nothing in between to cushion the prisms in any way in the event the instrument was sharply jarred or dropped. With the new method devised by Universal, a thin thermoplastic vinyl resin washer, slightly larger than the base of a prism, was inserted into the recess on a prism shelf and then heated to a temperature in excess of 140 degrees Fahrenheit until the plastic washer began to soften. A prism was then placed on top of the washer and slight pressure was exerted while adjusting the prism into its proper position. This action created a perfect impression of the prism's base on the plastic washer and once the washer had cooled, the impression remained permanent over a wide temperature range. At this point, the prism could be removed from the washer as often as necessary and then easily replaced to its former position on the washer before final assembly of the prism to the prism shelf *(Fig. 4-29)*. As a result of Universal's new mounting method, assembly and initial optical alignment of binoculars was speeded considerably and the necessity of repair and readjustment resulting from extreme shock or vibrations was lessened, as was the number of skilled workers previously required to perform these operations. More specific details of this new method were explained and illustrated in U.S. Pat.# 2,437,947 *(Fig. 4-30)* which was applied for on February 17, 1944 with Adin Daniel Falkoff, a Universal designer, being listed as the inventor.

After these and other modifications were incorporated into the Universal design binocular, production of the U.S. Army M13 binocular and the U.S. Navy Mark 33 Mod.0 binocular was discontinued and production of the improved model was started shortly after. This improved binocular became known as the U.S. Army M13 A1 binocular *(Fig. 4-31)* and the U.S. Navy Mark 33 Mod.1 binocular. Although U.S. Army M13 binoculars had generally been marked with a manufacturer's name and year, it appears that most U.S. Army M13 A1 binoculars were not. Some claim that U.S. Army M13 A1 binoculars were purposely manufactured without these markings to help expedite production and delivery at a time considered by many to be the height of the war. At one point during the war, Universal began applying decals bearing the "Universal Camera Corporation" name to U.S. Army M13 A1 binoculars *(Fig. 4-32)* produced at its plant. Evidently, this practice was short-lived — few examples are known to exist.

Universal applied for two patents on the improved 6x30 binocular — U.S. Design Pat.# 140,375, illustrating the binocular's overall ornamental design and, more specifically, the external configuration of the binocular's improved prism coverplates, and U.S. Pat.# 2,454,859, explaining in detail the internal and external design of these coverplates and the means used to waterproof this particularly critical area of a binocular. These two patents gave Universal exclusive patent rights on the commercial sale of this binocular once the war had ended, allowing Universal to be the only company to manufacture the U.S. Army M13 A1 binocular and the U.S. Navy Mark 33 Mod.1 binocular commercially as a civilian binocular after the war. The "Universal 6x30 Prismatic Binocular" *(Fig. 4-33)*, as it was termed in Universal's postwar advertisements, was identical in every respect to the U.S. Army M13 A1 binocular, except for the exclusion of the military reticle. The retail price of the binocular was $85.00 *(Fig. 4-34)*, including either a black or brown vinyl-covered carrying case marked "Universal Camera Corporation". Because production of the 6x30 commercial binocular at Universal had remained

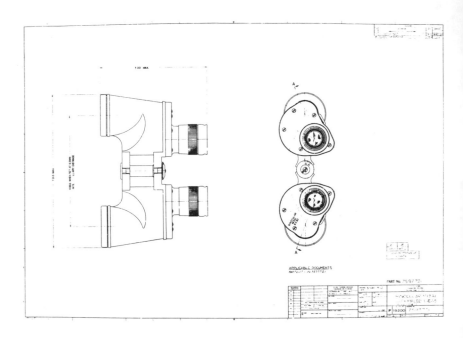

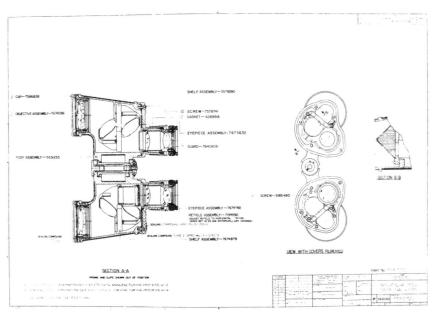

Fig. 4-31 Assembled, sectional and exploded views of the prism coverplate area of the U.S. Army M13A1 binocular, designed and patented by Universal Camera Corporation.

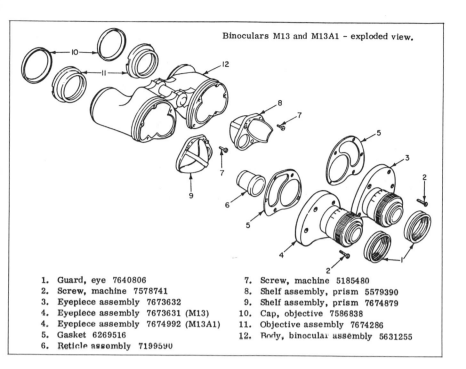

Binoculars M13 and M13A1 - exploded view.

1. Guard, eye 7640806	7. Screw, machine 5185480
2. Screw, machine 7578741	8. Shelf assembly, prism 5579390
3. Eyepiece assembly 7673632	9. Shelf assembly, prism 7674879
4. Eyepiece assembly 7673631 (M13)	10. Cap, objective 7586838
4. Eyepiece assembly 7674992 (M13A1)	11. Objective assembly 7674286
5. Gasket 6269516	12. Body, binocular assembly 5631255
6. Reticle assembly 7199590	

Fig. 4-32 Photo below shows one version of the U.S. Army M13A1 binocular. Universal also produced two other versions: one having no "Universal Camera Corp." marking; the other affixed with a rare "Universal Camera Corp." decal.

Fig. 4-33 The civilian 6x30 Universal prismatic binocular marketed solely by Universal in the immediate postwar years for $85.00 with carrying case. This binocular was identical to the U.S. Army M13A1 binocular produced by Universal during the war, with the exception of the military reticle. Below it is a Warranty Registration Card for the postwar Universal 6x30 Prismatic binocular.

essentially unchanged from wartime production of the military binocular, Universal was able to manufacture the instrument at an extremely low cost of $32.79). Compared to other binoculars on the postwar market, Universal's binocular was reasonably priced considering the fact that Bausch & Lomb's uncoated 6x30 individual focusing binocular (the first binocular produced by Universal during the war) appeared in a 1940 catalog at a retail price af $66.00. In addition to the improved waterproofing features of the Universal binocular, coated lenses and prisms were also included on the postwar binocular. As far as optical precision and durability were concerned, Universal's 6x30 binocular, both the military and postwar civilian versions, were rated quite highly by those in the military and, surprisingly so, by many in the optical industry. By the late 1940's though, financial difficulties developed for Universal and, as a result, the company's production standards and quality control declined sharply bringing about a noticeable reduction in the optical quality of the binoculars produced by Universal at that time.

UNIVERSAL CAMERA CORPORATION

DEALER PRICE LIST
Federal Excise Tax included where applicable.

Dated: January 20, 1947

ALL PRICES SUBJECT TO CHANGE WITHOUT NOTICE

UNIVERSAL CAMERA CORPORATION PERMITS NO 10% RETAIL PRICE CUT
YOU RECEIVE YOUR FULL MARGIN OF PROFIT
FAIR TRADE PROTECTED IN 45 STATES FOR FULL RETAIL PRICE

Catalog No.		Retail Price	Dealer Price
	UNIVERSAL MERCURY II And ACCESSORIES		
CX-27	MERCURY II With *f*2.7 Tricor Coated Lens	$82.90	$59.21
K-23	MERCURY II CASE	7.25	5.07
M-29	MERCURY PHOTOFLASH UNIT	7.30	5.43
M-30	MERCURY EXPOSURE METER	2.85	2.00
M-56	MASKS For MERCURY TRANSPARENCIES (50 to Pkg.)	.55	.38½
	UNIVERSAL METEOR AND ACCESSORIES		
PR-100	METEOR CAMERA	15.00	10.75
K-24	METEOR CASE	5.00	3.50
M-29	MERCURY PHOTOFLASH UNIT	7.30	5.43
	UNIVEX CANDID CAMERAS		
C&F15	UNIFLASH CAMERA & FLASH UNIT with Coated Lens	8.75	6.25
	UNIVEX FILM		
			Less Than 4 Doz. — 4 Doz.
00-C	"00" ULTRACHROME FILM	.15	.11 — .10½
			1-11 Pcs. — 1 Doz.
100-UP	#100 ULTRAPAN MOVIE FILM	1.10	.82½ — .77
236SS	35mm. ULTRAPAN SS (For Mercury I and Corsair I)	.62	.47 — .44
	MERCURY COPYING ACCESSORIES		
M-65	Complete Kit of 4 Extension Tubes and 1 Shim	7.35	5.13
M-66	Extension Tube #1	1.30	.92
M-67	Extension Tube #2	1.95	1.35
M-68	Extension Tube #3	2.55	1.79
M-69	Extension Tube #4	3.20	2.23
M-72	Shim .065" Thick	.35	.24
	UNIVERSAL CINEMASTER II		
G-835	CINEMASTER II WITH *f*3.5 LENS	51.90	37.06
G-825	CINEMASTER II WITH *f*2.5 LENS	66.65	47.61
G-819	CINEMASTER II WITH *f*1.9 LENS	96.75	69.13
K-22	CINEMASTER Eveready Carrying Case	4.95	3.47
	PROJECTORS and 8mm. MOVIE ACCESSORIES		
PC-500	UNIVERSAL 500 Watt Projector with Superlux Coated *f*2 Lens	69.50	46.34
B-82	HIGH INTENSITY LAMP FOR PC-12, P-8, P-300	.70	.52½
B-89	HIGH INTENSITY LAMP FOR PU-8, PU-300	2.20	1.65
UP-203	BELTS FOR PROJECTORS (TAKE-UP)	.17	.12¾
UP-201	BELTS FOR PROJECTORS (MOTOR DRIVE)	.17	.12¾
M-1	UNIVERSAL SPLICER	1.69	1.13
		List Price	Dealer Price
	UNIVERSAL PRISMATIC BINOCULARS		
BN	6x30 PRISMATIC BINOCULARS	85.00 (Plus 20% Federal Excise Tax Collected By Retailer)	59.50

Printed in U.S.A.

DP-4

Fig. 4-34 Postwar Universal camera and binocular price list verifying the fact that Universal was still marketing the 6x30 prismatic binocular on January 20, 1947.

155

The 7x50 "Anchor" Design Binocular

The third style of binocular produced in mass quantity by Universal was a 7x50 binocular originally designed and produced by the Anchor Optical Company. During the war, the Anchor binocular design was produced by three different companies — Anchor Optical Company, National Instrument Corporation and Universal Camera Corporation. The original design was produced by Anchor in 1942 and 1943 as the U.S. Navy Mk XXXII Mod.0 binocular *(Fig. 4-35a)*. This designation was later changed in mid 1943 to U.S. Navy Mark 32 Mod.0. About that time, the same binocular, albeit slightly improved, was produced by the National Instrument Corporation of Houston, Texas under the designation of U.S. Navy Mark 32 Mod.1 *(Fig. 4-35b)*. Universal commenced production of the Anchor design binocular in March 1944 under the designation of U.S. Navy Mark 32 Mod.2. Although there appears to be little, if any, noticeable difference in the overall design and construction of these three U.S. Navy Mark 32 binoculars, the "Mod.0", "Mod.1" and "Mod.2" markings indicate that various improvements were in fact made to the original Anchor binocular design when National Instrument Corporation and Universal Camera Corporation began production of the binocular.

On November 4, 1943, Universal entered into an agreement with the U.S. Navy for the production of 20,000 U.S. Navy Mark 32 Mod.2 binoculars. Naval Contract NXsx-41100 specified that the 7x50 binoculars were to be marked with assigned serial numbers and the year "1943". Peculiarly, two variations of the 7x50 U.S. Navy Mark 32 Mod.2 binocular are known to exist today — one version bearing a serial number and the year "1943" *(Fig. 4-35c)* and another version having neither a serial number or year marking *(Fig. 4-35d)*. The latter version appears to be somewhat less common. Under the terms of the contract, Universal was to deliver 20,000 finished 7x50 binoculars to the U.S. Navy within six months of the contract date. As it eventually turned out, Universal experienced various unexpected shipping delays consisting of, first and most importantly, the late shipment of government-owned machinery necessary to produce the larger binoculars and, secondly, numerous delays and interruptions in the shipment of raw materials. As a result, Universal made its final deliveries to the U.S. Navy in February and March 1945, approximately nine to ten months later than initially scheduled. Naval records show that Universal received a maximum of $123.75 for every 7x50 binocular it produced under the contract plus funds in the amount of $104,000 for the manufacture and/or purchase of machinery and equipment necessary to machine the larger-sized binocular bodies and to produce the necessary coverings and component parts needed for the final assembly of these binoculars. Additional funds were also paid to the company for the manufacture and/or purchase of optical production machinery, optical measurement and testing equipment, optical coating equipment and final inspection equipment used in the production of the 7x50 binocular. Universal worked around the clock, machining thousands of aluminum binocular bodies and metal binocular component parts — not to mention, grinding, polishing and coating all of the lenses and prisms which were later assembled into each binocular. In certain instances, when unexpected difficulties arose, subcontractors were called upon to assist Universal in machining metal binocular parts and to provide Universal with limited quantities of finished lenses and/or prisms.

One important concern involving the U.S. Navy Mark 32 binocular was the matter of optical lens coating. During the war, it was discovered that coated optics produced a marked reduction of light reflection and increased the amount of available light transmitted through a binocular by approximately 25%, making it particularly useful for viewing in low light situations.

156

Fig. 4-35a The 7x50 U.S. Navy Mark XXXII Mod. 0 binocular was designed and produced by the Anchor Optical Corporation. This same basic design was eventually put into production by the National Instrument Corporation of Houston, Texas and the Universal Camera Corporation of New York City.

Fig. 4-35b The 7x50 U.S. Navy Mark 32 Mod. 1 binocular was produced by the National Instrument Corporation, a Houston, Texas firm operating in wartime under the direction of the "Universal Management Group", formed by the Universal Camera Corporation at the request of the U.S. Navy.

Fig. 4-35c and d The 7x50 U.S. Navy Mark 32 Mod. 2 binoculars produced by Universal Camera Corporation — one version (above) shows the marking "1943" with an assigned serial number, the other version (below) has neither of these markings.

Fig. 4-36 Comparison photographs showing the external structural differences between the U.S. Navy Mark 28 binocular (above), originally designed by Bausch & Lomb, and the U.S. Navy Mark 32 binocular (below), originally designed by Anchor Optical. (Mark 28 - from the collection of Nathan T. Butcher).

By mid 1944, magnesium fluoride was being used as an anti-glare coating for lenses and prisms on almost all military binoculars made in the United States. Despite this fact, some 7x50 U.S. Navy Mark 32 Mod.2 binoculars were manufactured at Universal in 1944 and 1945 without this important feature. The U.S. Navy Mark 32 binocular was easily recognized by the distinctly contoured shape of its telescopes, each curving abruptly inward just beneath the prism coverplates, then flaring gradually outward toward the objectives. Inasmuch as waterproofing was concerned, the Anchor design U.S. Navy Mark 32 binocular was somewhat less desirable than, for instance, the 7x50 Bausch & Lomb design U.S. Navy Mark 28 binocular *(Fig. 4-36)* in full scale production at the time. Both binoculars incorporated some of the same waterproofing features — prism coverplates integrally cast with tubular metal eyepiece housings, rubber gaskets for fastening the prism coverplates to the binocular body and an improved sealant wax applied to these joints and the lens mounts. A heavy grease was also applied to the eyepiece cells. The major drawback of the Anchor design U.S. Navy Mark 32 binocular was the lack of deep-rimmed coverplates and auxiliary shoulders on the binocular casings themselves, a feature similar to that found on the 7x50 Bausch & Lomb design U.S. Navy Mark 28 binocular *(Fig. 4-37)* and

Fig. 4-37 Side views comparing the prism coverplate rim area of the Bausch & Lomb designed U.S. Navy Mark 28 binocular (above) and the Anchor Optical designed U.S. Navy Mark 32 binocular (below). (Mark 28 - from the collection of Nathan T. Butcher).

also the 6x30 Universal design U.S. Navy Mark 33 binocular. In combination with a good sealant wax and gaskets, the latter type of prism coverplates afforded extremely effective waterproof protection. Other aspects of the Anchor design — the eyepiece assembly, the hinge assembly and the optical system — were basically the same as the Bausch & Lomb design U.S. Navy Mark 28 binocular.

It would seem inappropriate to overlook the different carrying cases supplied with binoculars produced by Universal and other companies during and after World War II. Prior to 1943, carrying cases for American-made binoculars, including those produced by Universal, were constructed primarily of leather. During World War I, canvas was another material frequently used. Both materials had proven quite suitable for World War I usage, but when subjected to the high temperatures and humidity characteristic of World War II fighting in tropical climates, leather and canvas were totally inadequate. Under such weather conditions, these materials were extremely vulnerable, showing signs of rapid deterioration, warpage and fungi growth. Aside from this, leather had become one of many scarce wartime commodities. For these and other reasons, the U.S. Army and Navy began utilizing stitched vinyl-covered fiber board cases and molded plasticized vinyl cases in 1943. For example, the 7x50 U.S. Navy Mark 32 binocular was packed in a molded plasticized vinyl carrying case manufactured by Hood Rubber Company. Early in the production of the U.S. Navy 7x50 binocular, Universal experienced difficulty obtaining the new molded vinyl cases and requested permission from the U.S. Navy to substitute leather cases on a temporary basis. Universal was allowed to furnish the first 5,000 binoculars in leather cases, but the remaining 15,000 binoculars had to be furnished in the new molded plasticized vinyl type carrying cases. The leather case Universal used was identical in design to the molded vinyl case, having a long narrow strap which dropped down over the front of the case, fastening onto a small knob on the underside of the case. In the early 1950's, hard plastic cases were put into use by the military and were designated by the U.S. Army as the M62 series (6x30) and M63 series (7x50) carrying cases. Since World War II, the U.S. Army has supplied 6x30 binoculars in M17, M62 or M62 A1 carrying cases and 7x50 binoculars in M24, M44, M63 or M63 A1 carrying cases. For the most part, the carrying cases for U.S. Navy binoculars were basically the same in construction as the binocular carrying cases used by the U.S. Army.

The following chart provides information relating to the specific types and models of military binoculars produced by Universal Camera Corporation during the years 1942-1945. The chart lists only those Universal military binoculars that are known for certain to exist. Although this chart is considered relatively complete, the possibility does exist that Universal may have produced other models which are not documented here. Examples of such questionable models manufactured by Universal would be a 6x30 binocular bearing only British markings, a 6x42 U.S. Navy plastic binocular, or any binocular marked "1945". The Universal binoculars appearing on this chart have been categorized according to "year" — that is, the "year" marked on the prism coverplate. The year marking appears to reflect the actual year that a specific binocular contract was signed and executed. In many instances, production of binoculars under a specific contract extended well into the following year or even longer — in such cases, the binoculars most often continued to bear the original year marking as specified in the contract. In some instances, the year marking was omitted entirely.

UNIVERSAL MILITARY BINOCULARS

1942

Power	Produced for	Military Nomenclature	Basic Design*	Cover Screws	Coated Optics	Additional Information
6 x 30	US Army	M 3	B&L	2	No	Lt reticle
6 x 30	US Army	M 6	B&L	2	No	Rt reticle
6 x 30	US Army	M 8	B&L	2	No	Lt reticle
6 x 30	US Army	M 9	B&L	2	No	Lt reticle
6 x 30	US Navy	Mk XXIX Mod.0	B&L	2	No	
6 x 30	Canada	REL Canada Prismatic-2S	UCC	4	Yes	*See (1) below*

1943

Power	Produced for	Military Nomenclature	Basic Design*	Cover Screws	Coated Optics	Additional Information
6 x 30	US Army	M 13	UCC	5	No	Lt reticle
6 x 30	US Navy	Mk XXXIII Mod.0	UCC	4	No	Same as Mark 33. 0.
6 x 30	US Navy	Mark 33 Mod.0	UCC	4	No	Same as Mk XXXIII. 0.
6 x 30	US Navy	Mark 33 Mod.1	UCC	5	No	
7 x 50	US Navy	Mark 32 Mod.2	ANC	5	Yes/No	*See (2) below*

1944

Power	Produced for	Military Nomenclature	Basic Design*	Cover Screws	Coated Optics	Additional Information
6 x 30	US Navy	Mark 33 Mod.1	UCC	5	Yes	*(Fig. 4-38)*

Not Dated

Power	Produced for	Military Nomenclature	Basic Design*	Cover Screws	Coated Optics	Additional Information
6 x 30	US Army	M 13	UCC	5	Yes	Mfd 1943. Lt reticle
6 x 30	US Army	M 13 A1	UCC	5	Yes	Mfd 1943-45. Lt reticle Mfg mark: none, stamped, or decal.
6 x 30	US Marines	U.S.M.C.	B&L	2	No	Mfd 1942-43.
6 x 30	US Marines	U.S.M.C.	UCC	4	No	Mfd 1943-44.
6 x 30	US Navy	Mark 33	UCC	4	Yes	Mfd 1943.
7 x 50	US Navy	Mark 32 Mod.2	ANC	5	Yes/No	Mfd 1944-45. *See (2)*

Lend / Lease or Surplus

Power	Produced for **	Military Nomenclature	Basic Design*	Cover Screws	Coated Optics	Additional Information
6 x 30	USA/Britain	M 6, 1942 D↑D No2 MkII	B&L	2	No	Rt reticle. *See (3)*
6 x 30	USA/Surplus	M 9, 1942 USDA-FS	B&L	2	No	Lt reticle. *See (4)*
6 x 30	USN/Canada	Mark XXIX Mod.0, 1942 ↑CGB 53 GA	B&L	2	Yes	*See (5) below*
6 x 30	USN/Surplus	Mk XXXIII Mod.0, 1943 NPS	UCC	4	No	*See (6) below*

* The following abbreviations — B&L, UCC and ANC — appear under the "Basic Design" heading. They represent Bausch & Lomb Optical Company, Universal Camera Corporation and Anchor Optical Company, respectively.

** Under this particular heading, the abbreviations USA and USN represent the U.S. Army and the U.S. Navy, respectively.

NOTES FOR UNIVERSAL MILITARY BINOCULAR CHART

(1) Identical to the waterproof U.S. Army M13 and U.S. Navy Mark 33 binoculars Produced by Universal in 1943, this binocular was also produced by Universal for the Canadian government. The "1942" year marking suggests that the company entered into an agreement with the Canadian government sometime in 1942 for production of a 6x30 service binocular. Apparently, production under the Canadian contract was started mid-1943 after Universal had commenced retooling operations for its improved waterproof 6x30 service binocular. Canadian binoculars were most often marked "CANADA" or "REL-CANADA" — this particular binocular was marked REL-CANADA, the letters "REL" referring to "Research Enterprises Limited", a Toronto based company owned and operated by the Canadian government. During the war, Research Enterprises Limited began producing its own 6x30 and 7x50 binoculars. Although fabrication of most of the binocular parts was subcontracted out to other companies, Research Enterprises Limited performed fine machining of metal parts, in addition to the manufacture and assembly of the binoculars' optical elements and final testing of the finished instruments.

(2) By 1944, magnesium fluoride optical coating had become an important and indispensable anti-glare feature used on a wide variety of military optical instruments. All 6x30 binoculars produced by Universal in 1944 for the U.S. Army and U.S. Navy had an anti-glare lens coating but, for reasons unknown, optical lens coating was not done consistently on the 7x50 U.S. Navy Mark 32 Mod.2 binoculars produced at Universal during 1944 and 1945.

(3) This binocular, originally manufactured in 1942 by Universal for the US Army, was sent to Great Britain under the provisions of the Lend/Lease Act of 1941. The British government stamped this particular binocular on the right prism coverplate with the markings "D↑D" and "No2 MkII". The broad arrow symbol, "↑", was used to represent British government ownership — less frequently, it appeared on Canadian equipment. The capital letters "D D" are believed to represent the Department of Defense. "No2 MkII" was a military marking commonly seen on British binoculars. It appeared on the standard 6x30 binocular produced during World War II for the British Army by Kershaw, a world famous binocular manufacturer located in England. Great Britain was one of a number of allied countries receiving munitions and ordnance material from the United States during 1941 and 1942. Under the provisions of the Lend/Lease Act, representatives from the U.S. Army and U.S. Navy met regularly to consider orders for much needed equipment from allied nations and to decide where United States' surplus equipment should be sent. In addition to Great Britain, the United States provided ordnance materials to the following countries: Canada, Russia, Africa, China, India, Australia, New Zealand and several other countries. For this reason, some early Universal-made binoculars may have foreign military markings from any of the aforementioned countries in combination with American military markings.

(4) Obtained by the U.S. Forestry Service at a government surplus sale, this U.S. Army M9 binocular was used on the Yager Butte fire lookout at Custer National Forest from 1947 to 1967. In addition to the original military markings, the binocular was hand engraved "USDA-FS" (U.S. Department of Agriculture-Forestry Service) on the right objective cap.

(5) This Universal binocular was utilized in the Lend/Lease program and, as a result, it bears the foreign marking "CGB 53 G.A." with a large broad arrow symbol "↑" *(Fig. 4-39)*. The entire meaning of this marking is not known for certain, but the three letters "CGB" are believed to be an abbreviation for Canada & Great Britain.

(6) This U.S. Navy Mark XXXIII binocular was acquired by the National Park Service in the early 1950's for use at Yellowstone National Park by the Grizzly Bear Research Team. In addition to the original military markings, the binocular was hand engraved with the marking "NPS" (National Park Service).

162

Fig. 4-38 The 1944 U.S. Navy Mark 33 Mod.1 binocular.

Fig. 4-39 The 1942 U.S. Navy/Canada Mark XXIX Mod.0 : CGB 53 GA binocular.

In peacetime years, Universal gained a great deal of experience mass producing plastic cameras and accessories, experience which later proved helpful, if not invaluable, in the design of a compact and rugged 6x42 plastic binocular *(Fig. 4-40)*. In comparison to conventional aluminum binoculars in production at the time, the Universal plastic binocular seemed almost tailor-made for mass production — a minimal number of complex parts were involved in the design, very little machine work was necessary and an integrally molded embossed gripping surface eliminated the need for any separate body covering. Simple construction and ease of assembly made

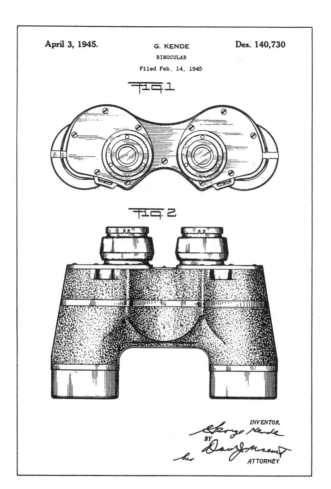

Fig. 4-40 Assembled view of the 6x42 Universal all plastic binocular design invented by George Kende, as depicted in U.S. Des. Pat. # 140,730.

the plastic binocular perfect for low cost mass production methods. Although radically different in design and construction from standard aluminum binoculars, accelerated service condition tests conducted by the U.S. Navy proved beyond a shadow of a doubt that Universal's 6x42 plastic binocular was equally, if not better, suited for use as an all-purpose U.S. Navy binocular than all other U.S. Navy binoculars in service use at the time. Test results indicated that the Universal 6x42 plastic binocular could be extremely useful for night, amphibious, tropical or submarine warfare.

The idea of a plastic service binocular came to light in April 1942 when the Joint Optics Committee of the Navy-Army Munitions Board met with officials of the U.S. Navy and U.S. Army to discuss the critical shortage of aluminum, used in large part for the production of binoculars, and to decide which type of material would best replace aluminum in the production of binoculars. Commdr. T.O. Brandon, Materials Officer for the U.S. Naval Observatory, suggested that various plastic materials be examined and tested for use in the production of service binoculars. With the approval of those present, a program was instituted under his direction at the U.S. Naval

164

Observatory in cooperation with the Organic Plastics Section and the Optical Instruments Section of the National Bureau of Standards. Representatives of the U.S. Government, the Society of the Plastics Industry, private optical manufacturing companies and private plastics manufacturing companies attended several meetings at the Naval Observatory to determine the best type of plastic material for the job. After much deliberation, seven plastic samples were submitted to the U.S. Navy and test binoculars were then fabricated from each sample using the molds from standard 7x50 U.S. Navy binoculars. The seven 7x50 plastic binoculars and one 7x50 aluminum binocular were subjected to accelerated service condition tests to demonstrate and compare the instruments' abilities to withstand impact and shock and also variations in temperature and humidity. According to the results of these tests, one plastic material proved superior over all the other plastics tested — it was identified as Bakelite BM-15060, a plastic technically referred to as "a thermosetting phenolic material containing a long-fiber asbestos filler". After an initial stabilization process, this particular plastic material exhibited excellent dimensional stability throughout a temperature range of -40 to 140 degrees Fahrenheit, not to mention an extreme resistance to various elements commonly associated with tropical combat situations — shock, moisture, water, corrosion and fungus. Good dimensional stability was, by far, the single most important factor to be considered in the development of a general purpose all plastic service binocular. As with almost any substance or material subjected to extreme temperature variations, a certain amount of expansion and contraction was expected. The extent to which these thermal reactions occurred depended on the particular type of material being used, the temperature, and the length of time the material was exposed to this temperature. Bakelite BM-15060 was chosen for use in fabricating the Universal 6x42 plastic service binocular because the actual degree of thermal expansion and contraction exhibited by this particular plastic material at any given temperature was significantly less than that of all the other plastics tested.

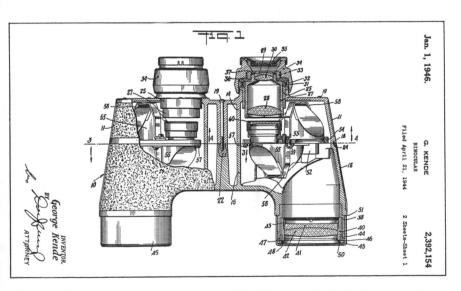

Fig. 4-41 Partial sectional view of the 6x42 Universal all plastic binocular design invented by George Kende, as depicted in U.S. Pat. # 2,392,154.

165

At the request of the U.S. Navy, George Kende, Universal's Chief Engineer, began the design work for a plastic service binocular in late 1943. Following completion and final development of Kende's design, Universal applied for and was granted the following patents — U.S. Design Pat. #140,730, applied for on February 14, 1945, covering the ornamental design of the plastic binocular and U.S. Pat. # 2,392,154, applied for on April 21, 1944, covering the structural features of the plastic binocular *(Fig. 4-41)*. Universal's 6x42 plastic binocular design included a number of features not found on other American-made service binoculars. One of the most unusual features of the plastic binocular was its solid, or "fixed", ocular bridge, as opposed to the "hinged" ocular bridge commonly found on all other handheld American-made binoculars. With a solid ocular bridge, interpupillary distance was not adjustable and so an average interpupillary distance setting of 65mm was automatically incorporated into the plastic binocular design. To accommodate users requiring different interpupillary distance settings, it was decided that the plastic binocular could be produced in three different versions with interpupillary distances of 62mm, 65mm and 68mm. The U.S. Navy had previously determined that interpupillary distance settings ranging between 62mm and 68mm would suitably accommodate approximately 87% of its service users. Another unusual feature of the plastic binocular was the elimination of eyepiece focusing. Each fixed focus eyepiece was preset with a center field diopter setting of -1.2 to provide the observer with a focal image distance of 0.85 meter, a range generally considered normal for the average user.

Instead of the usual right and left housing sections common to conventional hinged binoculars, the main housing sections of the 6x42 plastic binocular consisted of an upper portion, carrying both eyepiece assemblies, and a lower portion carrying both objective assemblies. There were no removable prism coverplates as in conventional binoculars — the prism clusters in the 6x42 plastic binocular were assembled directly onto the lower housing. The upper housing section was then assembled with the corresponding lower housing section using cement and several connecting screws to create a permanent seal against air and water. With fully coated optics and 7x50 Zeiss porroprisms, the 6x42 plastic binocular provided approximately the same field and light gathering power as the standard U.S. Navy 7x50 binocular. The 6x42 plastic binocular was an excellent spotting device because the body design afforded a rather large span between the objective lenses and the optical elements were arranged in a manner which enhanced the stereoscopic effect of the binocular. All things considered, the Universal 6x42 plastic binocular was a reliable optical instrument — rugged, compact, lightweight and extremely simple to use.

Universal submitted the design work for the 6x42 plastic binocular to the U.S. Naval Observatory where arrangements were immediately made to have molds constructed in accordance with the design drawings. The U.S. Naval Observatory contacted the Plastics Division of the General Electric Company regarding fabrication of these molds and subsequent construction of the binocular. Special metal inserts were employed in the design and construction of the plastic binocular for the purpose of securing the instrument's optical elements and to give the plastic binocular additional structural strength. The inserts were die cast from an aluminum-silicon alloy, a lightweight metal chosen specifically because its thermal expansion and contraction reaction closely paralleled the thermal expansion and contraction reaction of the plastic material used to fabricate the binocular body. Because thermal expansion and contraction was essentially the same in these two materials, there was little chance of the plastic material developing cracks or the optical component parts loosening or shifting, the latter being extremely important in maintaining proper optical alignment and collimation for the entire life of the instrument.

In February 1944, examples of the completed 6x42 plastic prototypical binocular were delivered to the U.S. Naval Observatory for study and testing. The 6x42 plastic binocular weighed 36 ounces as compared to the standard 6x30 aluminum binocular weighing 22 ounces and the standard 7x50 aluminum binocular weighing 44 ounces. At the U.S. Naval Observatory, accelerated service condition tests for temperature, shock, impact, water and fungus resistance were conducted on a group of five binoculars — Universal's 6x42 plastic binocular and four U.S. Navy binoculars consisting of a standard 6x30 aluminum binocular, a standard 7x50 aluminum binocular and two waterproof 7x50 aluminum binoculars. Interestingly enough, the 6x42 plastic binocular fared quite well against its aluminum counterparts in the accelerated service condition tests.

Temperature and Humidity Test - In this test, all five test binoculars were subjected to extreme variations in temperature and humidity equal to approximately three years of continuous service use. Slight dimensional changes occurred affecting the optical alignment of each binocular tested. The extent to which this occurred in the 6x42 plastic binocular was well within, approximately ⅓, the accepted tolerance limit for U.S. Navy binoculars.

Impact Test - The results of this test indicated that the 6x42 plastic binocular was able to retain optical alignment within accepted tolerance limits after being subjected to the impact of a 130 gram steel ball dropped from a height of 43 inches. This test was designed to simulate severe service use. The same test revealed aluminum binoculars could only retain optical alignment within accepted tolerance limits when the test ball was dropped from a height of 30 inches or less.

Fungus Test - The fungus test was conducted at the University of Pennsylvania where the 6x42 plastic binocular and a standard 6x30 binocular were placed for twelve weeks in a chamber containing fungus spores taken directly from the tropical region of Panama. To simulate tropical weather conditions, the temperature inside the chamber was kept between 70 and 90 degrees Fahrenheit and the relative humidity between 70 to 90 percent. After three weeks, the 6x30 aluminum binocular had started to develop internal fungus growth. Five weeks later, the fungus growth had spread considerably throughout the inside of the binocular, virtually ruining the optical performance of the instrument. During the entire twelve week period, there was absolutely no evidence of internal or external fungus growth in the 6x42 plastic binocular.

Water Immersion Test - Results of the water immersion test proved extremely favorable for the 6x42 plastic binocular. All five binoculars were placed in a water pressure tank for the purpose of determining their resistance to water leakage under varied water pressures. In this particular test, the 6x42 plastic binocular proved far superior to the four aluminum binoculars tested. Two of the aluminum binoculars, the standard 6x30 binocular and the standard 7x50 binocular, could only withstand a water pressure af 0.5 psi, equal to a water depth of 1.1 feet. The other two aluminum binoculars were considered waterproof instruments, but could only withstand a water pressure of 0.7 psi and 4.3 psi, equivalent to a water depth of 1.6 feet and 10.0 feet, respectively. The 6x42 plastic binocular managed to outperform all four of the other binoculars tested. Astonishing as it seems, signs of leakage in the plastic binocular were first observed at a water pressure of 45 psi, or a water depth of 103.6 feet.

Evaluation of the plastic binocular was completed in August 1944 and the instrument was given a satisfactory rating by the U.S. Navy as an all-purpose service binocular. U.S. Navy records uncovered by this author failed to indicate the specific U.S. Navy nomenclature ("Mark" and "Mod" number) assigned to the plastic binocular. Although production samples of the 6x42 plastic binocular were manufactured in 1944 for the service tests described above, it is not known for certain whether the 6x42 plastic binocular was ever really produced in mass quantity for the U.S. Navy and distributed to its servicemen. Production of all military binoculars was sharply curtailed by the U.S. Government in late 1944 — in view of this, it seems somewhat doubtful that the U.S. Government would have put the plastic binocular into full scale production at that particular point in time. A report from the U.S. Naval Observatory and the National Bureau of Standards, published late in 1944, indicated that the U.S. Navy was seriously intending to manufacture the plastic binocular to fulfill wartime needs. It was further noted that once wartime needs were filled, the plastic binocular would be available to civilians on the postwar commercial market. At the war's end, Universal considered bringing the low cost plastic binocular to market, along with a host of other new products, but many unforeseen problems developed, forcing the company to abandon its interest in this particular postwar venture. The 6x42 plastic binocular with its fixed focus eyepieces and solid ocular bridge seems to be an unknown species among binocular collectors today. After describing the plastic binocular to scores of binocular collectors and enthusiasts across the country, the author was unable to obtain an actual specimen of, or information substantiating the existence of, the 6x42 plastic binocular, whether it be the military or commercial version. None of the people interviewed had ever seen or heard of such a binocular.

In addition to successfully designing a 6x30 binocular with improved waterproofing protection and a 6x42 plastic binocular proven virtually leak-proof in water depths up to 103.6 feet, Universal managed to find solutions to other wartime problems associated with the design and construction of service binoculars. In 1942, Universal applied for a patent on the development of a new cementing compound to replace Canada balsam, a natural substance generally considered standard by the optical industry at the time for cementing optical elements inside binoculars. Formulated and tested at Universal by Adin Daniel Falkoff, the cementing compound was composed of two synthetic esters, chemically known as "diethylene glycol di-abietate" and "pentaerythritol tetra-abietate". Comparison tests showed that, in certain combinations, these two synthetic esters performed much better with respect to aging and weathering than Canada balsam when exposed to varying climatic conditions. In 1944, George Kende, Universal's Chief Engineer, and Sten Johanson, Universal's Chief Designer, one of the men responsible for the design of Universal's 6x30 binocular with improved waterproofing, combined their ingenious talents to develop a rather unusual piece of military equipment — a small, yet powerful, binocular and a special headgear unit onto which the binocular could be mounted for use without support from the user's hands or torso. This outfit was quite unique in the respect that most adjustments were easily made with the headgear and binocular in place. Interpupillary distance, eye distance (the distance between observer's eye and eye piece) and the up or down viewing angle of the binocular could be easily adjusted using just one hand. This special binocular did not have the conventional hinged ocular bridge — the right and left housing sections were mounted instead on a rigid shaft so each section could be moved away from or toward one another by means of a centrally located adjusting knob. Universal obtained two separate patents on the binocular and headgear designs — U.S. Pat.# 2,436,574, applied for on February 14, 1945, relating primarily to the design of the binocular and U.S. Pat.# 2,436,576, applied for on February 14, 1945, relating to both the binocular and headgear unit.

According to the recollections of former Universal employees, Universal supposedly never manufactured an instrument known as a monocular — despite these claims, such an instrument bearing the "Universal Camera Corporation" marking was eventually found. The design and construction of the Universal 6x30 monocular *(Fig. 4-42)* appears to be identical to that of the Universal 6x30 binocular with improved waterproofing first produced at the plant in 1943. This particular Universal monocular has no military markings and was found in a protective olive drab green canvas zippered case. In Universal's 1950 Annual Report to the Securities and Exchange Commission, Universal reported receiving a U.S. Army contract for the production of "monocular instruments". It appears that the monocular pictured here is undoubtedly an example of the monoculars produced by Universal under its 1950 U.S. Army contract.

Fig. 4-42 The 6x30 Universal monocular, believed to have been produced by Universal under a 1950 Army contract. (From the collection of Paul Sulc. Photo courtesy: Paul Sulc).

CHAPTER FIVE - PART ONE

1946-1948

THE MERCURY II -
"ESPECIALLY DESIGNED FOR COLOR"

The close of World War II signaled a new beginning for the Universal Camera Corporation. Wartime production of binoculars had given Universal considerable knowledge and experience in the field of optics, resulting in the company's ability to manufacture all of its own postwar camera and projection lenses. This was an obvious benefit to the company, since approximately 80% of Universal's prewar lenses had been purchased from other manufacturers. Universal managed to earn a sizable profit from its government contracts. In 1942, 1943 and 1944 Universal's net sales totaled over $15,000,000: war production accounted for 92% of these sales. It was through the fulfillment of these war production contracts that Universal managed an incredible financial turnaround that confounded many in the photographic industry. It was evident to all that the financially stricken Universal Camera Corporation was once again on the road to prosperity.

Many long months passed before amateur photographers were once again able to choose from a wide selection of new cameras and photographic equipment. Store shelves had long since been wiped clean of new cameras, quality used cameras and other related photographic supplies. The U.S. Government had prohibited the sale of new photographic equipment for civilian use since 1942, when an estimated 20 million cameras were in use by amateur photographers across the country. With the war finally at an end, the demand for cameras and photographic equipment was expected to grow to unbelievable proportions. Many of the 10 million men and women in the Armed Forces had acquired a certain degree of photographic skill while in the service; upon discharge, a large number of them decided to purchase new cameras of their own. Added to that were countless young people, all anxious to satiate their interest in photography with the long awaited purchase of a new camera. Photography was, after all, America's most popular spare-time activity. Photographic manufacturers began gearing up for record capacity production — a deluge of never-ending orders was certain to come.

Universal maintained some very favorable prospects for the immediate postwar photographic marketplace, one of which was the completed 35mm eye level SLR prototype that was shelved in 1941 because of the war. In 1944, Universal was granted a patent for the automatic diaphragm/shutter design used in the 35mm SLR prototype and also for its 2¼ inch square format waist level SLR model, both of which were designed and constructed

"I'm Not Ready for Reconversion"

NEITHER ARE WE . . .

He's still giving everything.

Until his job is done Universal's job is making the precision optical instruments he needs.

We're sticking to that job— 100%—until *he's* ready for us to reconvert.

BECAUSE HIS NEEDS COME FIRST *you'll have to wait for* MERCURY II, *the new camera we promised you "soon." It's worth waiting for—the* MERCURY II *is especially designed for color.*

UNIVERSAL CAMERA CORP.

NEW YORK • CHICAGO • HOLLYWOOD

There's only one flag we're prouder of!

Peacetime Manufacturers of Mercury, Cinémaster, Corsair Cameras and Photographic Equipment

Fig. 5-1 A Universal advertisement concerning reconversion to peacetime production, taken from "Popular Photography", March 1945.

in 1940. With these significant patents and the completed 35mm SLR prototype in hand, Universal had the option of introducing an entirely new and amazing 35mm eye level SLR design as its mainstay on the postwar photographic marketplace. Secondary to this was a new Speed Graphic type camera already in the advanced stages of design and planning. Not surprising though, Universal's managers, Githens and Shapiro, chose a different route — albeit, a more familiar one. They decided to resurrect a number of the company's prewar designs, particularly the well-known Mercury and Cinemaster cameras. Apparently, Githens and Shapiro felt, as they had in the past, more secure with this decision, essentially hoping to safeguard their newfound good fortune. For the time being, Universal's decision was not inconceivable. In order to speed reconversion efforts, many manufacturers reverted back to their prewar designs, usually with the addition of a few minor improvements. Under this plan, full scale peacetime production and distribution of photographic equipment could be a reality within only a few months time. Once store shelves were sufficiently stocked with new cameras and accessory equipment, manufacturers began turning their attention toward the development of more advanced designs.

Promotional ads for Universal's postwar line of products began appearing as early as June 1944 and continued steadily thereafter *(Fig. 5-1)*. In promoting its postwar products, Universal focused heavily on the concept of color photography. Kodachrome was understandably popular at the time; in addition to that, Eastman Kodak had introduced Kodacolor negative film for color prints just prior to the war in 1941. The emphasis was definitely on color — this was particularly evident in promotional ads representing Universal's

Fig. 5-2 The Universal Mercury II Model CX Candid Camera with standard coated 35mm f/2.7 Universal Tricor Lens.

172

Fig. 5-3 A die casting advertisement showing the three part Mercury II housing, taken from Die Casting, December 1945.

postwar headliner, the Universal Mercury II Model CX Camera *(Fig. 5-2)*, originally priced at $65.00 with a 35mm f/2.7 Tricor lens. The company boasted excellent results when the Mercury II was used in conjunction with color films: another vantage selling point was the economy of the camera's single frame format, producing 65 pictures from a standard 36 exposure 35mm cartridge. The new and improved minicamera was originally scheduled for production early in 1945 — but as the war lagged on, production was postponed until December, when the Mercury II Camera made its official debut. At the time, Universal boasted a production schedule of approximately 300 Mercury II cameras per day. The first Mercury II cameras off the production line were reserved for the U.S. Army, which had placed priority orders in excess of $1 million with a number of different camera concerns. Shortly after the war ended, large quantities of Mercury II cameras were shipped overseas and began appearing in Army PX stores everywhere.

The basic construction of the Mercury II consisted of a three-part aluminum alloy die cast housing, weighing only 7.2 ounces. The remaining parts used in the construction of the Mercury II were either die cast in aluminum or zinc alloy. Approximately 200 parts were mounted and assembled onto a zinc alloy frame, producing a complex camera mechanism that controlled the following features: shutter aperture, shutter speed, automatic film transport and lens focusing mount. The mechanism could be easily checked and inspected before emplacing it in the camera housing. Universal thought this particular aspect of the camera's design was particularly advantageous for achieving good quality control in mass production. When all 235 parts (lens not included) were combined with the three-part exterior housing, the total camera weight was only 18.5 ounces *(Fig. 5-3)*.

The major difference between the Mercury II and its predecessor, the Mercury I, was in the filmloads each camera used. As mentioned earlier, the Mercury I was designed to use a non-standard 35mm Univex #200 series filmload while the Mercury II was designed to use a standard 35mm film cartridge. After the collapse of Universal's film business in 1940, the company began to realize that the amateur photographer was growing less and less indulgent of non-standard filmloads and the problems commonly associated with them — at the same time, interest in the new color films was steadily increasing. Universal decided that "standardization" was essential if the company was to become a significant part of the postwar photographic market.

Several other differences between the Mercury I & II cameras are listed below.

Size - The Mercury II is ½ inch longer and ½ inch higher than the Mercury I. The film chambers on the Mercury II were enlarged to accommodate standard 35mm film cartridges.

Weight - Due to the difference in size, a 2.5 ounce weight difference exists between the two models (lens not included), the Mercury II being the heavier of the two.

Lenses - The Mercury II was sold with either a 35mm f/2.7 Universal-made Tricor lens or a 35mm f/3.5 Universal-made Tricor lens *(Fig. 5-4)*, the latter of the two being somewhat less common. It is unknown whether Universal ever manufactured postwar versions of the following prewar Mercury lenses — the 35mm f/2.0 Wollensak Hexar, the 75mm f/3.5 Ilex Telecor or the 125mm f/4.5 Wollensak. To date, this author has never seen any of these three lenses in a postwar "Universal-made" version. There is evidence, however, that in the

174

Fig. 5-4 Universal Mercury II Camera with uncommon coated 35mm f/3.5 Universal Tricor Lens.

immediate postwar years Universal applied anti-reflective coating to leftover prewar 35mm f/2.0 Wollensak Hexar lenses and then used these coated lenses for sale with the Mercury II camera. Consistent with war design standards, all postwar lenses manufactured in the Universal optical shops possessed the following advantages over lenses sold by Universal in prewar years — anti-reflective lens coating to increase light transmission efficiency, color correction, improved optical glass, and, for bonding lens elements, new synthetic cements capable of withstanding extremes in temperature.

Characteristic Features - The film exposure counter dial on the Mercury II was redesigned. An 18 exposure standard film cartridge registered 32 exposures on the dial, while a 36 exposure standard film cartridge registered 65 exposures on the dial. The film exposure counter dial on the Mercury I registered either 18 or 36 exposures when using either a UniveX #218 or #236 filmload, respectively.

The Mercury II featured the following range of shutter speeds - 1/20, 1/30, 1/40, 1/60, 1/100, 1/200, 1/300, 1/1000 second, plus T and B. (See Chapter 3 - Part 1 for speed settings on the two prewar Mercury models).

The shutter wind knob and shutter speed knob on the Mercury II were both enlarged, making them easier for the operator to use.

In designing the Mercury II, the neck cord loops were done away with entirely. The photographer was left to rely on a carrying case as the only means for supporting the camera around the neck.

Exterior Finish - A number of synthetic materials were used to cover the Mercury II instead of the genuine leather covering previously used on the

175

Mercury I. Leather was scarce immediately following the war, necessitating the use of synthetics for the first Mercury II cameras off the production line. Githens and Shapiro were quite pleased with the new synthetics — deeming them a suitable and less expensive substitute for the real thing.

George Kende, Chief Engineer at Universal and inventor of the Mercury Camera, described in detail the following process used in finishing the three-part exterior housing of the Mercury II. "Flat surfaces are satin-finished on wet belt sanders using 240 grit belts. The curved surfaces are polished by using string wheels on which Lea Compound 'B' is applied. For final polish Lea Compound 'A' is applied lightly over all exposed surfaces. The castings are then degreased in a trichlorethylene vapor degreaser, then washed and sprayed with clear Alkyd modified urea-formaldehyde resin and baked for one hour at 250 degrees Fahrenheit."

Generally speaking, the metal finish on the Mercury II lacked the luster and gleam that characterized the Mercury I. The finish of the Mercury II seemed to become dingy and dull within only a short time. Signs of heavy corrosion are extremely common on Mercury II models today, whereas many of the Mercury I models appear almost like new. Some former Universal engineers recalled the inferior finish of the Mercury II was due to the postwar use of magnesium metal in combination with the aluminum alloy normally used in die casting the Mercury housings. Magnesium had become quite popular during WW II and was being readily used by many other manufacturing companies in the postwar fabrication of their own products. The aluminum alloy used in the production of the Mercury I camera provided a more gleaming appearance than the combination of aluminum and magnesium used in the production of the Mercury II camera.

Accessory Equipment - The Mercury II was compatible with the following Mercury I accessories: enlarger, copying attachment, rangefinder, exposure meter, flash unit, normal or telephoto lenses, accessory optical viewfinders and UniveX No.11 Filters or Sunshade (the No.11 slip-on filter and sunshade were originally used on the prewar f/2.0 Hexar lens).

A postwar version of the Mercury exposure meter was made by Universal for use on the Mercury II *(Fig. 5-5)*. When designing the Mercury II, the accessory clip was moved to accommodate the addition of a rewind knob. The accessory clip was repositioned slightly inward and flush with the front of the camera, directly adjacent to the round protrusion housing the Mercury shutter. When the prewar exposure meter was slipped onto the accessory clip of the Mercury II, the meter's eyepiece was too far from the eye, making it difficult

Fig. 5-5 The Mercury II Exposure Meter (left) and Mercury I Exposure Meter (right).

176

to obtain an accurate reading. Universal decided to redesign the meter for the Mercury II. The tubular eyepiece on the postwar meter was lengthened substantially. The meter was not marked in any way, but it can be distinguished by observing the bottom back corners of the meter — one corner was literally cut off to provide a better fit on the Mercury II accessory clip.

Much like the prewar Mercury exposure meter, Universal's prewar rangefinder was somewhat difficult to use with the Mercury II, in that the rangefinder's eyepiece was far too short. Universal never marketed a postwar rangefinder for its Mercury II camera. Another photographic manufacturer, Spiratone Fine Grain Laboratories, introduced a similar clip-on rangefinder especially for the Mercury II in March 1947.

Due to the newly designed Mercury II film exposure counter and the enlarged shutter wind knob, the Mercury I rapid wind device was rendered incompatible with the Mercury II model. This author has never seen a Mercury II, or an advertisement for a Mercury II, equipped with a rapid wind device of any kind.

Fig. 5-6 Universal Mercury "Jiffy Masks" for mounting Mercury transparencies.

Universal began offering 2 x 2 Jiffy Transparency Masks *(Fig. 5-6)* in 1939 for mounting Mercury I transparencies. The demand for these masks increased dramatically when Universal introduced its standardized Mercury II. Most photofinishers refused to mount Mercury transparencies; therefore, Mercury II owners were faced with two choices — mounting their own slides or showing the uncut roll as a filmstrip. Universal included 12 free Jiffy masks with the purchase of a Mercury II camera. Otherwise they were sold, 50 to a box, at a cost of $.50. These gummed masks were produced in both orange and blue colors and each mask was marked "MERCURY Jiffy-Mask".

The Mercury II had its own leather carrying case, marked "Mercury II". Two basic versions of the Mercury II case exist — one is a front-opening type case in a burnt orange or dark brown (nearly black) color, while the other is a deluxe case, back-opening, lined and dark brown in color.

Other Features - Totally new on the Mercury II was a film reminder dial located on the rear cover next to the exposure calculator dial. The dial could be set for color film or any of three speeds of black & white film. In standardizing the Mercury II, these additional features were added: a film rewind knob, a rewind button, and a permanent film take-up spool.

While the Mercury II is well-known today as an "economical" single frame camera, there is a common misconception that its forerunner, the Mercury I, was a double frame format camera. The Mercury I film exposure counter

---

Calendar of PHOTOGRAPHIC EXHIBITIONS

*Conducted according to the recommended practices of Photographic Society of America.

7th Annual Vancouver International Salon of Pictorial Photography*, Vancouver Photographic Society.
On exhibition Oct. 22 to Nov. 10 in the Vancouver Art Gallery, 1145 West Georgia St., Vancouver, B.C., Canada.

X Salon Anual de Arte Fotografico Internacional, Foto Club Argentino.
On exhibition November 1946 in the Salon Peuser, Florida 750, Buenos Aires, Republica Argentina.

11th Annual Western Ontario International Salon of Photography, London Camera Club.
On exhibition Nov. 1 to Nov. 23 at the Elsie Perrin Williams Memorial Building, London, Ontario.

8th Annual Atlanta Salon of Photography*, Atlanta Camera Club.
On exhibition Nov. 1 to Nov. 15 at Rich's Inc., Atlanta, Ga.

9th Rhode Island National Salon of Photography*, Camera Club of Rhode Island.
On exhibition Nov. 1 to Nov. 18, R. I. School of Design Museum, Providence, R. I.

37th Chicago Camera Club Salon of Photography, Chicago Camera Club.
On exhibition Nov. 3 to Dec. 1 in the Club's exhibition room, 137 N. Wabash Ave.

32nd Scottish Salon of Photography, Scottish Photographic Federation.
On exhibition Nov. 30 to Dec. 15 at the Glasgow Art Gallery.

15th Annual Minneapolis Salon of Photography*, Minneapolis Camera Club.
On exhibition Dec. 1 to Dec. 31 at the Minneapolis Institute of Arts.

5th Sao Paulo Salon of Photographic Art (International)*, Foto Clube Bandeirante.
On exhibition December, The Prestes Maia Galleries, Sao Paulo, Brazil.

X Official Salon of Photography*, Club Fotografico de Chile.
Closes November 15.
Entry fee waived for foreign contributors.
Six prints allowed.
On exhibition Dec. 10 to Dec. 30 at the Palacio La Alhambra, Santiago.
For entry blank write to Senor Secretario, Club Fotografico de Chile, Calle Huerfanos 1223, Santiago, Chile.

2nd Salt Lake International Color Slide Exhibit*.
Closes November 17.
Entry fee $1.00.
Four 2 x 2 slides and/or larger transparencies allowed.
On exhibition Dec. 1 to Dec. 8 at the University of Utah.
For entry blank write C. E. Barrett, M. D., Salon Chairman, Box 246, Salt Lake City, Utah.

4th Montreal All-Canadian Salon of Photography*, Montreal Amateur Photographers' Club.
Closes November 18.
Entry fee $1.00.
Four monochrome and/or colored prints allowed.
On exhibition Nov. 30 to Dec. 15, Museum of Fine Arts, Sherbrooke St.
For entry blank write Geo. Fearnley, 1280 Bernard Ave., Montreal 8, Que.

December, 1946

6th International Focus Photo Salon, Amsterdam, Holland.
Closes November 19.
Entry fee $1.00 for black-and-white prints, $1.00 for color slides.
Four prints and six slides allowed.
On exhibition Sept. 21 to Oct. 6 at "Arti et Amicitiae" Art Gallery.
For entry blank write to International Focus Photo Salon, Zuider Stationsweg 33, Bloemendaal, Holland.

1st Hudson-Mohawk International Salon*, Albany Camera Club.
Closes November 19.
Entry fee $1.00.
Four prints allowed.
On exhibition Dec. 11 to Jan. 5 at the Albany Institute of History and Art.
For entry blank write Salon Secretary Mrs. E. Lehman, 445A First St., Albany, New York.

30th Annual International Salon of Pictorial Photography, Camera Pictorialists of Los Angeles.
Closes November 30.
Entry fee $1.00.
Four prints and four color slides allowed.
On exhibition Jan. 1947, in the Los Angeles Museum, Exposition Park.
For entry blank write Lynton Vinette, Los Angeles Museum, Exposition Park, Los Angeles 7, Calif.

9th Annual Springfield International Salon of Photography*, the George Walter Vincent Smith Art Museum.
Closes December 9.
Four prints allowed.
On exhibition Jan. 2 to Jan. 22, 1947, at the George Walter Vincent Smith Art Museum, Springfield, Mass.
For entry blank write Salon Secretary.

12th Annual Des Moines International Salon of Photography*, Y. M. C. A. Movie and Camera Club.
Closes December 10.
Entry fee $1.00.
Four prints allowed.
On exhibition Jan. 1 to Jan. 20, 1947, in the Hall of Photography, West Fourth St., at Keosauqua Way, Des Moines, Iowa.
For entry blank write Walter Vittum, Y. M. C. A., Des Moines, Iowa.

6th Chicago International Salon of Photography*, Chicago Historical Society.
Closes Jan. 15, 1947.
Entry fee $1.00.
Four prints allowed.
On exhibition Jan. 25 to Feb. 27, 1947, at the Chicago Historical Society.
For entry blank write Chicago Historical Society, Clark St. and North Ave., Chicago 14, Ill.

14th International Salon of Photography*, Delaware Camera Club.
Closes January 15, 1947.
Entry fee $1.00.
Four prints allowed.
On exhibition Feb. 2, to Mar. 2, 1947, Delaware Art Center, Park Drive and Woodlawn Ave.
For entry blank write Mrs. Wilbur Blair, 19 Bedford Drive, Edge Moor Gardens, Wilmington 261, Del.

2nd Chicago International Exhibition of Nature Photography*, Nature Camera Club.
Closes January 13, 1947.
Entry fee $1.00.
Four prints and four color slides allowed.
On exhibition Feb. 1 to Feb. 28 at the Chicago Natural History Museum.
For entry blank write H. J. Johnson 1614 W. Adams St., Chicago 12, Ill.

5th International Western Canadian Salon of Photography*, Manitoba Camera Club.
Closes January 18, 1947.
Entry fee $1.00.
Four monochrome prints allowed; four color prints (any process) allowed.
On exhibition Feb. 15 to Feb. 28, 1947, in the Winnipeg Art Gallery, Winnipeg Civic Auditorium.
For entry blank write Henry Bawden, Salon Secretary, 313 Smith St., Winnipeg, Man., Canada.

(Continued on page 106)

Fig. 5-7 Two Spiratone advertisements featuring various Universal products including the Mercury II Camera and a complete line of Mercury accessories and processing services, taken from "Popular Photography", December 1946 and December 1947.

179

was marked for a maximum of 36 exposures. Initially one might assume that the number "36" relates to double frame exposures. In all actuality though, the number relates to 36 single frame exposures. UniveX #200 series films were cut in lengths of 18 and 36 single frame exposures, as opposed to the standard 35mm film cartridges, which were cut in lengths of 18 and 36 double frame exposures. Nevertheless, a quick glance inside the camera instantly reveals and confirms the camera's single frame format; in addition, the 35mm focal length of the normal Mercury lens would indicate the existence of a single frame format.

One New York photographic distributor did much to promote the sale of Universal's postwar products, especially the Mercury II. Spiratone, located at 49 West 27th Street, New York City, began offering Mercury single-frame processing services immediately following Universal's introduction of the Mercury II in 1946. There was no apparent connection between the two companies. Within a few short months though, Spiratone's continuous advertising of "Mercury Services" had managed to spark the curiosity of those at Universal, as well as others in the photographic industry. Many of Universal's employees were Mercury owners, eventually discovering the convenience and dependability of the Mercury processing services that Spiratone provided. Other photofinishers were generally unwilling to process 35mm single-frame films, leaving Mercury owners with an exasperating problem. It was a successful combination of keen foresight and ingenuity that prompted Spiratone to begin offering specialized Mercury processing services. The overall acceptance of these photofinishing services influenced Spiratone to begin distributing a complete line of special accessory items for the Mercury camera. Ads promoting the Mercury II appeared monthly during 1946 and 1947 in Popular Photography, Modern Photography and other publications *(Fig. 5-7)*. A typical Spiratone ad usually read, "Always look to Spiratone for the latest, the best, the most reasonable in Mercury II accessories and services. Remember: SPIRATONE has the only COMPLETE SERVICE for EVERY MERCURY NEED!". In March 1947, Spiratone began circulating a free newsletter entitled "Mercury Photography News" and later "Mercury Bulletin", describing various accessories available from Spiratone for use with the Mercury II and how to obtain satisfactory results when using them. In the Fall 1948 "Mercury Bulletin", Spiratone announced its new coated Mercury Telephoto Lens and Mercury Wide Angle Lens, each priced at $19.95. Spiratone also offered the Esdy Rangefinder for use on the Mercury II. The rangefinder focused from 2½ feet to infinity and was available from Spiratone for $4.78. Mercury accessory equipment was just the beginning for Spiratone — a seed had sprouted. Spiratone discovered a profitable market distributing generalized photographic accessory equipment and soon began offering accessories for many other popular make cameras. Within a few years, Spiratone was well on its way to becoming one of today's most well-known distributors of general photographic accessory equipment.

Approximately 150,000 Mercury II cameras were sold the world over during the period 1946 through 1952. The prewar Mercury I possessed a quality look and feel that was far superior to that of the postwar Mercury II; in spite of this, the Mercury II sold well — the new improved coated lens and the standard 35mm filmload capability were points in its favor. At the original price of $65.00, the Mercury II was a relatively good buy for the amateur photographer. Surprising enough, by December 1946 the retail price of the Mercury II had skyrocketed to an unbelievable $82.90, making it a bit less attractive for many an interested buyer. The price remained stationary at that point until about 1951, when Mercury II cameras could easily be purchased at 50% off the regular price.

CHAPTER FIVE - PART TWO

1946-1948

"FOR PICTURES THAT CLICK ... CLICK A UNIVERSAL"

Fig. 5-8 The Universal Buccaneer Camera.

Six months into production, it was evident that sales of the Mercury II were falling behind those of other 35mm cameras on the market at the time. Cameras in the same price range featuring a rangefinder and double frame format, such as the Argus C 3, Clarus 35 and the Perfex 55, seemed to be the more popular choice. This prompted Universal to begin design work on a double frame 35mm camera with a built-in rangefinder and exposure meter.

In May 1947, Universal introduced the Universal Buccaneer Camera *(Fig. 5-8)* at a retail price of $65.00. Promotional advertisements for the Buccaneer proclaimed — "Never so much for so little!", "Universal's New Trail-blazer..." and "The ONE Minicamera That Gives You EVERYTHING!". Construction of the Buccaneer body began with the old Corsair dies. The combination viewfinder/exposure meter attachment previously used on the Corsair camera was replaced by a metal housing containing the Buccaneer's combination rangefinder/viewfinder and exposure meter. The metal housing made the Buccaneer somewhat top-heavy; consequently, Universal's engineers attempted to distribute the camera's weight more evenly by using metal (instead of plastic) in the construction of the rear cover. The remainder of the camera body was constructed of GE Textolite. Designed for use with standard 35mm film cartridges, the Buccaneer was equipped with a coated 50mm f/3.5 Universal Tricor lens, set in an auto-retractable lens mount, with a minimum focusing capability of three feet. Its built-in rangefinder (super-imposed images type) was coupled with the optical viewfinder to facilitate easy one step viewing and focusing. The built-in extinction type exposure meter was designed for use in conjunction with the camera's exposure calculator dial on the rear cover, much the same as the Mercury and Corsair cameras. The Buccaneer incorporated a five speed Universal Chromatic shutter with speeds from $\frac{1}{10}$ to $\frac{1}{300}$ second plus T and B, and aperture settings ranging from f/3.5 to f/16. Aperture and shutter speed settings were placed in front and also above the lens mount to facilitate exposure adjustment with the camera in its operating position. The Buccaneer incorporated these additional features: built-in photoflash synchronization, special shutter release lock to prevent double exposures, automatic film transport system, film type indicator, automatic exposure counter dial, cable release and tripod socket. A medium brown leather eveready case, marked "Buccaneer", was available at the additional cost of $7.25.

The Universal Cinemaster II Model G-8 Camera *(Fig. 5-9)* began appearing alongside the Mercury II in national magazines across the country as early as 1944. Actual distribution of the Model G-8 did not begin until

Fig. 5-9 Cinemaster II Model G-8 Cine Camera with special all chrome f/2.5 Univar Lens.

September 1946. Before peacetime production was even under way, Universal had already acquired over $2 million in orders for the Mercury II and the Model G-8 cameras. The Model G-8 was nearly identical in appearance to the prewar Model F-8. Other than the nameplate, the only noticeable differences were an improved run/lock button and some minor modifications to the film transport system. Universal's Advertising and Sales Departments tried to assure the public that "important" improvements had been made to the postwar model and that these changes warranted the higher postwar price tag. Equipped with an f/3.5 Universal Univar lens, the Cinemaster Model G-8 was priced at $51.90, compared to the prewar Model F-8 which sold for $32.50. The promotional campaign for the Model G-8 was by no means a failure — the Model G-8 proved to be one of Universal's best selling postwar cameras with sales in excess of 65,000 units.

Fig. 5-10 The 1½" f/3.5 Universal Univar Telephoto Cine Lens. A special Keystone and Revere adapter ring was included with this lens. (Courtesy: Al Nelson)

Fig. 5-11 Four uncoated prewar cine lenses manufactured for Universal by Ilex Optical and Wollensak Optical (left) and four coated postwar cine lenses manufactured by Universal in its own optical shop (right).

183

Universal manufactured a line of postwar coated cine lenses which included a ½" f/3.5 Univar, a ½" f/2.5 Univar, a ½" f/1.9 Univar and a 1½" f/3.5 Univar telephoto *(Fig. 5-10)*. All of these lenses were introduced in 1946, with the exception of the f/2.5 Univar lens. This lens was introduced in 1941 for use on the prewar Cinemaster line — it was one of the very first lenses manufactured by Universal. The f/2.5 Universal-made lens replaced the f/2.7 Wollensak lens previously used by the company since 1936 (except for their markings, the two lenses looked basically the same). Interestingly, Universal equipped approximately its first 5,000 Model G-8 cameras with special all chrome ½" f/2.5 Univar lenses. No manufacturer's name appeared on the lens, but it carried the marking "Made in U.S.A." *(Fig. 5-11)*.

Another prewar Universal design to resurface on the postwar market was the Universal Model PC-500 Projector *(Fig. 5-12)*, retailing at $63.50. Universal dropped the "UniveX" name which previously appeared on the prewar 500 watt projector (Model P-500) and replaced it with the "Universal" name instead. Universal discontinued use of the "UniveX" name almost entirely after the war. Universal also added a "C" to the model number of its new postwar 500 watt projector, most likely indicating one of two things — "color" or "coated" (lens). This "C" appeared later on other postwar Universal

Fig. 5-12 The Universal Model PC-500 Projector with coated 1" f/2 Universal Superlux Lens.

projectors which, like the PC-500, had evolved from designs marketed before the war. The 8mm Model PC-500 projector incorporated the same basic features as the prewar version with the addition of a coated, color-corrected 1" f/2 Universal Superlux lens, which was actually slower than the lens previously used on the prewar Model P-500 projector. As with other postwar Universal products, improvements on the Model PC-500 were relatively insufficient to warrant a $21.00 price increase over that of the prewar model. Ludicrous as it seems, Universal discontinued the postwar Model PC-500 in 1947, only to reintroduce it again as a "new improved" model in 1948 — this time with an even higher price tag than before! Advertisements for this "improved" model read, "Now better than ever!". Relatively scarce as a collectible, the 500 watt 8mm Universal Model PC-5 projector *(Fig. 5-13)* was identical in appearance to the Model PC-500 projector and retailed at the inflated price of $75.00. "Photography affordable to everyone" was the single principle on which the Universal Camera Corporation was founded in 1932. In its prewar years, Universal offered the amateur photographer many excellent values. For the most part, this was not the case in postwar years — Universal's products were extremely high priced, considering the fact that most of the company's alleged postwar product design improvements were in reality quite insignificant, failing to justify a higher price.

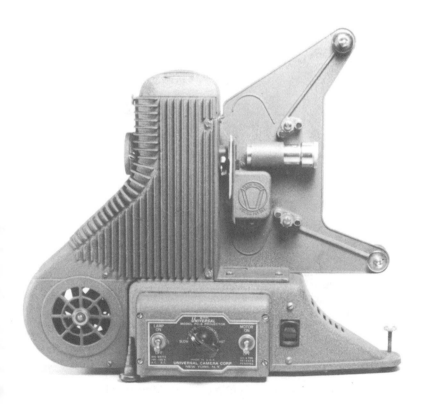

Fig. 5-13 The Universal Model PC-5 Projector with coated 1" f/2 Universal Superlux Lens.

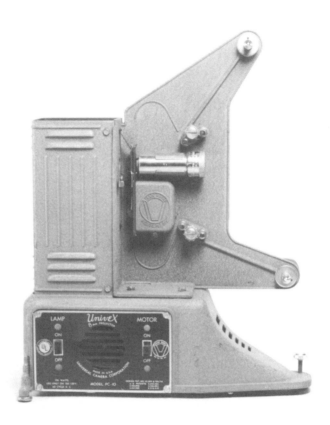

Fig. 5-14 The UniveX Model PC-10 Projector with coated 1" f/2 Universal Hi-Lux Lens.

Two low priced 8mm projector models were also introduced by Universal in 1946. The 100 watt UniveX Model PC-12 Projector, originally retailing at $35.25, was equipped with a 1" f/2 Universal Superlux lens. The Model PC-12 operated on AC current only, possessing virtually all of the same features as the 1941 prewar UniveX Model P-300 projector. With its crinkle-gray finish, the Model PC-12 projector was most often advertised as the low priced companion piece to the Model G-8 Cinemaster II camera. Shortly after, Universal introduced another similar projector model — the 100 watt UniveX Model PC-10 Projector *(Fig. 5-14)*, equipped with a 1" f/2 Universal Hi-Lux lens. This model did not carry the single frame projection feature found on the prewar Model P-300 and PU-300 projectors. The Model PC-10 was similarly finished in crinkle-gray enamel and retailed at $37.00. These two projector models are rarely seen on the collector's market.

Universal brought another familiar prewar design to the postwar marketplace in the summer of 1946 — the Uniflash Camera and Flash Outfit, reintroduced at the postwar price of $6.70. The Uniflash attracted little attention after the war because most photo enthusiasts had begun to develop an interest in the larger formatted films, such as the 120, 620, 116 and 616 sized rollfilms. Early in 1947, Universal's Engineering Department was concentrating heavily on several new camera designs which would utilize

Fig. 5-15 The Universal Meteor Camera, the original version with all chrome lens tube.

the larger 2¼ inch format that had grown so popular since the war. David C. Whitaker, Githens' personal advisor on camera construction, was the man responsible for the development of the Universal Meteor Camera *(Fig. 5-15)*, Universal's first, all new, postwar design for the domestic market. As for the originality of the design itself, there was one noticeable exception — the old Corsair viewfinder/exposure meter component was incorporated into the design of the Meteor. (Several years later, this same component part reappeared again on another Universal design). The Meteor, which retailed at $15.00, was introduced for the beginning photographer interested in low price and simplicity. A dark brown eveready case, marked "Meteor", could be purchased for an additional $5.00. The Meteor became one of the more popular low-priced cameras on the market during the late 1940's. Two distinctly different variations exist — the first has an all metal chrome lens tube, the other has a black plastic lens tube *(Fig. 5-16)*. The Meteor produced 12 exposures, 2¼x2¼" in size, on standard 620 rollfilm by means of a unique "film chamber loading" system. Not being the ordinary back-opening type camera, film was instead loaded into the bottom of the Meteor by means of a removable base plate. Integral with the camera's base plate was a metal framework, referred to as the "loading frame", onto which the film could be loaded. Once properly loaded, the "loading frame" was reinserted into the bottom of the camera until the attached base plate was firmly in place. In addition to the built-in combination viewfinder/exposure meter, the Meteor

Fig. 5-16 The Universal Meteor Camera, a later variation with black plastic lens tube.

featured an exposure calculator and built-in photoflash synchronization. All aluminum in construction, the Meteor was equipped with a coated 72mm f/11 Achromat doublet lens, set in a retractable mount, with a minimum focusing capability of five feet. With the lens in its innermost position, accidental exposures were prevented by means of a stop arm. The Meteor featured a single speed shutter (I (⅟₅₀), plus B) and apertures ranging from f/11 to f/32.

U.S. Design Pat.# 152,232 pertains to the ornamental design of the Meteor. As part of the record in this design patent, Whitaker cited two references (U.S. Design Pat.# 102,527 and U.S. Design Pat.# 103,700) in relation to the design of the Meteor — both were camera designs invented in the mid 1930's by Walter Dorwin Teague, a highly respected and well-known design engineer of the Eastman Kodak Company. One Kodak design is recognizable as the Bullet Camera with its telescoping tubular lens: in itself, the other design is unfamiliar — it does, however, bear a stark resemblance to the Meteor design. Both Kodak camera designs were of the back-opening type — therefore, it would seem that the "chamber loading system" of the Meteor was original in nature. (Author's Note: Scattered rumors exist among photographic collectors and historians that Universal manufactured a Meteor II — this author has found nothing to substantiate these claims).

Two completely new projector designs were introduced by Universal in 1947 — the 8mm Universal Cinematic Model P-750 Projector *(Fig. 5-17)*, retailing at $135.00, and the 16mm Universal Tonemaster Film & Sound

Fig. 5-17 (right) The Universal Cinematic Model P-750 8mm Projector with coated 1" f/1.6 Universal Superlux Lens.

Fig. 5-18 (below) The Universal Tonemaster 16mm Film and Sound Projector with coated 2" f/1.6 Universal Superlux Lens.

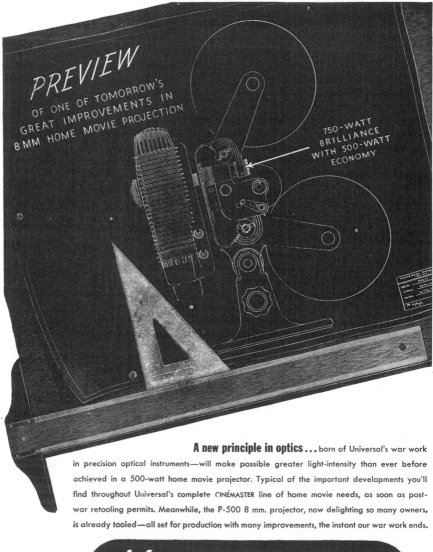

A new principle in optics... born of Universal's war work in precision optical instruments—will make possible greater light-intensity than ever before achieved in a 500-watt home movie projector. Typical of the important developments you'll find throughout Universal's complete CINÉMASTER line of home movie needs, as soon as post-war retooling permits. Meanwhile, the P-500 8 mm. projector, now delighting so many owners, is already tooled—all set for production with many improvements, the instant our war work ends.

UNIVERSAL CAMERA CORP.

NEW YORK • CHICAGO • HOLLYWOOD

Manufacturers of Mercury, Cinémaster, Corsair Cameras and Photographic Equipment

Fig. 5-19 A Universal advertisement showing a rough draft drawing of the Cinematic projector as first perceived by Joseph Pignone in 1941, taken from "Popular Photography", February 1945.

Projector *(Fig. 5-18)*, retailing at $350.00. A blueprint drawing of the Model P-750, as originally conceived, was first rendered in 1941 by Joseph Pignone, the engineer responsible for the design and invention of Universal's two prewar SLR models. This same drawing later appeared in magazine ads in 1945 as a promotion for the new postwar 750 watt Universal projector *(Fig. 5-19)*. Constructed almost entirely of die cast metal parts, the Model P-750 was completely gear-driven, requiring no chains or spring belts of any kind. The Model P-750, operated at 60 cycles on AC-DC current and boasted the following features: 750 watt projection, 400 foot reel capacity, a single clutch lever for fully geared forward, reverse, rewind and still picture projection, a self-locking easy-load film gate, a rheostat speed control for no flicker projection, blower and fins cooling, a separate power cord, and a removable condenser. Equipped with a coated 1" f/1.6 Universal Superlux lens, the Model P-750 also offered these convenience features: a built-in automatic pilot light, luminous controls which were visible to the operator in the dark, a carrying handle which was an integral part of the projector's die cast construction, and a sponge rubber cushion base. The Model P-750 was finished in antique bronze enamel and weighed approximately 15 pounds. Universal offered a wood-framed carrying case for the Model P-750 priced at $10.75. In the months immediately following the introduction of the Model P-750, a slew of inoperable projectors were returned to the Service Department at Universal. Of all the projectors ever manufactured by Universal, the Model P-750 earned the worst reputation for mechanical

Fig. 5-20 The Universal Cinematic Model P-752 8mm Projector with coated 1" f/1.6 Universal Superlux Lens.

problems. Many photographic retailers claimed it was not unusual for a new Model P-750 Cinematic to have gear problems, fresh out of the factory box. In an attempt to remedy an apparent weakness in the projector's fully gear-driven system, Universal developed and introduced a slightly modified version of the original Cinematic, the Universal Cinematic Model P-752 Projector *(Fig. 5-20)*, priced $20 less, at $115.00. At first glance, the only noticeable difference between the two Cinematic models was the new gray enamel finish. A closer look at the new Model P-752 revealed two separate projection controls — one labeled "Project" and "Rewind", and another labeled "Run" and "Still" — instead of the single lever previously used to control these different operations on the bronze Model P-750 projector. The 750 watt Cinematic models are seldom seen today. The high price tag on these two models put them out of reach for many amateur photographers.

The 1000 watt Tonemaster Sound Projector was introduced in November 1947. In 1948, Universal subcontracted for the production of over $1.5

Fig. 5-21 The Universal Roamer I Folding Camera, the original version.

million of these sound projectors. Determined to "come out ahead" on a project that had cost the company a small fortune, Universal established a separate sales division to manage the distribution and sale of the new Tonemaster projector. In a nationwide attempt to promote the sale of the Tonemaster, executives working out of this division focused their attention on different states across the country including New York, West Virginia, Louisiana, Ohio, Illinois and California. In comparing the features of the Tonemaster to those of other sound projectors on the market at the time, the $350.00 price tag seemed reasonable. Operating on AC-DC current, the Tonemaster's 2000 foot reel capacity provided approximately one full hour of running time without a film change. Single unit construction and a light-weight aluminum carrying case contributed to the projector's extreme portability. One unusual characteristic of the Tonemaster was its "armless design", whereby the film reels were mounted directly onto the unit itself, eliminating the need for conventional extension arms. Incorporated into the design of the Tonemaster were these additional features: a tri-blade shutter, a five tube amplifier, built-in microphone and record player connections, an

Fig. 5-22 The Universal Roamer II Folding Camera.

eight inch speaker operating between 50 and 6000 cycles, a 50 foot speaker cord, centralized controls including a single lever automatic motor-driven rewind control, sound and tone controls, semi-automatic tilting, reverse draft and blower cooling. Promotional material for the Tonemaster identified the projector's len as being a coated 2" f/1.6 Universal Superlux. One former Universal manager seemed relatively certain that Universal never commenced serial production of this particular projector model, claiming that only a small quantity of prototype models were manufactured. Interestingly, a Tonemaster was acquired by this author, equipped with a lens marked "NATCO, INC., Chicago, U.S.A. 2" E.F. f/1.6 Coated Lens" and marked with a "1457" serial number. Since that time, the author has been unable to locate any other examples of the Tonemaster. With only one known serial number available, it is virtually impossible to approximate production figures for the Tonemaster. Whatever the exact number produced, most Universal collectors will agree that the Tonemaster is, without a doubt, one of the rarest of all Universal projectors.

Fig. 5-23 The Universal Roamer 63 Folding Camera.

Fig. 5-24 Universal Accessory Flash Cable Attachment for use with the Roamer cameras.

Fig. 5-25 Universal Roamer I Folding Camera, the later version with variant lens mount.

During 1948, Universal introduced two entirely new lines of still cameras. First to be introduced was a line of folding cameras, producing eight exposures, 2¼x3¼" in size, on standard 120 or 620 film. This new line was comprised of three different models: the Universal Roamer I Camera *(Fig. 5-21)*, the Universal Roamer II Camera *(Fig. 5-22)* and the Universal Roamer 63 Camera *(Fig. 5-23)*. Certain features were common to all three models: aluminum die cast construction, an accessory shoe clip, eye level and waist level viewfinders, tripod and cable release sockets, and built-in photoflash synchronization. To obtain flash pictures with the Roamer cameras, the UniveX Mercury Photoflash Unit was used in combination with a special accessory hot shoe adapter, known as the Universal Flash Cable Attachment *(Fig. 5-24)*. First and least expensive in the series of folding cameras was the Roamer I, retailing at $29.75. The Roamer I was equipped with a 100mm doublet f/11 lens, coated and color corrected, with a minimum focusing capability of five feet. A single speed shutter (I (⅟50), plus B) was incorporated into the design of the Roamer I — exposures were accomplished by actuating the shutter release lever located on the shutter barrel. The more expensive Roamer models employed the use of a unique "shutter release trigger" conveniently located on the camera's front cover. This added feature provided

Fig. 5-26 The Universal Uniflex I Camera — the original version (left) with a squeeze-type cover latch and the later version (right) with a sliding lock catch (see bottom edge).

a much simpler, more accessible means of releasing the shutter. The Roamer I was constructed using the same shutter and lens mount originally used on the Meteor camera. A variant model of the Roamer I *(Fig. 5-25)* was also produced — the design of the lens mount was considerably different from the lens mount used on earlier Roamer I cameras. In all other respects, the two versions were identical.

The second in the folding camera series was the Roamer II, priced at $48.00. A coated 100mm Universal anastigmat f/4.5 lens, of triplet construction, provided the user with a minimum focusing capability of four feet, while a four speed Universal Synchromatic shutter provided speeds up to $\frac{1}{200}$ second, plus B. A few months later, Universal topped off its line of folding cameras with the introduction of the Roamer 63, priced midway between the Roamer I and Roamer II cameras. Except for the speed of the lens, the Roamer 63 displayed all the same characteristics as the more expensive Roamer II model. As the model name implies, the Roamer 63 was fitted with an f/6.3 lens, putting the retail price of this model at $38.00. A dark brown carrying case, marked only "UNIVERSAL", was available for use with any of the Roamer models at a cost of $7.50.

The twin lens reflex camera enjoyed a booming popularity in the mid and

Fig. 5-27 The Universal Uniflex II Camera, the original version (left) with squeeze-type cover latch and the later version (right) with sliding button latch mechanism.

late 1940's and Universal was right on cue with its new twin lens reflex line — the Universal Uniflex I Camera *(Fig. 5-26)* and the Universal Uniflex II Camera *(Fig. 5-27)*. Owing to its large format, coupled with the advantageous ability to view, compose and focus directly on the ground glass, the twin lens reflex camera had steadily become the preferred choice among amateur and professional photographers alike. Introduced in June 1948, the Uniflex I and Uniflex II provided 12 exposures (2¼x2¼" in size) on standard 120 or 620 rollfilm. Included on both models were the following features: aluminum die cast construction, built-in photoflash synchronization with hot shoe clip, a front surface reflex mirror, a direct vision viewfinder, single knob synchronized focusing of the viewing and taking lenses, a depth of field scale, cable release and tripod sockets, and two coated anastigmat lenses of triplet construction.

The Uniflex I, priced at $48.00, featured a 75mm Universal f/4.5 viewing lens and a 75mm Universal f/5.6 taking lens. The design also included a between the lens four speed Universal Synchromatic shutter providing a top speed of ½₀₀ second, plus B. The earliest Uniflex I & II cameras were equipped with a rear cover squeeze-type lock catch, located on the underside of the camera near the front. It was not uncommon for the user to inadvertently apply pressure to this lock catch while taking pictures, thereby causing the cover to open, ruining the film inside. Subsequently, later models were equipped with a sliding lock catch that could not be opened unintentionally. The Uniflex II, priced quite a bit higher at $75.00, offered a pair of slightly faster lenses — an f/3.8 viewing lens and an f/4.5 taking lens. In addition, a five speed shutter was added with a top speed of ½₀₀ second, plus T and B. Marked only "UNIVERSAL", a dark brown leather carrying case was available for both the Uniflex I & II models at a cost of $9.95. Universal produced two distinct versions of the Uniflex II. The earliest models produced had significantly more chrome trim than the later models, which are almost entirely black *(Fig. 5-28)*.

In less than three years time, from 1945 to 1948, Universal managed to introduce a rather substantial line of postwar products. Each of these products reflected Universal's relentless determination to recapture the successful stature it had known in years gone by. Despite a great deal of optimism and

Fig. 5-28 The Universal Uniflex II Camera, the final version showing much less chrome trim than the two earlier versions.

months of planning and hard work, a series of unfortunate incidents had already begun to develop at Universal. The collective adverse effects of these occurrences would eventually cast a shadow over many of Universal's popular postwar products, leaving Universal once again in a dismal situation.

Fig. 5-29 Employees of Universal's Tool and Model Shop, circa 1948.

CHAPTER SIX

1948-1952

"THE TREND IS UNIVERSAL!"

The majority of the photographic industry was completely unaware of the misfortunes encountered by Universal in the years immediately following the war. Hidden behind an array of new products was a company trying to overcome one major setback after another. Even today, very few people know the actual circumstances responsible for the eventual demise of the Universal Camera Corporation.

Universal was less than one year into peacetime production when the first of a long series of problems began. In August 1946, the union members of C.I.O., Local 165, went on strike against the New York Merchandise Company. Many of the striking workers had been with the company a good number of years and were well aware that Universal was a subsidiary of New York Merchandise. Because Universal occupied space in the same building as New York Merchandise, the strikers were able to cause considerable disorder to Universal's everyday business operations. As far as they were concerned, any financial difficulties incurred by Universal as a result of the strike would eventually be passed on, in one way or another, to New York Merchandise. The strike lasted seven long months. During that time, workers at Universal were generally permitted to cross picket lines, although incidents of harassment and vandalism were frequently reported. One of the major concerns of the striking workers was the arrival and departure of shipments at the West 23rd Street building. Consisting mainly of raw materials and finished goods, these shipments were the lifeline of both Universal and New York Merchandise — an obvious target for the strikers. The scene was generally chaotic whenever large shipments were scheduled in or out of the building. In some instances, as many as 200 police officers were called in to control disturbances created by the striking workers.

Less than two months later, the die casters in the area became involved in a strike which lasted several months longer than originally predicted. Universal had subcontracted with a number of these die casting firms to produce parts for its postwar camera and projector designs. Anticipating the timely arrival of these parts, Universal began hiring additional assembly workers for the job. As it turned out, the finished parts did not reach Universal until October 1947, approximately eight months later than originally scheduled. During this same period, more specifically in March 1948, one of the die casting firms subcontracted by Universal filed a voluntary petition for bankruptcy under Chapter X of the Bankruptcy Act. The company signed a contract with Universal in November 1947 for the production of $1.5 million worth of 16mm sound projectors. Several months prior to the signing of this contract, cash advances in excess of $90,000 were made to the die casting firm along with various shipments of tools and raw materials. To make matters worse, Universal had assumed financial responsibility for 50% of a bank loan taken out by the subcontractor in the amount of $115,000. Consequently, in July 1949, a Houston bank entered a third party judgment against Universal for $57,500. One problem compounded another until Universal found itself saddled with an operating loss of over $1 million for the year 1947. To keep the business going, sizable loans were needed — in 1947 alone, Universal took more than $950,000 in bank loans and an additional $265,000 in loans from the stockholders and officers of the company.

Once the die casters had returned to work, Universal began receiving regular shipments of finished camera and projector housings. Thousands of Universal cameras and projectors were quickly assembled for shipment to retailers across the nation. Not long after, Universal started receiving an unusually large number of returns from its Uniflex and Roamer camera lines. The

Fig. 6-1 Evidence of an adhesive problem affecting thousands of Uniflex and Roamer cameras during 1948.

cameras were virtually covered with dried adhesive and the synthetic covering had begun to lift up and curl at the corners *(Fig. 6-1)*. Universal immediately contacted the supplier of the adhesive, the Hood Rubber Company, a division of the B. F. Goodrich Company, who attributed the mishap to a recent change in adhesive formulas. Apparently when the cameras were subjected to even the slightest amount of heat, the glue would begin to liquefy and then ooze from underneath the synthetic covering. The problem usually occurred during shipment, although some cameras did manage to reach their destinations without any visible defects. Oftentimes retailers would display groups of cameras in storefront windows. With the warm sunlight beating against these windows, it wasn't long before the faulty adhesive on Universal's cameras began to melt, resulting in a dreadful sight that did little to compliment Universal or the retailer. Needless to say, many of Universal's cameras were quickly removed from public view.

In an attempt to remedy the situation, Universal immediately hired and trained a group of employees to work specifically on the restoration of these defective cameras. Before anything else could be done, the cameras had to

Fig. 6-2 Two Universal advertisements equally representative of Universal's extensive postwar promotional efforts, taken from "Popular Photography", August and September 1948.

be completely disassembled. The cleaning process that followed was both tedious and time-consuming. It involved scraping the crusted glue from each camera by hand with a razor blade. Afterward, the smooth metal surfaces were repolished and the camera's remaining surfaces were covered once again with new synthetic material. This salvage effort was continued well into 1949. Universal estimated the cost of this program in the tens of thousands of dollars. In June 1949, Universal initiated a lawsuit against the B. F. Goodrich Company for $1 million in damages which resulted from the use of the faulty adhesive. Word of the defective cameras eventually spread throughout the industry, after which time Universal experienced much difficulty selling the Uniflex and Roamer line of cameras. Consequently, the company found itself caught with huge inventories of finished cameras and spare parts. As time passed, it became increasingly clear that the faulty adhesive had cost Universal in many other ways. Universal, for instance, had invested hundreds of thousands of dollars into an advertising campaign for these cameras in 1948 — all of this was totally wasted. Photographs of certain influential photo and department store heads were included in many of Universal's 1948 magazine ads, along with their personal statements professing quality and dependability in Universal's products *(Fig. 6-2)*. The matter of the defective cameras prompted most of these store officials to contact Universal and request the immediate removal of their names, statements, and photographs from all Universal advertising. Many other retailers shared similar feelings, quickly severing their connections with Universal. Much expense was spent in an effort to retain the business of these customers, but to no avail. At this point in time, the retail industry wanted little to do with Universal. They were thoroughly disinterested, if not totally disgusted, with Universal's products. Ironically, one of Universal's most frequently used 1948 advertising slogans was "The Trend is UNIVERSAL!" — by the end of 1948, very few people were likely to agree. The entire situation proved highly embarrassing for the company and, as a result, Universal's reputation suffered badly.

Universal was understandably distressed by the mishap — a considerable amount of time and money had been spent on the development of the Uniflex line. Initially, management had instructed the Engineering Department to put

Fig. 6-3 Original drawing of the final production model of the Uniflex I Camera.

Fig. 6-4 Original drawing of the "automatic" Uniflex II Camera. Financial difficulties kept Universal from putting this model into production.

Fig. 6-5 Original drawing of the final production model of the Uniflex II Camera.

together a design for a reasonably priced twin lens reflex camera, similar in fashion to the popular Rolleicord camera. Two distinctly different working models were eventually completed and awaited management's approval for production. The working model of the Uniflex I *(Fig. 6-3)* was approved immediately for production. The working model of the Uniflex II *(Fig. 6-4)* incorporated a number of "automatic features". Serious financial indebtedness forced management to disapprove this particular model for production. As a less expensive alternative, the advanced features were removed from the original Uniflex II design and the production model that resulted was much the same as the Uniflex I, except for the addition of a faster lens and shutter *(Fig. 6-5)*.

The year 1948 brought an abrupt end to many of Universal's projects "still in the making". During the war years, Universal made plans to diversify its postwar line of photographic products with the introduction of an automatic record changer and a combination phonograph/radio unit. The automatic phonograph was invented early in 1945 by Frank M. Johnson. A cabinet to house the phonograph was later designed by George Kende *(Fig. 6-6)*.

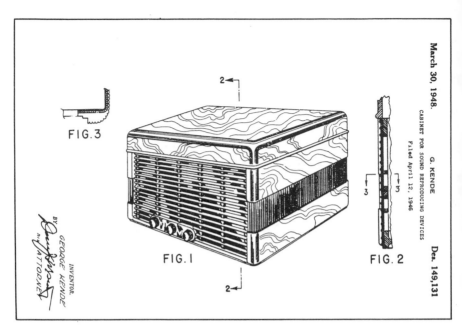

Fig. 6-6 U.S. Des. Pat. #149,131 showing George Kende's 1946 design of a cabinet for an automatic phonograph.

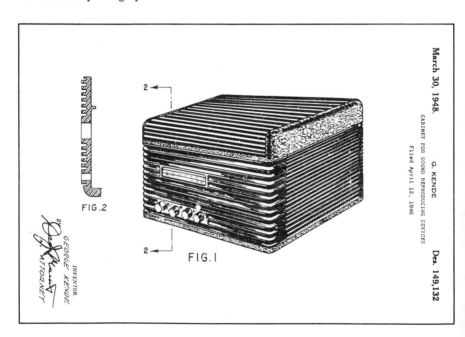

Fig. 6-7 U.S. Des. Pat. #149,132 showing George Kende's 1946 design of a cabinet for a combination phonograph/radio unit.

Another cabinet, very similar to the first, was designed to include a radio along with the phonograph *(Fig. 6-7)*. The main feature of Universal's automatic phonograph was its ability to play a group of records having different diameters. For instance, records of 10 inch and 12 inch diameter could be stacked together on this phonograph and the unit would automatically adjust for each different size record being played. The phonograph was to be marketed under the trade name "Ultravox". A great deal of money was channeled into Universal's Electronics Division to expedite the completion of the project. Universal obtained the following patents on its automatic phonograph — U.S. Design Pat.# 149,131 and U.S. Design Pat. #149,132, both applied for on April 12, 1946; and U.S. Pat.# 2,544,230, applied for on November 5, 1945. By the time the latter patent was granted on March 6, 1951, more than five years had passed and the phonograph project was long since abandoned due to Universal's failing financial state. Neither the phonograph unit or combination phonograph/radio unit ever reached serial production, although working prototype models of each were constructed at Universal.

While Universal struggled desperately to remain a part of the photographic industry, two other photographic companies gained immediate recognition with the introduction of their new products. In 1947, the David White Instrument Co. of Milwaukee, Wisconsin introduced the Stereo Realist, a precision made 35mm stereo camera. Although only a small number of these cameras were released for sale that year, in the years that followed, the Stereo Realist became extremely popular, creating a new revival of stereo photography. Approximately 20,000 Stereo Realists were sold in 1949 and sales figures were expected to double in the forthcoming year. About the same time, the world witnessed one of photography's most memorable and triumphant achievements. In February 1947, Dr. Edwin H. Land of the Polaroid Corporation announced and demonstrated the Polaroid Land Camera to the Optical Society of America. Two years later, in February 1949, the much talked about and long awaited Polaroid Land Camera, listing at $89.75, was finally released on the retail market. Truly an amazing photographic accomplishment, the world renowned "one minute picture process" succeeded in cornering a good share of the public's attention through the late 1940's. Skeptics in the industry originally thought the camera would never amount to anything more than a passing photographic novelty, but as the list of practical uses grew longer and longer, the Polaroid Land Camera soon became a standard piece of equipment for thousands of amateur and professional photographers, as well as countless business organizations across the country. During 1949, the retail trade industry estimated sales of the Polaroid Land Camera at approximately 10,000 units per month. During this same period, Universal's sales began to decline rapidly, dropping from $6 million in 1947 to $3.4 million in 1948, and continuing to fall even further to a low of $1 million in 1949. In the face of rising competition, it seemed that the overall popularity of Universal's photographic products had definitely diminished.

The atmosphere at Universal in the late 1940's and early 1950's was one of sheer disheartenment — the enthusiasm and excitement that once prevailed during Universal's earlier more successful years had disappeared from sight completely. In January 1947, Universal employed over 1200 people at its New York City plant alone. Since that time, hundreds of Universal's workers had been laid off and, as each year passed, Universal's financial condition grew continually worse. By January 1950, Universal's employment rolls had plunged below the 200 mark. There was no question about it — things had not gone well for Universal since the prosperous war years. Everything that could have gone wrong — did. March 10, 1949 was no exception. On that particular date in time, a triple murder/suicide scandal made the front pages of many New York area newspapers. As the story became public, it was learned that both murder victims were employed by the Universal Camera Corporation. One of the victims, a young woman, was the personal secretary of Otto Githens, Universal's President; the other, a young man, was one of the head production engineers with the company, in addition to being a close aide and consultant to Githens. Over the next few days, Universal's name was frequently mentioned as the story's shocking details began to unfold in news reports. Whether Universal's sales were adversely affected by this tragic incident would be difficult to say. One thing is for certain — the particular circumstances surrounding this tragedy did little to improve the company's already tarnished reputation.

Universal's situation seemed hopeless indeed. With insufficient working capital and several large debts still in arrears, it seemed as though there was little anyone could do to save the ailing camera company from almost certain bankruptcy. Universal's situation was one of total disarray, with virtually no solid chance of a successful or productive recovery in sight. Most of Universal's officers, directors and managers were thoroughly convinced their jobs would soon be a thing of the past. After giving much forethought to the state of affairs at Universal, George Kende, Universal's Chief Engineer and Optical Plant Manager, decided to resign from his position in December 1948. During his 13 year tenure with the company, Kende assigned a total of 39 U.S. patents to Universal. In prewar years, Universal allocated sufficient funding for general photographic research purposes and the expansion of its facilities. This funding, combined with Kende's competent direction and management, allowed Universal to conquer many obstacles associated with the manufacture of photographic and optical instruments. In the immediate postwar years, Universal's research and development funds were quickly depleted as the company began to encounter one unexpected problem after another — problems that were partly the result of pure misfortune and partly the result of mismanagement. With the financial situation as it was, Kende realized there was little more of consequence he could accomplish at Universal and was certain the company could never again rival its competitors, as it once had in prewar years. Several years after his resignation from Universal, Kende acquired the position of Vice President of Manufacturing at Wollensak Optical Company where he remained until 1963. He then joined the Bausch & Lomb Company as Chief Engineer of its Scientific Instrument Division where he became involved in the development and production of microscopes, fiber-optic instruments and other high-tech optical instruments. Further on in his career, Kende joined the Kollsman Instrument Corp., where he directed production of instruments for the Apollo Command Module and the Lunar Excursion Module. From 1972 until his retirement, Kende worked as a full time professional consultant, providing various corporations with technical information and advice on product design and manufacture.

Kende's resignation was, by far, the most devastating blow for Universal — only a few remnants of a once prosperous company remained. In the months following Kende's resignation, the general state of affairs at Universal showed no improvement whatsoever, resulting in several other important resignations. In November 1949, Milton M. Shaw, Secretary and Director of Universal since 1937, resigned from his position and returned full time to New York Merchandise where he concurrently held the position of President since 1941. Harry Millstein, a member of Universal's Board of Directors, resigned in March 1950. Three months later, in July 1950, Githens,

Universal's President, submitted his resignation, leaving his position as President to Shapiro, Universal's Vice President. After resigning, Githens continued to retain his stock holdings in Universal and his seat on the Board of Directors. Shapiro's former position of Vice President was delegated to John D. Cassidy, Universal's General Manager. Cassidy eventually resigned from the position as Vice President and left the company in August 1951. During the war, Cassidy was a Commander in the U.S. Navy assigned to the Office of the Inspector of Naval Materials in New York City. While serving in this capacity, Cassidy worked closely with Universal and other companies handling affairs related to the production and procurement of binoculars and other optical instruments for the U.S. Navy. After the war, in September 1945, he accepted a position with Universal.

Beginning in the late 1940's, a great number of enthusiastic camera fans became caught up in the photographic whirlwind known as the "spy camera era". There were literally dozens of inexpensive foreign and domestic ultra-miniature cameras on the market to choose from, the majority of which were highly inferior in construction, lacking the ability to produce pictures of any acceptable quality. Nevertheless, Universal saw this as a golden opportunity to gain back its long lost fame and fortune, a get rich quick scheme. The basic ingredients in Universal's plan consisted of an inexpensive small spy camera, a nonstandard filmload supplied by Universal and throngs of overly anxious amateur picture takers hard-pressed to walk away from "a good deal" — in all actuality, this was the identical formula used by Universal in 1933. Unfortunately, the amateur photographers of 1950 were not as easily satisfied as the millions of amateur photographers of 1933, who seemed reasonably content with their purchase of a simple UniveX Model A camera. By 1950, "spy" cameras were being discarded or tossed aside in large numbers, their

Fig. 6-8 The Universal Minute-16 Camera, the original version with 3 f-stops.

Fig. 6-9 The Universal Minute-16 Camera, the later version with 4 f-stops and other minor design changes.

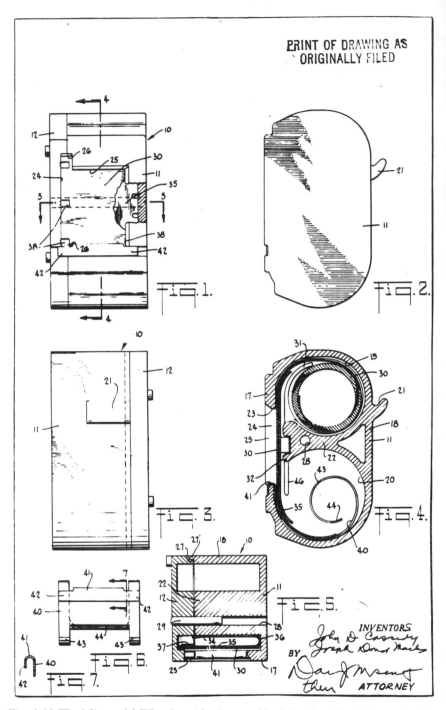

Fig. 6-10 The Minute-16 Film Cartridge invented by John Cassidy, Universal's Vice-President, and Joseph Marks, Universal's General Manager, as depicted in U.S. Pat. # 2,673,500.

owners quickly realizing that consistently poor pictures were a common characteristic of the cheaper models. By this time though, Universal had already invested approximately $2 million into the design and production of a new 16mm ultraminiature camera, its special film cartridge and related accessory equipment. To finance the new project, Universal obtained several large bank loans plus additional funding provided by New York Merchandise. Approximately 30,000 pieces of Universal's finished inventory stock — cameras, projectors, and binoculars — were used as collateral in 1948 to secure a total of $223,000 in loans from New York Merchandise earmarked specially for the Minute-16 project. Even Shapiro, Universal's Vice President, made personal loans to the company on several occasions during that period. One loan in particular was quite substantial, in the amount of $112,500 — this, too, was secured by finished inventory. Aside from the usual design and production costs for Universal's new ultraminiature camera, additional funds were necessary to establish photofinishing plants specially geared to process the camera's reusable plastic film cartridges. Universal opened labs for processing its new ultraminiature films in New York, Chicago and Hollywood; as it eventually turned out, dwindling funds forced Universal to close the Chicago and Hollywood labs less than a year later. Universal continued to maintain post office boxes in each of the three cities to accept mail orders for its ultraminiature film processing. Film processing orders were picked up daily at all three postal stations and forwarded to Universal's New York main photofinishing facility for processing.

The Universal Minute-16 Camera (Fig. 6-8) arrived on the market in November 1949, just in time for the Christmas season. Universal boasted pre-production orders in excess of $1 million. Originally priced at $7.95, the Minute-16 was equipped with a 30mm (1.3") f/6.3 coated, color corrected lens and a single speed (⅟50 second) rotary shutter. Weighing just under six ounces, the Minute-16 featured zinc alloy die-cast construction, a direct vision optical viewfinder, an automatic exposure counter, an automatic film transport system and built-in photoflash synchronization (X-synch). Additional features included a built-in lens shade, double exposure prevention and a tripod socket. Two distinct versions of the Minute-16 are known to exist. The first and original version of the Minute-16 camera featured three aperture settings (f/6.3, f/11, f/16) in a sliding plate and a bright chrome-plated finish. A second version of the Minute-16 camera, manufactured approximately

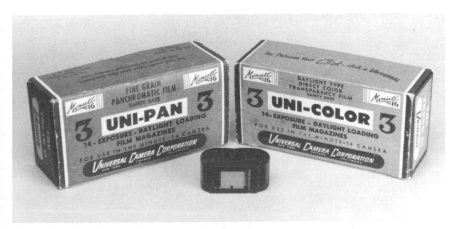

Fig. 6-11 Universal Minute-16 Cartridge Film in a special three-pack carton.

one year later, was marked for four aperture settings (f/6.3, f/8. f/11, f/16), instead of the three found on the original Minute-16 *(Fig. 6-9)*. The improved diaphragm, still controlled by a single lever, consisted of two perpendicular V-shaped openings which allowed intermediate stops and avoided potential problems. An improper or intermediate placement of the diaphragm lever of the early model would have resulted in blockage of the light. This later version was not as attractive in appearance as the original Minute-16 due to a matte zinc finish which was rather dark and dull in comparison to the bright chrome-plated finish found on the original version. One other noticeable characteristic of this later version of the Minute-16 was a modified viewfinder, featuring a spring-type catch allowing the viewfinder to "pop up" with the simple press of a fingertip.

The Minute-16 was designed to use a patented reusable daylight loading film cartridge providing 14 exposures, 11x14 mm in size *(Fig. 6-10)*. Basically, the cartridge consisted of two molded plastic parts — a main body section and a light-tight cover piece. When assembled, the two parts were held together by a force-fitting pin. After exposing the filmstrip inside, the cartridge was sent to Universal's processing lab where it was opened, the film removed for processing and new film inserted into the cartridge for future distribution. A metal film guide and metal retaining spring facilitated proper movement of the film from the loading chamber into the receiving chamber. As part of the cartridge design, one side of the film's sprocket holes were exposed for the purpose of transporting the film through the cartridge. When the cartridge was inserted in the camera, the camera's internal film transport mechanism engaged with the exposed sprocket holes and the film was advanced in this manner. No spools, take-up or otherwise, were employed in the design of this cartridge — the film was simply inserted as a coil and removed as a coil after exposure. Despite a rather ingenious concept, one major flaw remained to plague the Minute-16 film transport system and the company's engineers were never quite able to resolve it completely. Universal's main concern at the time was to conserve whatever cash funds were still on hand and to rush production and distribution of the Minute-16 camera and film cartridge, which appeared reasonably functional for the most part. However, much to the customer's dismay, film jams frequently occurred due to the troublesome design flaw that remained and this eventually hampered future sales of the camera. Minute-16 film cartridges were supplied in two types — Universal Uni-Color, a direct color transparency film rated at ASA 10, and Universal Uni-Pan, a black and white negative film rated at ASA 32. Both films were sold in special

Fig. 6-12 The Universal Minute-16 Camera, Film and Flash Unit.

212

Fig. 6-13 The Universal Minute-16 Viewer and Film Mount.

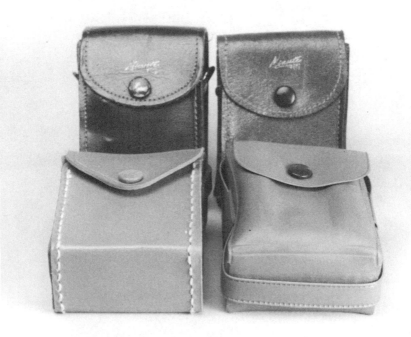

Fig. 6-14 Different examples of the Minute-16 Carrying Case.

three-pack cartons *(Fig. 6-11)* priced at $1.00 each, or by the single roll for only $.35. The processing charge for Minute-16 film was $1.00. The Gevaert Co. supplied 16mm film to Universal in bulk form on 600 ft. spools. At Universal's factory, the bulk film was cut, loaded and sealed into the reusable cartridges and then placed into metal canisters for final packaging. Essentially this was a new operation for Universal — in previous years, all of Universal's other nonstandard films, UniveX #00, #100 and #200, were purchased almost exclusively in precut, prepackaged form.

Universal introduced a line of Minute-16 accessory items — the Minute-16 Flash Unit, the Minute-16 Multi-Mount Transparency Viewer, the Minute-16 Multi-Mount, and the Minute-16 Carrying Case. All of these items were sold separately and packaged in blue cartons, characteristic of the Minute-16 product line. Priced at $3.95, the Minute-16 Flash Unit *(Fig. 6-12)* was a three-part affair consisting of a reflector, a battery case, and a camera bracket — all of which could be assembled or disassembled quickly and easily for the purpose of portability. The all metal flash unit was powered by two Penlite batteries and required bayonet-based photoflash bulbs. Priced at $1.00, the all plastic handheld Multi-Mount Transparency Viewer *(Fig. 6-13)* featured a

Fig. 6-15 The Universal Minute-16 Combination Outfit. The outfit included the following: camera, carrying case, flash, transparency viewer, transparency mounts, picture frame, film, flash bulbs and instruction books. This Universal outfit was introduced in December 1950; consequently, some outfits included a Christmas display card such as the one shown.

"fine-ground" viewing screen and a lens providing 5X magnification. The patented Minute-16 Multi-Mount *(Fig. 6-13)* was approximately 5½" in length and constructed of clear polystyrene. Priced two for $.25, the Multi-Mount was designed to hold a strip of Minute-16 transparencies containing a maximum of seven frames. With the transparency strip sandwiched tightly between the two sections of the Multi-Mount, the mount could then be inserted into the Multi-Mount Transparency Viewer for direct vision viewing. Universal supplied several different carrying cases for the Minute-16 *(Fig. 6-14)*. Originally, the cases were marked "Minute-16" and constructed entirely of genuine leather. Later examples did not carry the "Minute-16" trade name and were made from various imitation leather materials. A cheap vinyl/plastic case was eventually made during Universal's final years in business. The cases were made in a variety of colors, from dark brown to light beige.

Approximately one year after the Minute-16 reached the market, Universal began offering a rebate on the total purchase price of every Minute-16 camera sold, subject to the following condition. Universal provided a customer with a special rebate coupon every time a roll of Minute-16 film was sent in for processing. After a total of 30 coupons were accumulated, the customer sent the coupons back to Universal and the full purchase price of the camera was refunded. Another promotional gimmick appeared in the form of a gift outfit. Priced at $16.95, the Minute-16 Combination Outfit *(Fig. 6-15)* consisted of the following: a Minute-16 camera, a carrying case, a flash unit, a transparency viewer, four transparency mounts, three rolls of film, three flash bulbs, a self-standing picture frame and instruction booklets. Introduced in December 1950, the gift outfit was packaged in a large (12¾x11¼x2½") blue box marked "Minute-16 Combination Outfit". Another less common Minute-16 outfit was supposedly marketed by Universal and is said to contain a camera, lens cap, flash unit, transparency viewer, transparency mounts and a small metal tripod. Either of these outfits would definitely be a rare acquisition for a photographic collector — most outfits found today are almost always incomplete.

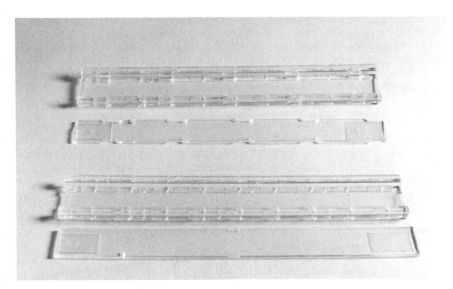

Fig. 6-16 The Minute-16 Multi-Mounts — the original version (above) developed by Wallace Ward, a Universal Designer, and the improved version (below) redesigned by Joseph Marks, Universal's General Manager.

The Minute-16 camera and related accessory equipment were the combined efforts of three men — Wallace W. Ward, a Universal designer, John D. Cassidy, Universal's Vice President, and Joseph David Marks, Universal's General Manager. Ward was the man chiefly responsible for the camera's original design and preliminary production tooling. Cassidy directed and monitored all phases of the project closely and, after serious consideration, decided to hire another person to assist Ward in eliminating many of the "bugs" associated with the Minute-16 project. Marks was hired by Cassidy in 1949 and immediately began work on the Minute-16 project. Since both the Minute-16 camera and cartridge had already been tooled for mass production before joining the staff at Universal, Marks was somewhat limited in his efforts to correct whatever problems became manifest. Costs had to be kept to a minimum and so only minor design and tooling changes were possible. One of the many minor changes made by Marks pertained to the design of the Multi-Mount. Upon Marks' arrival, the original Multi-Mount involved an interlocking latch-type cover slide *(Fig. 6-16)* already tooled for production. It was soon discovered that this Multi-Mount developed striations which were quite noticeable when projected. To eliminate this problem, Marks developed a Multi-Mount having a straight-edged, or "stripping" cover slide as it was called. In addition to the Minute-16 accessories already discussed, an electric slide projector *(Fig. 6-17)* was designed for use with the Minute-16 Multi-Mount. The projector was designed with a die cast metal base for strong support, a light weight sheet metal housing to accommodate the projection lamp and the light condensing system, and a rotatable slide mount with an attached focusing lens. A loaded Multi-Mount was inserted through one side of the projector and the special rotatable slide mount feature allowed the operator to turn any one of the seven frames 90 degrees to the left or right, or completely upside down if so desired. These adjustments could be performed during the viewing process, without ever having to remove the Multi-Mount from the projector. This feature was extremely useful whenever a combination of vertically and horizontally composed pictures were contained on the same transparency strip. Only a few examples of the Minute-16 electric slide projector were produced and these were used for inspection by distributors. Shortly after, Universal abandoned the entire prospect of bringing this particular Minute-16 accessory to market — interest in subminiature photography was beginning to wane somewhat and Universal was hardly in the position, financial or otherwise, to attempt the volume production and widespread marketing of this last somewhat costly Minute-16 accessory.

Meanwhile, the U.S. Government was taking steps to bring the postwar recession to an end. Additional money was being pumped into the system in an effort to increase spending and decrease unemployment. During this period, Universal managed to sell hundreds of thousands of Minute-16 cameras. The company's financial report for 1950 indicated a significant increase in product sales which was largely credited to the new Minute-16 line. Universal's sales figures for that year increased about 53% from the previous year's sales figures, putting an end to the drastically declining sales of the three previous years. At the same time, Universal's operating loss was substantially reduced by more than 63%, leaving the company with an operating loss of $347,499 as compared to $951,840 from the previous year.

In addition to the sale of the Minute-16 camera, one other factor contributed to Universal's financial upswing in 1950. Universal decided to liquidate the bulk of its finished inventory stock at cost. The only finished inventory retained by the company were Minute-16 related items. As previously mentioned, Universal had secured several loans in 1948 and 1949 using

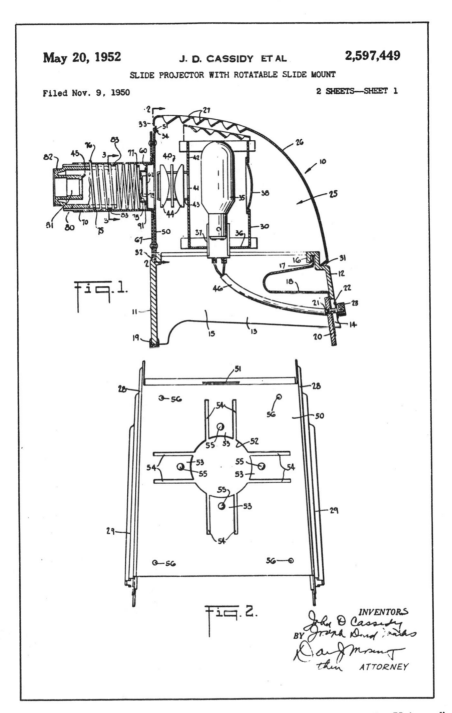

Fig. 6-17 The Minute-16 electric slide projector invented by John Cassidy, Universal's Vice-President, and Joseph Marks, Universal's General Manager, for use with the seven frame Minute-16 Multi-Mount transparency holder, as depicted in U.S. Pat. #2,597,449.

217

Fig. 6-18 An Abe Cohen's Exchange, Inc. advertisement showing Universal's products offered at low discount prices — up to 50% off original list price, taken from "Modern Photography", June 1951.

large quantities of finished and unfinished cameras as collateral. Upon repayment of these loans, the cameras and camera parts were returned to Universal and, not surprising, the company found itself caught with huge inventories of cameras that most retailers refused to carry in their stores. The recent faulty adhesive problem had left many in the retail industry steaming. The few retailers that were willing to carry Universal's products were well aware of the company's unstable situation; consequently, they realized Universal would probably accept far less than full wholesale price for its overstocked items and Universal did just that.

The majority of Universal's inventory stock was bought up by a few large retail and/or wholesale photographic firms. One such firm, known as Abe Cohen's Exchange, Inc., was located at 142 Fulton Street in New York City. Universal's cameras and projectors were advertised in Abe Cohen's ads *(Fig. 6-18)* at up to 50% off the original retail price. The Universal line was regularly featured between August 1950 and August 1951, suggesting that a rather large quantity of merchandise had been purchased by the retailer at that time. Another firm involved in this same deal was the Davega Stores Corp., an affiliate of Abe Cohen's Exchange. In 1951, Davega Stores owned and operated a chain of 25 New York and New Jersey area retail stores specializing in the sale of large household appliances, sporting goods, electronics and photographic equipment. Like Abe Cohen's, Davega Stores was also selling Universal products at prices up to 50% off the original retail value and still making a profit doing so. (Interestingly, soon after Universal filed bankruptcy in 1952, Davega filed a claim in the amount of $32,480.75 against the bankrupt company. Apparently, this figure represented damages

Fig. 6-19 The Universal Vitar Camera.

219

incurred or expected to be incurred by Davega as a result of Universal's failure to uphold the original terms of its warranty agreement on the merchandise sold to Davega.) Many retailers across the country were outraged as they learned of the huge price cuts on Universal's products. They, after all, had paid full wholesale price for the same merchandise. Once consumers discovered there were large retail stores advertising Universal's products at 50% off list price, the smaller retailers were unable to sell their remaining Universal stock at original list prices, resulting in little or no profit on these Universal products.

In an effort to further improve the company's financial picture in 1950, Universal began taking certain measures to reduce its overhead costs. All service repair and photofinishing work was promptly discontinued at the Chicago and Los Angeles branch offices and operations were instead channeled to the New York office. Additional cutbacks were made in the area of advertising. Universal decided to employ its own advertising and sales promotion manager in an effort to avoid the costly expense of hiring an advertising agency. After 1949, most of Universal's promotional activities were aimed at distributors and dealers, with next to no direct consumer advertising. Late in 1950, Universal also decided it would be profitable to introduce a number of "new" cameras, each constructed entirely from spare parts, parts that were otherwise destined in all likelihood for the trash receptacle. With this thought foremost in mind, Universal's Engineering Department began design work on a 35mm camera, a 2¼ x 2¼ twin lens reflex camera and an 8mm movie camera. In all actuality, the three cameras that resulted from this effort were anything but "new".

The basic design of the 35mm Universal Vitar Camera *(Fig. 6-19)* began with the old Corsair/Buccaneer body and the Corsair combination view-finder/exposure meter with flash hot shoe clip. Added to that was a retractable lens barrel and shutter housing taken from the Buccaneer. All of the miscellaneous hardware (knobs, counter, film transport system, etc.) was also taken from the Buccaneer. The lens and shutter appeared to be a contribution from the Uniflex/Roamer line of cameras. The Vitar featured an uncoupled shutter; in other words, the user had to first advance the film by turning the film wind knob, then make the exposure by pressing the shutter release lever on the

Fig. 6-20 The Universal Uniflex III Camera.

lens mount. A body mounted shutter release button was impossible if Universal's engineers were to make the most from the spare parts available to them. The Vitar was equipped with a coated 50mm f/3.5 Universal Tricor lens, set in an auto-retractable mount, with a minimum focusing capability of three feet. The camera also featured a four speed Flash Chronomatic shutter, with speeds ranging from ½₅ to ½₀₀ second, plus B. Aperture settings ranged from f/3.5 to f/16. Other features of this model included double exposure prevention and built-in photoflash synchronization. The Vitar reached the market in June 1951 with an original list price of $41. A medium brown carrying case, marked "Vitar", was available. The Vitar was produced in limited supply and is considered somewhat scarce by collectors today.

The 2¼ x 2¼ format Universal Uniflex III Camera *(Fig. 6-20)* was another prime example of a "spare parts" camera, manufactured solely for the purpose of liquidating finished cameras and/or camera parts that still remained in the plant. Produced in extremely small quantity, the Uniflex III camera appeared similar to the Uniflex II originally introduced in 1948, except for a less desirable four-speed (plus B) Flash Chronomatic shutter instead of the five-speed (plus T and B) shutter originally found on the Uniflex II. The settings of ½₀ second and "T" found on the Uniflex II were not included on the Uniflex III shutter. The lens speed and top shutter speed of ½₀₀ second remained the same on both models. Universal never announced or advertised the Uniflex III publicly, therefore its original retail price is unknown. This was probably Universal's most frugal effort to construct a camera entirely from spare parts. Even the nameplate on the Uniflex III was a spare part — it was originally a Uniflex II nameplate with Roman numeral "I" engraved adjacent to the Roman numeral "II".

The last so-called "spare parts" camera manufactured by Universal was the 8mm Universal Cinemaster Model H-8 Camera *(Fig. 6-21)*. Originally, the key feature of the Cinemaster line was the special "Dual-8" system which allowed the photographer his choice of using either UniveX Single-8 film or Standard Double-8 film. On this, the last and final Universal cine camera, the Dual-8 film system was totally eliminated, replacing it with a new film system designed specifically for Double-8 film use only. Inasmuch as the Cinemaster Model G-8 design remained untouched since its introduction in 1946, there seemed to be only one possible reason warranting the change in film systems from Dual-8 to Double-8. In 1951, Universal indicated it was still offering several varieties of special UniveX films *(Fig. 6-22)*. By 1952, supplies of these films had diminished

Fig. 6-21 The Universal Cinemaster Model H-8 Camera with f/2.5 Universal Univar Lens.

UNIVERSAL CAMERA CORPORATION

Makers of PRECISION PHOTOGRAPHIC AND OPTICAL INSTRUMENTS

28 WEST 23ᴿᴰ STREET, NEW YORK 10, N.Y., U.S.A.
TELEPHONE: OREGON 5-5100

July 3, 1951

Dear Madam:

Thank you for your recent inquiry regarding film.

We are currently producing five types:

1 - OOC Ultrachrome - priced at 15¢ per roll - for use in our Candid type cameras.

2 - UNI-PAN & UNI-COLOR - Price: Either type film magazine 35¢ each - 3 for $1.00 - for use in the MINUTE-16 Camera.

3 - #236SS - 35mm film - 36 exposures, priced at 63¢ per roll - for use in the Mercury I and Corsair I cameras.

4 - #100UP Ultrapan Movie Film - priced at $1.10 per roll.

5 - #100S Standard Movie Film - priced at 85¢ per roll.

All orders for film must be accompanied by money orders or checks to the correct amounts. It is inadvisable to send cash, because cash can be easily lost in the mails.

In order to avoid delays, it is suggested that, before ordering directly from us, you contact your local camera dealers. They are receiving regular shipments of our films.

Yours very truly,

UNIVERSAL CAMERA CORPORATION

By *Simon Weil*
Simon Weil
Sales Department

SW/YM

NEW YORK · CHICAGO · HOLLYWOOD

Fig. 6-22 A 1951 letter written in response to a Universal customer's query regarding UniveX film availability.

222

significantly — apparently, retailers were not ordering them on a regular basis and Universal had grown more and more inconsistent in its efforts to provide the special films to retailers. In all likelihood, the Double-8 Cinemaster Model H-8 camera was introduced because UniveX Single-8 films were no longer readily available. According to Universal, "current defense needs for raw materials" warranted the Januray 1951 introduction of the Model H-8 camera. Ironically, the Vitar, the Uniflex III and the Cinemaster Model H-8 cameras became candidates for the discount shelf before ever leaving Universal's plant — by the time they reached the market, Universal's other products had already been marked 50% off the list price.

In 1951, business for Universal continued on a slow, but upward trend. By June 1951, the company was once again under contract with the U.S. Army — this time for production of binocular component parts, monocular instruments and bombsights. Universal was unable to perform the specialized optical work required on the bombsights; consequently, that portion of the job was subcontracted to a New York area optical manufacturing firm, A. Jaeger. This subcontractor was reportedly one of a select few optical companies qualified to produce the special lens used in the bombsights. In 1951 alone, government contract work consumed 60% of Universal's business operations. In 1952, Universal acquired additional defense work involving the production of reflector assemblies for the U.S. Army Ordnance Department. The acquisition of government contracts in 1950, 1951, and 1952 was surely a stroke of good luck for Universal, since the company was still $600,000 in arrears on unsecured bank loans from 1948 and 1949. Universal's accounts were handled by two large New York banks, the Chase National Bank of New York and the Chemical Bank & Trust Company. By June 1951, both banks had become somewhat distressed over the general status of Universal's unpaid accounts, insisting that the company assign all future government contracts directly to them. Reluctantly, Universal agreed. Nevertheless in the months that followed, the banks continued to grow increasingly impatient over the company's remaining past due accounts. On December 18, 1951, a mutual decision was made by the banks to call in the balance on Universal's unsecured loans. Cash funds on deposit and equity in assigned contracts totaling $192,670.54 were confiscated by the banks. In one day's time, Universal was totally wiped out, with no working capital to speak of. Meanwhile, Universal was being pressured by the optical firm subcontracted to produce the bombsight lenses. In a December 21, 1951 transaction, Universal managed to persuade A. Jaeger to accept 1500 Minute-16 cameras in exchange for payments still due. To say the least, this was a curious transaction since A. Jaeger was strictly a manufacturer of precision optics. Nevertheless, this agreement made it possible for Universal to continue government contract work through April 1952.

On March 28, 1952, at a meeting of Universal's Board of Directors, all present agreed that the business should discontinue all operations unless a satisfactory agreement could be reached between Universal and the two banks. In the weeks that followed, no such agreement ever materialized. On April 16, 1952, Universal filed a voluntary petition for reorganization under Chapter XI of the Bankruptcy Act. The following day, an involuntary petition to have Universal adjudged bankrupt was filed in the same court by Lawrence Kleinberg, Superintendent of Manufacturing at Universal, and two other creditors. By decision of the court, the involuntary petition was stayed until a further decision was reached regarding Universal's tentative plan for reorganization. At the first meeting of Universal's major creditors, the plan for reorganization was proposed and rejected. Consequently, Universal was adjudged bankrupt on June 24, 1952. Shortly after, Joseph H. Frier was appointed trustee in bankruptcy for the Universal Camera Corporation.

BANKRUPTCY SALE – Large Stock Assets

Universal Camera Corporation, Bankrupt

CAMERA MANUFACTURER

UNDERWRITERS SALVAGE COMPANY OF N. Y.
OFFICIAL U. S. AUCTIONEER, SOUTHERN DISTRICT OF N. Y.

Sell Tuesday, Aug. 19th, 1952
AT 11:00 A.M. AT
28 WEST 23rd STREET, NEW YORK CITY

OPTICAL DEPARTMENT — Machinery, precision tools, accessories and equipment for all operations in the manufacture of optical lenses on a high production basis.

FABRICATION DEPARTMENT — Machinery, tools and equipment for the manufacture of camera housings, projectors and component parts on a high production basis.

Factory maintenance, employee and shipping room facilities; Paint Spraying Department, Air Conditioning Systems.

OFFICE — Equipment including executive and clerical office furniture, stenographic and office machines.

(Above Assets Located at 28 W. 23rd St., New York City)

LARGE STOCK — Component camera parts, cases, shipping boxes and steel shelving.

(These Assets Located at 509 W. 38th St., New York City)

DEVELOPING DEPARTMENT — Developing apparatus with auxilliary accessories, laboratory fixtures, enlargers, office furniture and fixtures.

(These Assets Located at 11 E. 22nd St., New York City)

TRADE NAMES AND TRADE MARKS

ALL THE FOREGOING WILL BE SOLD ON BULK BID OR OTHER UNITS AT THE DISCRETION OF THE TRUSTEE, BUT NOT IN SINGLE LOTS.

FINISHED GOODS — Large stock of cameras, projectors, carrying cases, film and other photographic articles.

(These Assets Located at 28 W. 23rd St., New York City)

WILL BE SOLD AS A UNIT ON BULK BID ONLY)

INSPECTION: August 15th, and 18th, 1952 from 9:30 A.M. to 4:30 P.M.

JOSEPH H. FRIER, Trustee
7 Dey Street, New York 7, N. Y.

(See Reverse Side for Terms of Sale)

Fig. 7-1 Official notice of the August 19, 1952 private bankruptcy sale of Universal's assets.

224

CHAPTER SEVEN

1952-1964

THE FINAL YEARS

In the early 1950's, there was little demand for Universal's cameras, all of which lacked the technological advancements characteristic of the newer, more popular, models on the market at the time. Amateur photographers had begun setting their sights on more sophisticated foreign and domestic cameras. It was obvious that Universal could no longer successfully compete with its rivals in the ever-changing photographic business. At this point in time, Universal's only possibility of survival was entirely dependent on the continuous acquisition of government contract work. Without it, Universal would most certainly cease to exist.

In the months preceding Universal's bankruptcy, production activities at the plant were limited to the Minute-16 line and government contract work. Processing and respooling of Minute-16 films was also being done, along with some minor repair work. At the time, the majority of Universal's work force seemed totally unconcerned, almost oblivious, as to the uncertainty of Universal's future. Most of Universal's original employees from prewar years had already left the company in search of better jobs offering more security. For those that remained, it was a total shock when the banks announced their refusal to cash Universal's payroll checks. Outraged by this occurrence, most of these remaining workers decided to seek employment elsewhere. Universal had little choice but to file bankruptcy.

During the next few months, appraisers were called upon to estimate the value of Universal's assets, which consisted mainly of finished and unfinished goods, metal fabrication tools and machinery, optical shop tools and machinery, and assorted photofinishing equipment. Trade marks, trade names, and patents were also up for bid. On August 19, 1952, a private bankruptcy sale *(Fig. 7-1)* was held at Universal's West 23rd Street location by Underwriter's Salvage Company of New York, the Official U.S. Auctioneer for the Southern District Court of New York. The assets involved in this particular sale were available by bulk bid only and were not to be sold in single lots *(Fig. 7-2)*. Universal's remaining property was auctioned off during a three day public sale which began on September 16, 1952 *(Fig. 7-3)*. Shortly after, a private sale was held in Chicago to liquidate the property remaining at Universal's branch office.

With assistance from a few close business associates, two rich and prominent brothers from Vermont, D. Henry Werblow and Robert M. Werblow, purchased the entire lot of Universal's trade names, trade marks and patents

PAUL B. SOMMERS, CHAIRMAN OF THE BOARD

ALFRED G. MARTIN, PRESIDENT

JOHN G. McCLURE, JR., VICE-PRESIDENT AND
GENERAL MANAGER

LLOYD F. HARJES, SECRETARY AND TREASURER

ROBERT P. STEPHENSON
REFEREE IN BANKRUPTCY

NEW YORK 13, N. Y.

August 19th, 1952

Hon. Robert P. Stephenson
Referee in Bankruptcy
United States Court House
Foley Square, New York

Re: Our Lot No. B-6551
Universal Camera Corp.
In Bankruptcy No. 88601

Honorable Sir:

In accordance with the bankruptcy rules, we are enclosing a copy of the catalogue of sale, in the above subject bankruptcy matter, constituting an itemized statement of the property sold, the name of each purchaser and the unit price received for each item.

Respectfully yours,

W J Slick

MANAGER BANKRUPTCY DEPARTMENT

ep

Fig. 7-2 The cover letter (above) and an itemized statement (right) of property sold at the August 19th private bankruptcy sale.

and the bulk of Universal's finished and unfinished goods stock. A relatively good share of Universal's tools, machinery and office equipment were also bought up by this group. Robert Werblow was the former President of Polygraphic Company of America, Inc., a lithographic printing firm that originated in Brooklyn, New York and later relocated to Bennington, Vermont. His brother, D. Henry Werblow, was also an executive of the same firm. Most in the industry presumed that Universal's assets would be bought up and used to supplement another business — little did anyone know that the Werblow brothers' intentions were to establish a "new" Universal Camera Corporation, which they would later refer to quite simply as, "the successor to the bankrupt firm by the same name". It was a little known fact that Universal continued conducting business after 1952, although on much more of a limited basis than before. Spokesmen for the new Universal company insisted that their new firm was in no way associated or connected with the bankrupt camera company. A number of factors contrary to this indicated that a rather substantial link did indeed exist between the post-1952 Universal Camera Corporation and the original company of the same name. As the story progresses, these factors will become evident.

In the early morning hours of September 24, 1952, four large trailer trucks loaded with equipment, supplies and merchandise stock from the original Universal Camera Corporation departed, heading north, from New York City. Later that day, the trucks arrived at their final destination — two old textile mills located at 264 Union Street, North Adams, Massachusetts *(Fig. 7-4)*. The mills were commonly known as the North and South Hoosac Mills, originally the home of the Hoosac Mills Corp., a manufacturer of cotton and silk cloth. In 1947, the North Hoosac Mill was sold to the Gevaert Co., who used the building primarily as a storage warehouse and rental property. A number of small firms — a lumber company, furniture company and printing company — leased portions of the four story building. Universal obtained a lease for the entire second floor of the building, providing the

	UNIVERSAL CAMERA CORP. 28 West 23rd Street New York, New York		August 19th, 1952 11:00 A.M.	
Lot #-				
Columbo Trad. Co.	1	All of the finished goods contained in finished goods room on second floor.		12,000.00
Columbo Trad Co.	2	All unfinished and raw materials located in this building and warehouse West 38th Street		12,500.00
Marcus	3	Developing department - Everything contained in 12 East 22nd Street		2,700.00
Wm. J. John	4	All Machinery and tools of Bankrupt including Air Contioning units - excluding repair department.		75,000.00
Columbo Trad Co.	5	Office furniture - not to include metal cabinets or desks in shop department and not to include steel shelving - on this floor and on second floor.		3,700.00
Columbo Trad Co.	6	Trade names and patents and copy rights.		5,000.00
Spro Machine Tool	7	Repair department on second floor.		1,000.00
(Arthur Albert Co.		Bulk Bid $156,000.00)		$111,900.00

Fig. 7-3 A public bankruptcy sale notice appearing in the New York Times on September 7, 1952. A three day public auction was to be held on September 16, 17, and 18 to dispose of Universal's remaining assets.

Fig. 7-4 The Universal Camera Corporation, Production Facility, 264 Union Street, North Adams, Massachusetts, 1952-1957. Aerial view shows old North Hoosac Mill, owned by Gevaert from 1947 to 1957, where Universal occupied the entire second floor. Another view looks toward Union Street where the old North Hoosac Mill is seen in the upper left corner. (Photos Courtesy: The Transcript, North Adams, Massachusetts)

229

Fig. 7-5 The Universal Camera Corporation, Main Offices, 175 Fifth Avenue, New York City, 1952-1964. (Photo Courtesy: Bill Stone Photography.)

company with approximately 20,000 square feet of floor space. At the same time, Universal was given an option to buy the building, if its business would somehow begin to show promise once again. While Universal was still involved setting up shop at the North Adams facility, Gevaert decided to sell its nearby Williamstown manufacturing plant to the Remington Rand Co.. The Williamstown plant had been operating since 1940. Gevaert began moving its supplies and equipment into the old North Hoosac Mill in North Adams, under the same roof as Universal. Since 1932, when Universal first began doing business with Gevaert, the relationship that ensued between the two companies was hardly without incident. Despite numerous difficulties, the two companies managed to remain on amicable terms. Needless to say, this was much to Universal's benefit at the time because the company required supplies of bulk film again and few companies were willing to risk doing business with Universal. As it had in the past, Gevaert agreed to provide Universal with the necessary film supplies.

The new Universal company established its main sales and service offices in the "Flatiron" building at 175 Fifth Avenue, New York City *(Fig. 7-5)*, just one block from the old firm's West 23rd Street location. A number of people previously employed with the original Universal company — officers, managers and various clerks — accepted positions with the new Universal company. Interestingly enough, Jacob Shapiro retained his former position as President. Simon Weil, General Sales Manager for Universal since 1950, continued working in the same capacity for the new company. Together Shapiro and Weil handled sales and related affairs directly from Universal's main office in New York City. D. Henry Werblow was named Vice President and Plant Manager of the new company, with much of his time being spent at the North Adams plant, primarily as an overseer of production activities. Of the dozens of former Universal employees interviewed for this book, only three were aware of the fact that Universal had continued in the camera manufacturing business beyond 1952. Information provided by these and other former Universal employees, along with information from several North Adams newspaper reports, helped paint the following picture, which in itself essentially confirms the fact that Universal did indeed have some rather definite, well-laid plans for continuing its camera manufacturing business after initiating bankruptcy proceedings. Early in 1952, a small number of Universal's employees were asked, under somewhat discreet circumstances, to staff the company's new production facility, which they were told would open later that year in North Adams, Massachusetts. Essentially, all of the employees chosen were well-experienced at their specific jobs and would later form the nucleus of Universal's new production facility. In addition, the North Adams production plant would require approximately 100 unskilled laborers to perform light production work — all of these job positions were to be filled by area residents. As an industrial newcomer to the North Adams area, Universal's idea to create 100 new jobs for area residents was an ideal way for the company to promote goodwill. As an added benefit, most of the workers from Universal's original New York plant would never know of the company's continued existence beyond 1952. All things considered, one point seems very clear: while members of Universal's executive staff were deep in the throes of dismantling and liquidating the original company, well-guarded plans for a "successor" Universal Camera Corporation were definitely in the making.

Approximately two months time was spent readying the North Adams plant for production. Fifteen men from the old Universal company arranged equipment, inventoried stock and set up machinery in the new plant. Universal's first objective was to bring back the Minute-16 line of products.

The new company had approximately 2000 finished Minute-16 cameras on hand from the bankruptcy auction. While this stock was being distributed, Universal began producing additional units. The North Adams plant handled all Minute-16 film spooling, processing and printing operations. D. Henry Werblow spoke of reviving other Universal cameras from the past, particularly the Roamer, Mercury, Uniflex and Cinemaster lines. Werblow also made brief mention of resurrecting Universal's three 8mm projectors and the 6x30 prismatic binocular originally produced by Universal in 1943. As founder of the new Universal company, Werblow was firmly convinced that the company would once again see profitable times — so much so, that he spent several weeks in Japan, late in 1952, in an attempt to rekindle Universal's long lost prewar foreign trade business. Werblow's optimistic attitude was extremely short-lived. Much to everyone's surprise, early in 1953, Werblow denounced his interest in the firm entirely. Shortly after, he became involved in the oil business through the purchase of a Texas oil company. About the same time, his brother, Robert, made a similar decision

Fig. 7-6 The Universal Steré-All Camera and Flash Unit.

to abandon his interests in Universal. Not long after, Leo H. Stuckens, a former official of the Gevaert Co., succeeded as Vice President and Assistant General Manager of Universal.

Early in 1953, word had reached the photographic industry that Universal would soon be distributing a new type of color film. The project presumably fell through because no such Universal film ever reached the market. It is unknown whether the film would have been a standard format color film or a new type of color film cartridge intended for use in the Minute-16 camera. Evidence regarding this new Universal color film product was found to exist in the form of a trade name, "Nu-Color", which Universal filed with the U.S. Patent and Trademark Office in February 1953.

The New York Photographic Show opened in New York in February 1953 and, without a doubt, the Japanese Nikon and Canon 35mm precision cameras captured a lion's share of attention from those in attendance. The advanced technology and quality that was built into the design of these new camera models was so impressive that it put them in direct competition with the already well-accepted German-made Contax and Leica cameras. Another design which enjoyed a large audience at the show was the 35mm stereo camera and related accessory equipment, represented by a number of domestic and foreign photographic manufacturing firms. The introduction of these exciting new products, and many others yet to come still beckoning on the horizon, soon brought the inexpensive ultraminiature camera craze to an end. Some camera enthusiasts did, however, acquire a lasting devotion toward ultraminiature photography. They eventually purchased one of the more expensive precision-made ultraminiature models such as the German-made Minox, the Italian-made GaMi or the Austrian-made Minicord. All of this seemed to put Universal's products years behind the times — the very thought of Universal attempting to reintroduce any other past products was, in itself, totally absurd.

In light of rising competition from both the domestic and foreign trade markets, the need for a totally "new" Universal camera design was all too clear. Universal's investors realized there was only one possible way for the company to get back in the running. Everyone agreed — Universal would have to design and produce a standard format camera, essentially something that would compete directly with other manufacturers' models currently on the market. In April 1954, Universal introduced what would ultimately be the company's last design — the Universal Steré-All Camera *(Fig. 7-6)*. Originally listing at $49.95, the Steré-All was one of the last entries to join the ongoing stereo boom, already on the decline after reaching its peak a year or two before. The Steré-All was designed sometime around 1950, at Universal's New York plant, by a Universal designer named George Frost. If Universal had found some way to finance the production of the Steré-All in 1950 or 1951, the camera would have enjoyed a much heartier reception than it did in 1954. The Steré-All, constructed almost entirely of plastic, featured a pair of matched 35mm f/3.5 Tricor coated lenses, apertures ranging from f/3.5 to f/16, an automatic film transport system coupled to a one-speed shutter (1/50 second) and built-in photoflash synchronization. Other characteristics of this model were the parallax corrected optical viewfinder, filter retaining rings to accommodate slip-on filters, an automatic exposure counter, an exposure guide on the camera's rear cover and double exposure prevention. The camera accepted the standard 35mm film cartridge.

Universal offered a number of accessory items for use with the Steré-All camera — the Steré-All Flash Unit, the Steré-All Slide Viewer and the Steré-All Carrying Case. Priced at $8.00, the Steré-All Flash Unit *(Fig. 7-6)* was imported from Germany and was completely unmarked, except for the

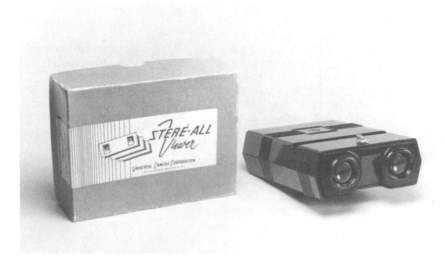

Fig. 7-7 The Universal Steré-All Slide Viewer.

legend "Made in Germany". The flash unit featured a five-inch parabolic reflector, a black bakelite battery compartment with a black metal slip-on rear cover and a safety on and off switch. The flash unit, bearing a marked resemblance to the Stereo Realist Flash Unit, required the use of three penlight batteries and standard bayonet-type flash bulbs. The Steré-All Slide Viewer *(Fig. 7-7)* was an all plastic unit operating on two "D" cell batteries. Like the Steré-All flash unit, the lightweight hand held viewer was similarly marked "Made in Germany", reportedly a product of the Steiner Co. in Germany. Priced at $12.50, the viewer featured two achromatic lenses which could be focused simultaneously for sharp 3-D slide viewing, an interocular adjustment lever and automatic illumination, whereby the unit would automatically illuminate when a slide was inserted and automatically shut off when the unit was set down. The Steré-All Camera, Viewer, and Flash Unit were packaged in green and white cartons, characteristic of the Steré-All product line. Since the Steré-All Flash Unit and Viewer do not carry the "Universal" name, they may be somewhat difficult for the collector to obtain. The Steré-All Carrying Case, originally priced at $7.50, was medium brown in color and marked "Steré-All" on the front.

Universal's financial backers could see that their recently acquired enterprise had not panned out as originally planned. There were no significant losses, but there were certainly no operating profits to speak of. It had been less than three years since the original Universal company discontinued its business operations, essentially nothing had changed. Universal's products were still considered inadequate for the times, even for the average amateur photographer. It appeared there was no way to alter Universal's ill-fated course. Most retailers remained reluctant to trust a firm that sold out its entire inventory at cost to a few large New York outfits less than five years earlier. The resentment and distrust that still lingered did little to help Universal in its meager attempt for a comeback.

In May 1957, Gevaert decided to sell the old North Hoosac Mill on Union Street, where Universal had carried on its production activities for nearly five years. The mill was sold to a local firm, the Sprague Electric Co., after Gevaert decided to discontinue operations in the North Adams area. Sprague intended to use all four floors of the building for its own storage purposes, leaving Universal and the other businesses in the building no other choice but to seek factory space elsewhere. A few weeks later, Universal found suitable quarters in a nearby building, known as the old Norad Mill *(Fig. 7-8)*, located at 1 Massachusetts Avenue, Braytonville (North Adams), Massachusetts. Universal leased approximately two-thirds of the building's third floor, totaling about 15,000 square feet of floor space.

Fig. 7-8 The Universal Camera Corporation, Production Facility, 1 Massachusetts Avenue, (Braytonville) North Adams, Massachusetts, 1957-1960. Although this photo was taken in the 1890's, the building remains unchanged. (Photo Courtesy: The Transcript, North Adams, Massachusetts)

Universal's activities in the North Adams area survived about three more years. During that time, Universal's production activities withered to almost nothing. Universal's only remaining operations during the late 1950's and early 1960's consisted of Minute-16 film spooling and processing *(Fig. 7-9)* and a very limited amount of camera repair work. Layoffs at the North Adams facility had started as early as 1954 and continued steadily until 1958, when only seven employees remained working at the plant. Finally, on January 5, 1960, a public auction *(Fig. 7-10)* was held at the Universal plant by Aaron Posnick & Co., Auctioneers of Springfield, Massachusetts. All of Universal's unused equipment and machinery was auctioned off, piece by piece. Shortly after, Universal packed up the remaining unsold stock and equipment and vacated the premises of the old Norad Building. It is uncertain what happened after this. The Postmaster of North Adams was able to recall a time in the early 1960's, when parcels addressed to Universal, presumably containing cameras for repair work, continued arriving even after Universal had left North Adams. All of the parcels had to be returned because Universal disappeared without leaving a forwarding address. Local residents

As of February 1 1961 the new price for processing
Minute 16 Unipan film is $1.50 per roll.

They are now individual pictures, hand developed,
on imported double weight paper.

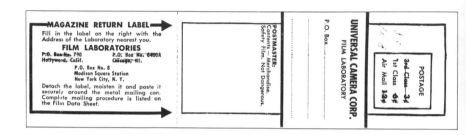

*Fig. 7-9 Evidence of Universal's meager existence continuing into the early 1960's.
Informational inserts packaged with Universal's Minute-16 film included typewritten
slips informing customers of a February 1, 1961 price increase on Minute-16 film
processing. Another slip, a film mailing label, indicated Universal was still using Post
Office Box 8, Madison Square Station, New York City — the same post office box
number used by the original company since the mid 1930's.*

recalled various rumors at the time alleging that Universal had moved a
small scale operation into a private home in the area. This is not so difficult
to believe when one considers Universal's history from the very beginning.
Despite an astoundingly successful start in the photographic business some
25 years earlier, it seemed as if Universal was, more often than not, somewhat
unprepared for whatever future competition it would have to face in the
years ahead. More than once, a lack of foresight caused the company severe
financial problems — each time though, Universal managed to recover to a
certain degree. From the beginning, Universal's founders were extremely
reluctant to accept the failure of their camera business. After nearly 20
years in steady decline, there were virtually no remaining pieces left to work
with, a totally irreversible situation ... and so it was, the final years of the
Universal Camera Corporation came to an end.

Universal's main office in New York closed in 1964. That same year,
bankruptcy proceedings for the original Universal company came to an
official close. After 1964, the Manhattan Telephone Directory no longer
carried the Universal listing. All other traces of activity relating to the
Universal Camera Corporation ceased to exist.

PUBLIC AUCTION SALE

Machinery • Tools • Equipment

To Be Sold Piece by Piece on the Premises
1 Massachusetts Avenue (3rd Floor, Old Norad Mill)
North Adams, Mass.

Tuesday, January 5, 1960
At 1:00 P. M.

MACHINERY consisting of:—Porta Cable 5 H. P. Belt Sander ● Curtiss 25 H. P. Air Compressor 6'½ x 5 Water Cooled ● Derk Milling Machine with '2 H. P. Motor ● South Bend Quick Change Precision Lathe Model A with '2 H. P. Motor ● 6 Bench Master '3 H. P. Punch Presses ● 2 Delta Bench Type Drill Presses with 4 Position Turrett Drill Heads '3 H. P. Motors ● 2 Delta '3 H. P. Bench Type Drill Presses with High Speed Tapping Attachments ● 2 Royal Bench Type Drill Presses '3 H. P. Motors ● Sterling 10 KVA Welder ● Black Diamond Precision Drill Grinder with '4 H. P. Motor ● 8 Famco No. 1 Arbor Presses ● 4 Taylor Spring Presses No. O ● U. S. 5 H. P. Heavy Duty 3-Speed Double End Buffer ● U. S. 1'2 H. P. Double End Buffer ● 8 Bench Type Chicago Air Presses ● J. B. No. 1 Tap Grinder with '4 H. P. Motor ● 2 Mead Impact Hammers ● Di-Arco Bench Type Precision Shear Cutter No. 1 ● Di-Arco Bench Type Bender ● Air Wrenches ● 2 Flexible Sanders.

MISCELLANEOUS EQUIPMENT:—2 Paasche Spray Booths ● Wheelco Oven with Motor & Fan ● Blower System ● 3—21'2x 21'½ 30 Gal. S. S. Tanks ● 3 Multi Drill Heads ● U. S. Eyelet Machine ● 20 Steel Benches ● Fluorescent Lights ● Steel Shop Chairs ● Fire Extinguishers ● Bench Vises ● Steel Parts Cabinet ● BX Wire ● Switch Boxes ● Galv. Pipe ● Desk Lamp ● High Speed Drills & Cutters.

OFFICE EQUIPMENT:—2 Royal Typewriters ● Monroe 8-Bank Calculator ● Burroughs Adding Machine ● Kenmore Electric Fan.

Terms of Sale—Cash or Certified Check
SALE PER ORDER OF OWNER
NO CONFIRMATION — IMMEDIATE REMOVAL
FOR FURTHER INFORMATION
WRITE   PHONE   WIRE
AARON POSNIK & CO.

(Auctioneers)

1214 Main Street   RE 3-5238   Springfield. Mass.

Fig. 7-10 A public auction notice appearing in The Transcript on December 31, 1959. A sale to liquidate Universal's unused shop equipment and machinery was held on January 5, 1960.

CONCLUSION

The story of Universal Camera Corporation drew to a final close on May 15, 1964 at the Southern District Court of New York. Lengthy bankruptcy proceedings, initiated by Universal 12 years earlier, were officially at an end. By this time, only a few scant operations remained at Universal — service work, mail order film processing and respooling empty film cartridges — all of this was discontinued shortly following adjudication of the bankruptcy case. After 32 years as a manufacturer and supplier of amateur photographic products, Universal quietly closed its doors, relinquishing its tiny niche in America's rapidly expanding photographic industry.

Numerous factors contributed to the demise of the Universal Camera Corporation — some are obvious in themselves, others have been, and will continue to be, the subject of discussion and supposition for many years to come. The one factor most commonly associated with Universal's ill-fated existence was the company's decision to build a foundation based entirely on a concept generally frowned upon by the photographic industry — nonstandard filmloads. Even during the 1930's, when Universal was busy selling millions of its nonstandard filmloads to amateur photographers everywhere, the well seasoned photographer avoided these films entirely. For this reason, many photographic retailers and distributors were reluctant to carry the UniveX line. In addition, Universal's products were often overshadowed by derogatory reports of unethical business conduct on the part of the executive staff. Universal soon became a familiar object of rumor within the industry — more often than not though, the rumors were unfounded or grossly exaggerated. All of this proved detrimental to the well-being of the company. A poor reputation plagued Universal through all of its years in business and, surprisingly, signs of it still linger today. Of the present day camera shop owners still in business since the 1940's and 1950's, some remain clearly hard-pressed for kind words when confronted with the subject of Universal Camera Corporation.

Despite its disparaging history, Universal's contribution to photography should never be underestimated. Compared to similar products on the market at the time, Universal's products were unique in design and, for the price, well constructed. In its prewar years, Universal was unparalleled in providing sturdy, reliable amateur photographic equipment at an unbeatably low price. Immediately prior to World War II, Universal's accounts totaled over 5000. UniveX cameras and accessories were readily available in countless photographic stores, drug stores, five and dime stores, jewelry stores, smoke shops and department stores throughout the United States and Canada and, to a lesser degree, stores in other foreign countries. Well-known department stores everywhere carried the UniveX line — for instance, Sears Roebuck & Co., Montgomery Ward & Co., R.H. Macy & Co., Marshall Field & Co., J.C. Penney Co. and Bloomingdales. Some other retail outlets carrying the UniveX line were United Cigar Whelan Co., Hook Drug Co., Owl Drug Co., Walgreen Drug Co., McKesson and Robbins, National Tea Co., Grand Union

Tea Co., Willoughby's, Bass Camera Shop and Kay Jewelry Co. As one can see, UniveX cameras were within a hand's reach of most people and, more importantly, they were priced to sell. People previously unable to afford photography were seemingly drawn toward it by the appeal of a small $.39 camera. In an effort to broaden their newly acquired photographic skills, many of these beginning photographers were later compelled to purchase one of the better quality cameras on the market. Universal's first camera, the UniveX Model A, was a radical new departure from other amateur cameras on the market at the time. Relatively good results were obtained from its postage stamp negative format and this, in itself, is believed to have been a contributing factor to the overall acceptance of the 35mm negative format, thus setting the stage for the 35mm minicamera craze soon to sweep the United States. During its short period in business, Universal managed to popularize inexpensive cameras on a large scale basis, both still and home movie — for this, the industry should be infinitely grateful...

Fig. 8-1 The Registered Trademark of the Universal Camera Corporation.

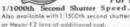

UNIVEX
VIEWING FILTER
Souvenir from New York World's Fair
MERCURY
With Built-In Photo Flash Synchronizer
For Day or Night Photography

1/1000th Second Shutter Speed.
Also available with 1/1500th second shutter
or Hexar f2 lens at additional cost.

● The UniveX Mercury is the fast-est American made super-speed can-did at a price within the reach of everyone. A camera that turns night into day, "impossibles" into simple shots. Incorporated in this remark-able camera are features usually found in expensive foreign models many times its price.

INSTRUCTIONS: This viewing filter will help you to get better pictures by showing in advance how the light tones will appear in the finished picture. Just look at the subject through the blue filter window. Then shoot picture only when you see good light grada-tions on subject. Many profes-sional photographers use this method.

PRINTED IN U.S.A.

UNIVERSAL CAMERA CORP., New York · Chicago · Hollywood

The Univex Viewing Filter promoted good photography as well as advertising the Mercury camera at the 1939-1940 New York World's Fair.

APPENDIX A

UNIVERSAL CAMERA CORPORATION
OFFICERS AND MANAGERS

PRESIDENTS
Otto W. Githens, 1933-1950
Jacob J. Shapiro, 1950-1964

VICE-PRESIDENTS
Jacob J. Shapiro, 1933-1950
John D. Cassidy, 1950-1951
D. Henry Werblow, 1952-1953
Leo J. Stuckens, 1953-

GENERAL MANAGERS
Percival H. Case, 1937-1945
John D. Cassidy, 1945-1949
Joseph David Marks, 1949-1952

SECRETARIES
Isaac B. Cohen, 1933-1937
Milton M. Shaw, 1937-1949
Victor Tropp, 1949-1952

TREASURERS
Simon Wain, 1934-1941
John F. Bruns, 1941-1943
Michael Tatkin, 1943-1952
W. V. A. Waterman, 1952-

CHIEF ENGINEER & OPTICAL PLANT MANAGER
George Kende, 1935-1948

PRODUCTION MANAGERS
Jesse Norden, 1935-1948
Charles Biasi, 1948-1952

GENERAL SALES MANAGERS
F. G. Klock, 1934-1940
Harry L. Shapiro, 1940-1947
Morton M. Schwartz, 1947-1949
Simon Weil, 1949-1964

ADVERTISING MANAGERS
Jacob J. Shapiro, 1933-1934
L. Hirschhorn, 1934-1935
F. G. Klock, 1935-1941
William B. Newman, 1941-1942
L. Provsky, 1942-1943
Morton M. Schwartz, 1943-1948
Seymour Walter, 1948-1949
C. J. Spinatelli, 1949-1951

APPENDIX B

UNIVERSAL CAMERA CORPORATION FACILITY LOCATIONS

MAIN SALES, PRODUCTION AND SERVICE FACILITY
521 Fifth Avenue, New York City, 1933
32 West 23rd Street, New York City, 1933-1938
28 West 23rd Street, New York City, 1938-1952
175 Fifth Avenue, New York City, 1952-1964

MAIN FILM PROCESSING FACILITY
12 East 22nd Street, New York City, 1936-1954

BRANCH SALES, DISTRIBUTION AND FILM PROCESSING FACILITIES
223 West Jackson Boulevard, Chicago, Illinois, 1937-1939
330 South Wells Street, Chicago, Illinois, 1939-1952
6058 Sunset Boulevard, Hollywood, California, 1937-1940
5910 Sunset Boulevard, Hollywood, California, 1940-1950

BRANCH PRODUCTION AND SERVICE FACILITY
264 Union Street, North Adams, Massachusetts, 1952-1957
1 Massachusetts Avenue, North Adams, Massachusetts, 1957-1960

DURING THE YEARS 1940-1950
UNIVERSAL MAINTAINED THE FOLLOWING ADDITIONAL FACILITIES

SALES FACILITIES
Atlanta, Georgia
Kansas City, Missouri
Dallas, Texas

PRODUCTION FACILITIES
932 Broadway, New York City
559 Sixth Avenue, New York City *
372 Johnson Avenue, Jersey City, New Jersey

STORAGE FACILITIES
34-36 West 22nd Street, New York City
509 West 38th Street, New York City

FILM PROCESSING MAILING ADDRESSES IN THE UNITED STATES AND CANADA

Universal Camera Corporation Laboratories
P.O. Box 8, Madison Square Station, New York City
P.O. Box 6400-A, Chicago, Illinois
P.O. Box 8110-A, Chicago, Illinois
P.O. Box 790, Hollywood, California
and
Postal Station B, Toronto, Canada

(*) Used by Universal during the war as an additional production facility. After the war, Chromex Film Laboratories was established at this location. Chromex was an affiliate of Universal during 1947 and 1948, but discontinued its operations after this period.

DURING THE YEARS 1936-1939
UNIVEX 8MM FILM AND PROCESSING SERVICES
WERE PURPORTEDLY AVAILABLE IN THE FOLLOWING
FOREIGN COUNTRIES

Algiers	Indochina
Argentine	Italy
Australia	Jamaica
Austria	Japan
Belgian Congo	Latvia
Belgium	Madagascar
Brazil	Malta
British India	Manchuria
Canaries	Mexico
Ceylon	Morocco
Chile	Netherlands Indies
China	New Zealand
Columbia	Norway
Cuba	Palestine
Czechoslovakia	Peru
Denmark	Philippine Islands
Dutch Indies	Poland
Ecuador	Portugal
Egypt	South African Union
Finland	Spain
France	Straits Settlements
Germany	Sweden
Great Britain	Switzerland
Greece	Syria
Guatemala	Turkey
Holland	Uruguay
Hungary	Venezuela
Iraq	Yugoslavia

UNIVERSAL CAMERA CORPORATION
U.S. DESIGN PATENTS

PATENT	DESIGN	INVENTOR	APPLICA-TION DATE	PATENT GRANTED
89,888	Model A ("Sunburst") Camera	Githens	Feb 23 33	May 16 33
91,228 *	Norton Camera	Whitlock	Oct 30 33	Dec 19 33
99,124	Model AF Camera	Githens/Norden/ Mannerberg	Jul 31 35	Mar 31 36
99,544	Model A-8 Cine Camera	Githens/Kende	Mar 23 36	May 5 36
101,956	Model P-8 Projector	Kende/Porter	Aug 7 36	Nov 17 36
109,716	Incandescent Projection Lamp	Kende	Mar 30 37	May 17 38
110,027	Variant Mercury	Kende/Brownscombe	Apr 2 38	Jun 7 38
110,028	Iris Camera	Kende/Yevick	Apr 14 38	Jun 7 38
110,323	Mercury Camera	Kende/Brownscombe	Mar 30 38	Jun 28 38
111,986	Model A ("Geometric") Camera	Milne	Jun 19 34	Nov 1 38
112,633	Mercury Photo Flash Unit	Cazin	Nov 2 38	Dec 20 38
117,174	Uniflash Camera	Githens/Kende	Aug 18 39	Oct 17 39
119,941	Model C-8 Turret Cine Camera	Robinton	Jul 25 39	Apr 16 40
120,583	Corsair Camera	Cazin	Mar 20 40	May 14 40
120,735	Twinflex Camera	Kende	Mar 26 40	May 28 40
121,155	Mercury Exposure Calculator	Brownscombe/Kertesz	Nov 2 38	Jun 25 40
121,816	Model P-500 Cine Projector	Kende/Salvatore	Dec 16 39	Aug 6 40
140,375	Binocular, 6x30 Hinged Bridge	Case/Johanson	Oct 25 44	Feb 20 45
140,730	Plastic Binocular, 6x42 Solid Bridge	Kende	Feb 14 45	Apr 3 45
145,364	Electric Slide Projector	Rubin	Oct 10 45	Aug 6 46
145,498	16mm Film and Sound Projector	Ward	Oct 10 45	Aug 27 46
149,131	Cabinet for Automatic Phonograph	Kende	Apr 12 46	Mar 30 48
149,132	Cabinet for Combined Radio and Phonograph	Kende	Apr 12 46	Mar 30 48
152,232	Meteor Camera	Whitaker	Apr 27 48	Dec 28 48
160,351	Minute-16 Camera	Ward	Aug 4 49	Oct 3 50
164,901	Minute-16 Transparency Mount	Cassidy/Marks	Nov 9 50	Oct 23 51

* - This Design Patent was assigned to Norton Laboratories, Portland, Maine.

APPENDIX C - PART 2

UNIVERSAL CAMERA CORPORATION
U.S. LETTERS PATENTS

PATENT	INVENTION	INVENTOR	APPLICA-TION DATE	PATENT GRANTED
2,029,474	Model A Camera, #00 Film Spool	Githens	Mar 7 33	Feb 4 36
2,029,475	Model A Camera, Shutter Mechanism	Githens	Aug 4 33	Feb 4 36
2,029,476	Model A Camera, #00 Film Spool	Githens	Mar 10 34	Feb 4 36
2,040,935	Model A Camera, Finder	Githens	Mar 10 34	May 19 36
2,078,432	Norton Camera, Film Spool	Whitlock	Aug 23 34	Apr 27 37
2,093,480	Simple Box Camera & Film Holder	Platt	Nov 7 32	Sep 21 37
2,093,500	Model A & Norton Cameras, Finders	Whitlock	Aug 14 34	Sep 21 37
2,133,743	Model A-8 Camera, Film Chamber & #100 Film Spool	Githens/Kende/Porter	Jan 28 37	Oct 18 38
2,164,061	Model AF Camera	Githens/Norden/ Mannerberg	Jul 12 35	Jun 27 39
2,167,713	Model A-8 Camera, Film Feed and Shutter Mechanism	Githens/Kende/Porter	Jan 21 37	Aug 1 39
2,172,348	Model A-8 Camera, Carrying Case	Githens/Lawson	Dec 15 36	Sep 12 39
2,174,155	Model A-8 Camera, Motor & Speed Control Mechanisms	Githens/Kende/Porter	Apr 7 37	Sep 26 39
2,190,658	Model P-8 Projector, Film Feed & Shutter Mechanism	Githens/Kende/Porter	Jun 3 37	Feb 20 40
2,208,797	Iris Camera	Kende	Oct 27 38	Jul 23 40
2,211,466	Model A-8 Camera, Governor	Kende	Mar 25 39	Aug 13 40
2,218,915	Corsair Camera, Body Mount Shutter Release Button	Kende/Cazin	Oct 28 39	Oct 22 40
2,221,089	Model P-8 Projector, Film Reel & Mounting Shaft	Githens/Kende/Porter	Dec 21 39	Nov 12 40
2,224,383	Model A-8 Camera, Film Footage Indicator	Githens/Kende/Porter	Jul 19 39	Dec 10 40
2,226,245	Variant Mercury, Rotary Shutter	Kende	Dec 3 37	Dec 24 40
2,233,389	Mercury Camera, #200 Film Spool	Kende/Brownscombe	Apr 25 38	Feb 25 41
2,233,390	Mercury Camera	Kende/Brownscombe	Dec 13 38	Feb 25 41
2,236,069	Model C-8 Turret Camera	Robinton	May 31 39	Mar 25 41
2,242,452	Mercury Camera, Clip-on Rangefinder	Cazin	Dec 29 39	May 20 41
2,242,464	Model P-8 Projector, Constructional Features	Githens/Kende/Porter	Dec 21 39	May 20 41
2,246,034	Mercury Camera, Rapid Winder	Elison	Jul 4 39	Jun 17 41
2,252,563	Model A-8 Camera, Constructional Features	Githens/Kende/Porter	Mar 3 37	Aug 12 41
2,260,672	Micrographic Enlarger	Johanson	Apr 1 40	Oct 28 41
2,260,673	Electric 2x2 Slide Projector	Kende	Jul 30 40	Oct 28 41
2,267,794	Twinflex Camera, Shutter Mechanism	Kosken	Jun 24 40	Dec 30 41
2,267,811	Buccaneer Camera, Combined Viewfinder & Rangefinder	Brownscombe	Apr 19 40	Dec 30 41
2,270,311	Mercury Camera, Constructional Features	Kende/Brownscombe	Jul 10 40	Jan 20 42
2,271,562	Uniflash Camera, Shutter Mechanism	Lotz	Jan 24 40	Feb 3 42
2,274,707	Mercury Camera, Shutter Mechanism	Kende/Brownscombe	May 9 40	Mar 3 42
2,277,233	Mercury Camera, Flash Synch & Flash Unit	Kende/Brownscombe	Jan 6 39	Mar 24 42
2,282,850	Uniflash Camera, Flash Synch	Brownscombe	Apr 1 40	May 12 42
2,282,863	Model P-8 Projector, Fire Shutter Mechanism	Githens/Kende/Porter	Dec 21 39	May 12 42
2,287,430	Mercury Camera, Exposure Calculator	Kende/Brownscombe	Dec 3 38	Jun 23 42
2,309,382	Corsair Camera	Cazin	Mar 26 40	Jan 26 43
2,309,403	Twinflex Camera	Kosken/Brownscombe	Jul 20 40	Jan 26 43

PATENT	INVENTION	INVENTOR	APPLICA-TION DATE	PATENT GRANTED
2,317,465	Iris Camera, Flash Synch	Kende/Cazin	Sep 12 39	Apr 27 43
2,319,318	Model P-8 Projector, Intermittent Film Feed	Githens/Kende/Porter	Dec 21 39	May 18 43
2,320,423	Uniflash Camera, Constructional Features	Githens/Kende	Jun 5 40	Jun 1 43
2,350,237	Cinemaster, Combined Viewfinder & Exposure Meter	Kende/Johanson	Dec 18 41	May 30 44
2,352,551	Automatic Prism Grinding Machines	Kende/Elison/Johanson	Mar 2 42	Jun 27 44
2,356,880	Single Lens Reflex Camera, Waist Level	Pignone	Aug 21 40	Aug 29 44
2,358,696	Optical Assembly Cement	Falkoff	Jun 29 42	Sep 19 44
2,380,610	Single Lens Reflex Camera, Auto Shutter/Diaphragm Mechanism	Pignone	Aug 21 40	Jul 31 45
2,392,154	Plastic Binocular, 6x42 Solid Bridge	Kende	Apr 21 44	Jan 1 46
2,436,574	Binocular for Mounting on Headgear	Johanson	Feb 14 45	Feb 24 48
2,436,576	Headgear for Binocular	Kende/Johanson	Feb 14 45	Feb 24 48
2,437,947	Method of Mounting Optical Prisms in Binoculars	Falkoff	Feb 17 44	Mar 16 48
2,454,859	Water & Moistureproofing Binoculars	Case	Oct 25 44	Nov 30 48
2,519,251	Electric Slide Projector, Shutter Dissolve	Johanson	Aug 2 46	Aug 15 50
2,544,230	Automatic Phonograph	Johnson	Nov 5 45	Mar 6 51
2,597,449	Minute-16 Electric Slide Projector	Cassidy/Marks	Nov 9 50	May 20 52
2,673,500	Minute-16 Camera, Film Cassette	Cassidy/Marks	Nov 9 50	Mar 30 54

APPENDIX C - PART 3

UNIVERSAL CAMERA CORPORATION
U.S. TRADEMARKS

SERIAL NO.	TRADEMARK	REGIST. NO.	FIRST USED	APPLICATION DATE	PUBLICATION DATE
340,244	Univex	308,159	Jul 5 33	Jul 29 33	Sep 12 33
340,245	Ultrachrome	308,158	Jul 5 33	Jul 29 33	Sep 12 33
340,246	"V"	319,692	Jul 5 33	Jul 29 33	Sep 25 34
389,202	Aristocrat	347,650	Oct 21 36	Feb 20 37	Apr 20 37
404,967	Silverlux	-	Dec 36	Apr 6 38	Jun 7 38
404,968	Univar	359,405	Sep 36	Apr 6 38	Jun 7 38
408,137	Univex Iris	378,225	Apr 6 38	Jul 1 38	Mar 26 40
408,588	Mercury	364,387	May 9 38	Jul 16 38	Nov 22 38
408,628	Vitar	-	May 9 38	Jul 18 38	Nov 22 38
413,968	Microtomic	-	Nov 16 38	Dec 16 38	Aug 1 39
414,169	Cinemaster	369,618	Dec 8 38	Dec 23 38	May 23 39
414,170	Hexar	-	Dec 8 38	Dec 23 38	May 23 39
417,631	Tricor	369,979	Nov 16 38	Mar 29 39	May 30 39
419,214	Apex	371,008	Mar 27 39	May 8 39	Jul 4 39
419,319	Comet	-	Mar 27 39	May 11 39	Aug 22 39
419,352	Meteor	372,407	Mar 27 39	May 12 39	Aug 22 39
419,353	Zenith	372,408	Mar 27 39	May 12 39	Aug 22 39
422,918	Micrographic	380,896	Jun 29 39	Aug 23 39	Sep 3 40
423,514	Uniflaoh	379,095	Jul 6 39	Sep 11 39	Apr 23 40
425,440	Univex Ace	-	Mar 9 39	Nov 8 39	Jan 9 40
425,539	Supar	-	Nov 4 39	Nov 10 39	Feb 13 40
425,713	Rayflex	-	Oct 10 39	Nov 16 39	Mar 5 40
425,823	Uniflex	377,742	Oct 16 39	Nov 18 39	Mar 5 40
426,382	Twinflex	377,969	Nov 20 39	Dec 8 39	Mar 12 40
426,675	Shur-O-Matic	-	Nov 17 39	Dec 16 39	Mar 12 40
427,447	Superflex	378,770	Nov 14 39	Jan 13 40	Apr 9 40
428,843	Corsair	379,024	Dec 16 39	Feb 23 40	Apr 16 40
438,558	Cinematic	393,841	Oct 23 40	Dec 5 40	Mar 3 42
498,952	Minivex	431,724	Feb 21 46	Mar 25 46	May 13 47
498,955	Ultravox - Class 21	440,685	Feb 4 46	Mar 25 46	May 13 47
498,956	Ultravox - Class 26	443,138	Feb 4 46	Mar 25 46	Sep 28 48
498,957	Ultravox - Class 36	440,769	Feb 4 46	Mar 25 46	May 27 47
498,958	Unitron	431,725	Feb 27 46	Mar 25 46	May 13 47
509,055	Buccaneer	432,533	Jul 19 46	Sep 13 46	Jun 10 47
510,552	Roamer	432,547	Aug 9 46	Oct 9 46	Jun 10 47
514,231	Beacon	435,889	Sep 19 46	Dec 13 46	Aug 26 47
518,570	Chronomatic	435,538	Jul 19 46	Mar 5 47	Sep 30 47
519,107	Tonemaster	443,851	Oct 15 46	Mar 15 47	Oct 26 48
562,422	Range-Viewer	593,138	Jul 19 46	Jul 28 48	Jul 27 54
583,896	Minute 16	542,501	Jun 9 49	Aug 23 49	May 15 51
587,153	Cavalier	544,823	Sep 19 46	Sep 29 49	Apr 10 51
609,324	Uni-Color	552,566	Jul 19 49	Jan 26 51	Aug 14 51
609,325	Uni-Pan	552,567	Jul 19 49	Jan 26 51	Aug 14 51
609,747	Jiffy Mask	560,852	Feb 46	Feb 7 51	Apr 1 52
642,430	Nu-Color	592,874	Oct 1 52	Feb 18 53	Jul 20 54
666,234	Steré-All	604,834	Apr 1 54	May 12 54	Jan 18 55

APPENDIX C - PART 4

UNIVERSAL CAMERA CORPORATION
UNIVERSAL PATENTEES

Philip J. Brownscombe	East Orange, New Jersey
Percival H. Case	New York, New York
John D. Cassidy	Riverside, Connecticut
Otto K. Cazin	Hoboken, New Jersey
Eli Elison	Jackson Heights, New York
Adin Daniel Falkoff	Brooklyn, New York
Otto W. Githens	New York, New York
Sten Johanson	New York, New York
Frank M. Johnson	New York, New York
George Kende	Dobbs Ferry, New York
Carl Kertesz	Long Island City, New York
Wilho A. Kosken	New York, New York
William L. Lawson	New York, New York
Richard K. Lotz	Brooklyn, New York
Edward G. Mannerberg	Brooklyn, New York
Joseph David Marks	West Orange, New Jersey
James D. Milne	Pittsfield, Massachusetts
Jesse Norden	Astoria, New York
Joseph Pignone	Brooklyn, New York
Samuel C. Platt	New York, New York
Everett Melbourn Porter	Brooklyn, New York
Frank A. Robinton	Hartford, Connecticut
Lewis Jay Rubin	New York, New York
Roland Salvatore	Lyndhurst, New Jersey
Wallace W. Ward	Bloomfield, New Jersey
David C. Whitaker	New York, New York
Carl H. Whitlock	Lockport, New York
William E. Yevick	Brooklyn, New York

APPENDIX D

**UNIVERSAL CAMERA CORPORATION
NET SALES AND PROFITS**

YEAR	NET SALES	NET PROFITS
1933	$ Unknown	$ Unknown
1934	Unknown	Unknown
1935	400,000 *	Unknown
1936	677,525	17
1937	2,771,775	135,301
1938	1,725,255	47,678
1939	2,142,709	83,360
1940	1,250,930	(125,403)
1941	1,121,597	(103,518)
1942	3,779,109	311,757
1943	5,505,162	171,236
1944	5,784,496	100,140
1945	4,538,238	78,162
1946	6,219,011	460,722
1947	6,074,913	(516,897)
1948	3,413,780	(1,589,790)
1949	1,061,494	(951,840)
1950	1,621,349	(347,499)
1951	2,951,082	56,393
1952	Bankrupt	Bankrupt
1953-1964	Unknown	Unknown

* Approximate figure.

( ) Denotes loss.

APPENDIX E

UNIVERSAL CAMERA CORPORATION
CONDENSED CHRONOLOGICAL PRODUCT HISTORY

CIRCA	PRODUCT	MODEL #	FILM SIZE
1933	Standard Model A Box Camera	A	Univex #00
1935	AF Folding Camera	AF	Univex #00
	Norton Univex Box Camera	NU	Univex #00
1936	AF-2 Folding Camera	AF-2	Univex #00
	AF-3 Deluxe Folding Camera	AF-3	Univex #00
	Standard Cine 8 Camera	A-8	Univex #100
	Projector, Univex (100 or 150 watt - AC only)	P-8	8mm
1937	Projector, Univex (200 watt - AC/DC)	PU-8	8mm
1938	Exposition Cine 8 Camera	C-8	Univex #100
	AF-4 Folding Camera	AF-4	Univex #00
	AF-5 Minicam Folding Camera	AF-5	Univex #00
	Iris Deluxe Candid Camera	CD-79	Univex #00
	Iris Standard Candid Camera	C-79	Univex #00
	Mercury I Camera	CC	Univex #200
	Projector, Univex (100 watt, 6 volt - DC only)	P-806	8mm
	Projector, Univex (100 watt, 32 volt - DC only)	P-832	8mm
1939	Corsair I Camera	C-514	Univex #200
	Iris Standard Flash Candid Camera	C-279	Univex #00
	Mercury I Superspeed Camera	CC-1500	Univex #200
	Trueview Cine 8 Camera	B-8	Univex #100
	Turret Cine 8 Camera	CT-8	Univex #100
	Zenith Candid Camera	Z-45	Univex #00
	Zenith Candid Flash Camera	Z-245	Univex #00
	Projector, Univex (500 watt - AC/DC)	P-500	8mm
1940	Corsair II Camera	C-525	Std 35mm
	Iris Deluxe Flash Candid Camera	CD-279	Univex #00
	Twinflex Camera	T-025	Univex #00
	Uniflash Camera & Flash	CF-15	Univex #00
1941	Cinemaster Standard Camera	D-8	Dual 8mm
	Cinemaster Special Camera	E-8	Dual 8mm
	Cinemaster Jewel Camera	F-8	Dual 8mm
	Projector, Univex (100 watt - AC only)	P-300	8mm
	Projector, Univex (200 watt - AC/DC)	PU-300	8mm
1946	Binocular, Prismatic (6x30)	BN	
	Cinemaster II Camera	G-8	Dual 8mm
	Mercury II Camera	CX	Std 35mm
	Projector, Univex (100 watt - AC only)	PC-12	8mm
	Projector, Universal (500 watt - AC/DC)	PC-500	8mm
1947	Buccaneer Camera	FF-535	Std 35mm
	Meteor Camera	PR-100	620
	Projector, Cinematic (750 watt - AC/DC)	P-750	8mm
	Projector, Tonemaster Sound (1000 watt - AC/DC)	P-1000	16mm
	Projector, Univex (100 watt - AC only)	PC-10	8mm
1948	Roamer I Camera	FC-111	120/620
	Roamer II Camera	FC-245	120/620
	Roamer 63 Camera	FC-363	120/620
	Uniflex I Camera	RC-560	120/620
	Uniflex II Camera	RC-450	120/620
	Projector, Cinematic (750 watt - AC/DC)	P-752	8mm
	Projector, Universal (500 watt - AC/DC)	PC-5	8mm
1949	Minute-16 Camera		16mm cassette
1951	Cinemaster Camera	H-8	Double-8
	Uniflex III Camera	RC-	120/620
	Vitar Camera		Std 35mm
1954	Steré-All Camera		Std 35mm

250

APPENDIX F

POPEYE
---25 Foot---

Shipwrecked	8201	Training Camp	8208
Dry Land Sailor	8202	The Bouncer	8209
Sleep Baby Sleep	8203	Saved By a Tree	8210
Olivoil Entertains Popeye	8204	Some Anchor	8211
The Strong Man	8205	Red Hot	8212
In the Water Barrel	8206	Shooting the Shoots	8220
Exercising the Bull	8207	The Boat Builder	8221

---50 Foot---

Indian Fighter	8101	Popeye the Champ	8112
The Nursemaid	8102	King of the Jungle	8113
The Circus Man	8103	Wagon Works	8114
Bluto the Bandit	8104	Spinachville	8115
The Butcher	8105	Horse Shoes	8116
At the Rodeo	8106	Flim Flam Fireman	8120
At the Carnival	8107	High Steppers	8121
Train Buster	8108	Free Lunch	8122
Fancy Skaters	8109	The Lumberjack	8123
Snowball Battle	8110	Lots of Baloney	8124
Gets the Works	8111	Apache Dancers	8125

MICKEY MOUSE
---25 Foot---

Mickey's Musicians	926-Z	Mickey the Castaway	932-Z
Mickey's Marathon	927-Z	Mickey and the Gorilla	933-Z
Mickey's Jungle Pals	928-Z	Mickey the Cook	934-Z
Mickey's Best Girl	929-Z	Mickey Fishes Around	935-Z
Mickey's Turkey	930-Z	Mickey and Pluto	936-Z
Mickey's Playmates	931-Z	Mickey's Mixup	937-Z

---50 Foot---

Mickey's Barn Dance	901-A	Mickey Goes Hunting	907-A
Mickey's Finish	902-A	Mickey the Duck Hunter	908-A
Mickey's Olympic Games	903-A	Mickey the Moose Hunter	909-A
Mickey's Bicycle Race	904-A	Mickey the Messenger	910-A
Mickey's Barnyard Melodies	905-A	Mickey Goes Courting	911-A
Mickey's Mad Dog	906-A	Mickey and the Dog Catcher	912-A

ELMER RABBIT
---25 Foot---

Elmer Catches Cold	26-Z	Elmer Gets Soaked	30-Z
Kitchen Antics	27-Z	House of Magic	31-Z
Home Run Oswald	28-Z	Oswald the Boxer	32-Z
The Speed Cop	29-Z		

---50 Foot---

Dog Team Race	1-A	Beauty and The Beast	8-A
Beauty Shop	2-A	Doctor Oswald	9-A
Soft Ball Game	3-A	Sniffs and Sniffles	10-A
Alaska Mush	4-A	The Slumberland Express	11-A
Play Ball	5-A	Adventures in Dreamland	12-A
The Duck's Birthday	6-A	G-Man Oswald	13-A
Barnyard Quints	7-A	Bo Peep's Sheep	14-A

OUR GANG
---25 Foot---

Amateur Engineer	81101	Watermelon Feast	81107
Stolen Train	81102	At the Races	81108
Baby Stunts	81103	Baby Parade	81109
Imitations	81104	Flea Circus	81110
New Lodge Member	81105	Bus Driver	81111
Starting School	81106	Fresh Cocoanuts	81112

---50 Foot---

Bold Pirates	81001	Frying Pan Special	81007
Babies and Gypsies	81002	Baby Laundry	81008
Let's Go Fishin'	81003	Bandits in the Well	81009
Country Fair	81004	Cowboys and Indians	81010
Hot-Dogs-Lemonade	81005	Wild Animals	81011
Wild Auto Ride	81006	Kiddie Wedding	81012

BETTY BOOP
---25 Foot---

The Speed King	8601	Birthday Gifts	8609
The Show Girl	8602	Spirit of '76	8610
The Fortune Teller	8603	Magic Maid	8611
Impersonations	8604	Betty's Banquet	8612
The Stenographer	8605	Betty & Dragon	8613
Flying to the Moon	8606	Daily Dozen	8614
Spider's Web	8607	Some Picnic	8620
Mystery Cave	8608		

---50 Foot---

Stopping the Show	8501	In Midgetville	8512
Betty Boop's Express	8502	Cannibal Island	8513
The Auto Race	8503	Lunch Wagon	8514
Mystery Island	8504	Wheat Cakes	8515
Fairytales	8505	Dr. Hoakem	8516
S. O. S.	8506	Caught in the Act	8517
Land of Boop a Doop	8507	Bed Time Story	8518
In Rubber Land	8508	Kat for Sale	8519
May Queen	8509	Doggy Troubles	8520
Witch's Clutch	8510	Bad Bad Baby	8521
Magic Mirror	8511		

MISCELLANEOUS TITLES
---50 Foot---

The Story of Santa Claus ... 126-A   Air Stunts 292-A
Savages of the South Seas ... 132-A   Evolution of a Butterfly 1021-A
Capturing a Shark 163-A

MISCELLANEOUS SUBJECTS

---Cartoons---
Barney Google
Donald Duck
Farmer Al Falfa
Krazy Kat
Puddy Pup
Scrappy

---Comedies & Westerns---
Stepin Fetchit
Lloyd Hamilton
Lupino Lane
Rex Lease
Bob Steele

---Others---
Aesop's Fables
Air Thrillers
Art Subjects
G-Men
Scenic
Travel

APPENDIX G

UNIVERSAL CAMERA CORPORATION
GENERAL ELECTRIC AND SLYVANIA PROJECTION BULBS
FOR USE IN UNIVERSAL PROJECTORS

PROJECTOR	TYPE OF BULB
Cinematic P750, P752	DDB/DDW - CZX/DAB
Tonemaster (sound) P1000	DFD, BFT
Universal PC5, PC500	CZX/DAB
Univex P8, PC10, PC12, P300	BWY
Univex P500	CZX/DAB
Univex PU8, PU300	CGD

APPENDIX H

UNIVERSAL CAMERA CORPORATION
COMPREHENSIVE RECORD OF UNIVEX PRODUCTS
WITH COLLECTIBLE RATING GUIDE

The next several pages contain a definitive reference source encompassing all known UniveX products — undoubtedly, it is the most thorough and complete record of UniveX products ever compiled and printed. In an effort to be as precise and conclusive as possible, the list includes various camera/lens and projector/lens combinations as they were originally sold. Original prices and catalog numbers for some items could not be obtained — these areas have been left blank. The list gives a brief, but specific, description of each product, including its original price and the year it was first introduced. Universal's original catalog numbering system was used in the preparation of this list. It proved useful in differentiating various camera/lens combinations and, at the same time, provided a more specific means of identifying each product. Catalog numbers are generally not the same as product model numbers; although in certain instances, a product's model number comprised a portion of the catalog number. Similarities between these numbers will eventually become evident. Catalog numbers were almost always found printed on the product's original factory box, with the exception of products marketed after 1948.

A special "Collectible Rating Guide" has been incorporated into this product listing and should prove quite useful in ascertaining which UniveX products are commonly seen on today's photographic marketplace, and which are not. Several things were considered in determining a rating for each of the items listed. The original price of a product, the length of time it was marketed, the quantity produced and its general appeal were all important factors in rating the scarcity of a particular product. Each item has been assigned a rating number from "1" to "5". These rating numbers signify the following: 1) EXTREMELY COMMON 2) COMMON 3) UNUSUAL 4) RARE 5) EXTREMELY RARE. The "Collectible Rating Guide" makes an overall comparison of every known UniveX product, pinpointing for the reader or collector the relative scarcity of each individual UniveX product. By no means is this intended as a price guide for obtaining the value of a collectible item; consequently, no attempt has been made to indicate the monetary value of any collectible item listed here. Excellent price guides are available for this particular purpose. Even though the value of a collectible constantly changes, the "Collectible Rating Guide" should maintain its accuracy indefinitely.

Note: Before using the "Collectible Rating Guide", please consider the following example: the UniveX Model A-8 Cine Camera with an f/1.9 Wollensak Univar lens is rated "4" or "RARE". In this particular case, "RARE" is intended to show that this is a rare camera/lens combination and that the collector would be hard-pressed to find this combination as it was originally sold. The f/1.9 lens alone is rated 4 or "RARE". The Model A-8 camera with a standard f/5.6 Univar lens is rated 1 or "EXTREMELY COMMON".

1) EXTREMELY COMMON   2) COMMON   3) UNUSUAL   4) RARE   5) EXTREMELY RARE

PRODUCT	CAT NO.	ORIG COST	CIRCA	RATING
Battery Pack, Eveready	M-750	$ .20	1939	5
Binoculars, Prismatic - 6x30	BN	$85.00	1946	3
Booklet, "How to Make Movies"	M-024	$ .25	1938	4
Cable Release	M-026	$ .35	1938	4
Camera, Buccaneer - Tricor(Univ) f/3.5/50mm Lens	FF-535	$65.00	1947	2
Camera, Corsair I - Univex f/4.5/50mm Lens	C-514	$16.75	1939	3
Camera, Corsair II - Univex f/4.5/50mm Lens	C-525	$19.75	1940	3
Camera, Iris Deluxe - Vitar(Ilex) f/7.9/50mm Lens	CD-079	$ 7.50	1938	4
Camera, Iris Deluxe Flash - Vitar(Ilex) f/7.9/50mm Lens	CD-279	$ 8.50	1940	4
Camera, Iris Standard - Vitar(Ilex) f/7.9/50mm Lens	C-079	$ 5.95	1938	2
Camera, Iris Standard Flash - Vitar(Ilex) f/7.9/50mm Lens	C-279	$ 6.95	1939	2
Camera, Mercury Model CC - Hexar(Woll) f/2.0/35mm Lens	C-620	$59.50	1939	4
Camera, Mercury Model CC - Tricor(Woll) f/2.7/35mm Lens	C-627	$37.50	1940	5
Camera, Mercury Model CC - Tricor(Woll) f/3.5/35mm Lens	C-635	$25.00	1938	1
Camera, Mercury Model CC-1500 - Hexar(Woll) f/2.0/35mm Lens	CS-620	$65.00	1939	5
Camera, Mercury Model CC-1500 - Tricor(Woll) f/2.7/35mm Lens	CS-627	$42.50	1940	5
Camera, Mercury Model CC-1500 - Tricor(Woll) f/3.5/35mm Lens	CS-635	$29.75	1939	5
Camera, Mercury II Model CX - Hexar(Univ or Woll) f/2.0/35mm Lens	CX-020	$103.25	1946	5
Camera, Mercury II Model CX - Tricor(Univ) f/2.7/35mm Lens	CX-027	$65.00	1946	1
Camera, Mercury II Model CX - Tricor(Univ) f/3.5/35mm Lens	CX-035	$51.75	1946	3
Camera, Meteor - Achromat f/11 Lens	PR-100	$15.00	1947	2
Camera, Minute-16 - 1.3" f/6.3 Lens		$ 7.95	1949	1
Camera, Model A	A	$ .39	1933	1
Camera, Model AF Folding	AF	$ 1.00	1935	2
Camera, Model AF-2 Folding	AF-002	$ 1.50	1936	1
Camera, Model AF-3 Deluxe Folding	AF-003	$ 2.50	1936	3
Camera, Model AF-4 Folding	AF-004	$ 1.95	1938	3
Camera, Model AF-5 Minicam - Achromar(Ilex) f/16/60mm Lens	AF-005	$ 3.50	1938	3
Camera, Model A-8 Standard Cine - Univar(Woll) f/1.9 Lens	C-019	$47.25	1937	4
Camera, Model A-8 Standard Cine - Univar(Woll) f/2.7 Lens	C-027	$27.50	1937	5
Camera, Model A-8 Standard Cine - Univar(Woll) f/3.5 Lens	C-035	$19.95	1937	3
Camera, Model A-8 Standard Cine - Univar(Ilex) f/5.6 Lens	C-056	$ 9.95	1936	1
Camera, Model B-8 Trueview Cine - Univar(Woll) f/3.5 Lens	B-835	$19.95	1940	3
Camera, Model B-8 Trueview Cine - Univar(Ilex) f/5.6 Lens	B-856	$ 9.95	1939	2
Camera, Model C-8 Exposition Cine - Univar(Woll) f/1.9 Lens	C-819	$47.25	1938	4
Camera, Model C-8 Exposition Cine - Univar(Woll) f/2.7 Lens	C-827	$27.50	1938	5
Camera, Model C-8 Exposition Cine - Univar(Woll) f/3.5 Lens	C-835	$21.50	1938	2
Camera, Model C-8 Exposition Cine - Univar(Ilex) f/4.5 Lens	C-845	$15.00	1939	2
Camera, Model C-8 Exposition Cine - Univar(Ilex) f/5.6 Lens	C-856	$12.50	1938	3
Camera, Model C-8 Turret Cine - Univar(Woll) f/3.5 Lens	CT-835	$29.95	1939	4
Camera, Model C-8 Turret Cine - Univar(Woll) f/4.5 Lens	CT-845	$25.00	1939	4
Camera, Model D-8 Cinemaster Standard - Univar(Ilex) f/4.5 Lens	D-845	$19.95	1941	5
Camera, Model D-8 Cinemaster Standard - Univar f/6.3 Lens	D-863	$15.95	1941	5
Camera, Model E-8 Cinemaster Special - Univar(Woll) f/1.9 Lens	E-819	$57.50	1941	5
Camera, Model E-8 Cinemaster Special - Univar(Univ) f/2.5 Lens	E-825	$39.50	1941	5
Camera, Model E-8 Cinemaster Special - Univar(Woll) f/2.7 Lens	E-827	$37.50	1941	5
Camera, Model E-8 Cinemaster Special - Univar(Woll) f/3.5 Lens	E-835	$27.50	1941	5
Camera, Model F-8 Cinemaster Jewel - Univar(Woll) f/1.9 Lens	F-819	$62.50	1941	5
Camera, Model F-8 Cinemaster Jewel - Univar(Univ) f/2.5 Lens	F-825	$44.50	1941	5
Camera, Model F-8 Cinemaster Jewel - Univar(Woll) f/2.7 Lens	F-827	$42.50	1941	5

PRODUCT	CAT NO.	ORIG COST	CIRCA	RATING
Camera, Model F-8 Cinemaster Jewel - Univar(Woll) f/3.5 Lens	F-835	$32.50	1941	4
Camera, Model G-8 Cinemaster II - Univar(Univ) f/1.9 Lens	G-819	$96.75	1946	4
Camera, Model G-8 Cinemaster II - Univar(Univ) f/2.5 Lens	G-825	$66.65	1946	1
Camera, Model G-8 Cinemaster II - Univar(Univ) f/3.5 Lens	G-835	$51.90	1946	4
Camera, Model H-8 Cinemaster - Univar(Univ) f/1.9 Lens	H-819		1951	5
Camera, Model H-8 Cinemaster - Univar(Univ) f/2.5 Lens	H-825		1951	5
Camera, Model H-8 Cinemaster - Univar(Univ) f/3.5 Lens	H-835		1951	5
Camera, Norton Univex	NU-001	$ .50	1935	3
Camera, Roamer 63 - Universal(Univ) f/6.3/100mm Lens	FC-363	$38.00	1948	2
Camera, Roamer I - Achromat f/11/100mm Lens	FC-111	$29.75	1948	2
Camera, Roamer II - Universal(Univ) f/4.5/100mm Lens	FC-245	$48.00	1948	2
Camera, Steré-All - Tricor(Univ) f/3.5/35mm Lens		$49.95	1954	2
Camera, Twinflex	T-025	$ 4.95	1940	3
Camera, Uniflash & Flash Unit - Vitar(Univex) 60mm Lens	CF-015	$ 4.95	1940	1
Camera, Uniflex I - Universal(Univ) f/5.6/75mm Lens	RC-560	$48.00	1948	2
Camera, Uniflex II - Universal(Univ) f/4.5/75mm Lens	RC-450	$75.00	1948	2
Camera, Uniflex III - Universal(Univ) f/4.5/75mm Lens	RC-		1951	5
Camera, Vitar - Tricor(Univ) f/3.5/50mm Lens		$41.00	1951	4
Camera, Zenith - Univex f/4.5/50mm Lens	Z-045	$12.50	1939	5
Camera, Zenith Flash - Univex f/4.5/50mm Lens	Z-245	$15.00	1939	5
Case, Buccaneer	K-025	$ 7.25	1947	3
Case, Cinemaster	K-022	$ 4.95	1941	3
Case, Corsair	K-020	$ 2.75	1939	4
Case, Exposure Meter (tubular)	K-007	$ .35	1938	1
Case, Iris (flash)	K-016	$ 2.00	1940	4
Case, Iris (non-flash)	K-009	$ 2.00	1938	4
Case, Mercury - Deluxe	K-010	$ 5.00	1938	4
Case, Mercury - Standard	K-015	$ 3.00	1938	2
Case, Mercury II	K-023	$ 7.25	1946	2
Case, Meteor	K-024	$ 5.00	1947	2
Case, Minute-16	K-029		1949	2
Case, Model A-8 Cine - Deluxe	K-002	$ 2.95	1938	3
Case, Model A-8 Cine - Standard	K-001	$ 2.00	1936	1
Case, Model AF	K-004	$ .25	1936	5
Case, Model AF-5	K-005	$ 1.00	1938	5
Case, Model B-8 Cine	K-012	$ 2.50	1939	5
Case, Model C-8 Turret Cine	K-017	$ 5.00	1939	5
Case, Projector (500 watt)	K-011	$ 5.50	1939	5
Case, Projector - Cinematic	K-028	$10.75	1947	5
Case, Projector - Deluxe	KD-006	$ 3.95	1938	4
Case, Projector - Standard	K-003	$ 2.95	1936	2
Case, Roamer	K-026	$ 7.50	1948	2
Case, Steré-All	K-031	$ 7.50	1954	3
Case, Titler (automatic)	K-013	$ .50	1940	5
Case, Twinflex	K-021	$ 1.50	1940	5
Case, Uniflash	K-019	$ 1.95	1940	5
Case, Uniflex	K-027	$ 9.95	1948	2
Case, Vitar	K-030	$ 7.00	1951	5
Case, Zenith	K-018	$ 3.00	1939	5
Cement, Film	M-002	$ .25	1938	5
Cleaner & Preservative, Film	M-003	$ .25	1938	5
Copying Stand Arm Only, Mercury	M-085	$12.50	1940	5
Copying Stand, Mercury	M-073	$17.50	1939	5
Counter Display "Theatre" & Demo Film	M-015	$ .75	1937	5
Developing Kit, Photocrafter (with camera & film)	001	$ 1.69	1938	5
Developing Kit, Photocrafter (without camera & film)	002	$ 1.20	1938	5
Easel	M-		1939	5
Editor & Viewer, Film	M-008	$ 1.95	1938	5
Enlarger, Micrographic	M-063	$27.50	1939	5
Exposure Meter, Candid (tubular)	M-012	$ 1.95	1938	2
Exposure Meter, Cine (tubular)	M-011	$ 1.95	1938	2
Exposure Meter, Mercury	M-030	$ 2.00	1938	3

PRODUCT	CAT NO.	ORIG COST	CIRCA	RATING
Exposure Meter, Mercury II	M-030	$ 2.85	1946	4 *
Extension Piece for Model A-8 Cine Cases	M-028	$ .75	1938	4
Extension Tube Kit, Mercury	M-065	$ 5.75	1939	5
Extension Tube No. 1, Mercury	M-066	$ 1.00	1939	5
Extension Tube No. 2, Mercury	M-067	$ 1.50	1939	5
Extension Tube No. 3, Mercury	M-068	$ 2.00	1939	5
Extension Tube No. 4, Mercury	M-069	$ 2.50	1939	5
Extension Tube Shim, Mercury	M-072	$ .25	1939	5
Film Cartridge, Daylight Loading	M-200	$ .60	1939	4
Film Cassette, Minute-16 UNI-COLOR	16-C	$ .35	1949	3
Film Cassette, Minute-16 UNI-PAN	16-P	$ .35	1949	3
Film Roll, #00 6-exp. ULTRACHROME	00-C	$ .10	1933	3
Film Roll, #00 6-exp. ULTRAPAN	00-P	$ .15	1938	3
Film, #100 8mm STANDARD	100-S	$ .60	1936	3
Film, #100 8mm ULTRAPAN	100-UP	$ .90	1936	3
Film, #100 8mm ULTRAPAN SUPERSPEED	100-UP	$ 1.10	1941	3
Film, #200 35 mm DUFAYCOLOR	218-D	$ .90	1939	5
Film, #200 35 mm MICROTOMIC	218-M	$ .35	1938	5
Film, #200 35 mm MICROTOMIC	236-M	$ .45	1938	5
Film, #200 35 mm ULTRACHROME	218-C	$ .30	1938	5
Film, #200 35 mm ULTRACHROME	236-C	$ .40	1938	5
Film, #200 35 mm ULTRAPAN SUPERSPEED	218-SS	$ .40	1938	5
Film, #200 35 mm ULTRAPAN SUPERSPEED	236-SS	$ .50	1938	4
Filter Kit with Filters (Cine) - Set/3 (M-33,41,42) - No.3	M-062	$ 7.25	1938	5
Filter Kit with Filters (Mercury) - Set/5 (M-47,48,49,50,51) - No.11	M-058	$17.00	1939	5
Filter Kit with Filters (Mercury) - Set/5 (M-35,36,37,38,43) - No.9	M-057	$12.50	1939	5
Filter Kit with Filters (Mercury II) - Set/3 - No.11	M-	$ 3.75	1946	5
Filter Kit without Filters (Cine) - No.3	M-079	$ 1.00	1938	5
Filter Kit without Filters (Mercury) - No.11	M-060	$ 1.25	1939	5
Filter Kit without Filters (Mercury) - No.9	M-059	$ 1.25	1939	5
Filter, Green (Mercury) - f/2.0 - No.11	M-050	$ 2.75	1939	5
Filter, Green (Mercury) - f/3.5 (& LT-035) - No.9	M-038	$ 2.00	1939	3
Filter, Green (Corsair I & II) - No.15	M-090	$ 1.75	1939	4 **
Filter, Polarized (Cine) - f/3.5, 2.7, 1.9 (& LT-135) - No.3	M-033	$ 3.00	1938	3
Filter, Polarized (Cine) - f/4.5 - No.2	M-034	$ 3.00	1938	5
Filter, Polarized (Mercury) - f/2.0 - No.11	M-051	$ 6.00	1939	5
Filter, Polarized (Mercury) - f/3.5 (& LT-035) - No.9	M-043	$ 4.50	1939	3
Filter, Red (Mercury) - f/2.0 - No.11	M-049	$ 2.75	1939	5
Filter, Red (Mercury) - f/3.5 (& LT-035) - No.9	M-037	$ 2.00	1939	3
Filter, Red (Corsair I & II) - No.15	M-089	$ 1.75	1939	4 **
Filter, Yellow 2X (Cine) - f/3.5, 2.7, 1.9 (& LT-135) - No.3	M-041	$ 1.75	1938	3
Filter, Yellow 2X (Cine) - f/4.5 - No.2	M-039	$ 1.50	1938	5
Filter, Yellow 2X (Mercury) - f/2.0 - No.11	M-047	$ 2.50	1939	5
Filter, Yellow 2X (Mercury) - f/3.5 (& LT-035) - No.9	M-035	$ 1.75	1939	3
Filter, Yellow 2X (Corsair I & II) - No.15	M-087	$ 1.50	1939	4 **
Filter, Yellow 4X (Cine) - f/3.5, 2.7, 1.9 (& LT-135) - No.3	M-042	$ 1.75	1938	3
Filter, Yellow 4X (Cine) - f/4.5 - No.2	M-040	$ 1.50	1938	5
Filter, Yellow 4X (Mercury) - f/2.0 - No.11	M-048	$ 2.50	1939	5
Filter, Yellow 4X (Mercury) - f/3.5 (& LT-035) - No.9	M-036	$ 1.75	1939	3
Filter, Yellow 4X (Corsair I & II) - No.15	M-088	$ 1.50	1939	4 **
Flash Cable Adapter, Roamer	M-091	$ 1.95	1948	4
Flash Tester	M-045	$ .35	1939	5
Flash Unit, Minute-16	M-	$ 3.95	1949	2
Flash Unit, Steré-All	M-	$ 8.00	1954	5
Flash Unit, Univex/Mercury/Univex Mercury	M-029	$ 3.95	1938	1
Humidifier Solution	M-004	$ .25	1938	5
Humidor Can	M-007	$ .40	1936	2
Lamp, Photo Flood - Uniflood #2	B-002	$ .50	1938	5
Lamp, Projection - 6 vt.	B-006	$ .50	1938	5
Lamp, Projection - 32 vt.	B-032	$ 1.50	1938	5
Lamp, Projection - 8 vt. Std 40 watt	B-081	$ .50	1936	2

PRODUCT	CAT NO.	ORIG COST	CIRCA	RATING
Lamp, Projection - 8 vt. Hi-Int 50 watt	B-082	$ .60	1936	3
Lamp, Projection - Std 125 watt	B-088	$ 1.50	1936	4
Lamp, Projection - Hi-Int 150 watt	B-089	$ 1.95	1936	4
Lamp, Projection - 115 vt. Hi-Int 500 watt	B-500	$ 4.20	1939	2
Lens Adapter, Argus - Enlarger	M-084	$ 4.50	1939	5
Lens Adapter, Contax - Enlarger	M-083	$ 6.50	1939	5
Lens Adapter, Leica - Enlarger	M-082	$ 5.00	1939	5
Lens, Cine - Univar f/6.3	L-		1941	5 ***
Lens, Cine - Univar(Woll) f/1.9	L-019	$39.75	1936	4
Lens, Cine - Univar(Univ) f/1.9	L-019	$45.00	1946	3 *
Lens, Cine - Univar(Univ) f/2.5	L-025	$22.00	1941	5
Lens, Cine - Univar(Univ) f/2.5	L-025		1946	1 *
Lens, Cine - Univar(Woll) f/2.7	L-027	$20.00	1937	2
Lens, Cine - Univar(Woll) f/3.5	L-035	$ 9.95	1936	1
Lens, Cine - Univar(Univ) f/3.5	L-035	$12.45	1946	4 *
Lens, Cine - Univar(Ilex) f/4.5	L-045	$ 5.00	1939	2
Lens, Cine - Univar(Ilex) f/5.6	L-056	$ 2.45	1936	1
Lens, Cine Telephoto - Univar(Ilex & Woll) 1" f/3.5	LT-135	$10.95	1939	4
Lens, Cine Telephoto - Univar(Woll) 1 1/2" f/3.5	LT-035	$37.50	1936	5
Lens, Cine Telephoto - Univar(Univ) 1 1/2" f/3.5	LT-035	$42.00	1946	5 *
Lens, Enlarging - Univar(Ilex) 2" f/4.5/50mm	LM-245	$ 7.50	1939	5
Lens, Mercury - Hexar(Woll) f/2.0/35mm	L-062	$45.00	1939	3
Lens, Mercury - Hexar(Univ or Woll) f/2.0/35mm	L 062	$77.76	1046	6 *
Lens, Mercury - Tricor(Woll) f/2.7/35mm	L-067	$20.00	1940	4
Lens, Mercury - Tricor(Univ) f/2.7/35mm	L-067	$34.50	1946	1 *
Lens, Mercury - Tricor(Woll) f/3.5/35mm	L-063	$12.00	1938	1
Lens, Mercury - Tricor(Univ) f/3.5/35mm	L-063	$20.75	1946	3 *
Lens, Mercury Telephoto - Telecor(Ilex) 3" f/3.5/75mm	LT-335	$19.95	1939	4
Lens, Mercury Telephoto - (Woll) 5" f/4.5/125mm	LT-545	$65.00	1939	5
Lens, Projection - Hi-Lux(Ilex) 1" f/2	L-020	$ 3.95	1936	3
Lens, Projection - Hi-Lux(Univ) 1" f/2	L-020		1946	4 *
Lens, Projection - Hi-Lux(Simp) 1" f/1.6	L-516	$ 7.50	1939	2
Lens, Projection - Hi-Lux(Simp) 3/4" f/1.65	L-165	$ 4.95	1936	3
Lens, Projection - Hi-Lux(Univ) 3/4" f/1.65	L-165		1946	5 *
Lens, Projection - Standard 1" f/3 (1941 version - f/2.7)	L-003	$ 1.20	1936	1
Lens, Projection - Superlux(Univ) 1" f/2	L-020		1946	2 *
Lens, Projection - Superlux(Univ) 1" f/1.6	L-516		1946	4 *
Lens, Projection - Superlux(Univ or Natco) 2" f/1.6	L-		1947	5 ***
Mask Plate, Enlarging (use with #00 film)	M-070	$ 1.95	1939	5
Mask Plate, Enlarging (use with 1/2 vest pocket film)	M-071	$ 1.95	1939	5
Masks, Transparency - Mercury	M-056	$ .50	1939	5
Minute-16 Combination Outfit		$16.95	1950	5
Mounts, Transparency - Minute-16	M-	$ .13	1949	3
Movie Films, Short Subject - 25 Foot	SS-025	$ .60	1938	3
Movie Films, Short Subject - 50 Foot	SS-050	$ 1.00	1938	3
Movie Films, Short Subject - 100 Foot	SS-100	$ 1.95	1938	4
Movie Films, Short Subject - 200 Foot	SS-200	$ 3.75	1938	5
Neck Cord	M-055	$ .25	1939	5
Oil, Projector	M-005	$ .25	1938	5
Projector Belt, Motor Drive	UP-201	$ .15	1937	1
Projector Belt, Take-up	UP-203	$ .15	1937	1
Projector, Model P-8 Univex - Hi-Lux(Simp) 3/4" f/1.65 Lens	P-081	$19.70	1937	4
Projector, Model P-8 Univex - Hi-Lux(Ilex) 1" f/2 Lens	P-082	$18.70	1937	3
Projector, Model P-8 Univex - Standard 1" f/3 Lens	P-083	$12.50	1936	1
Projector, Model P-8 Univex (6 vt. DC) - Standard 1" f/3 Lens	P-806	$17.95	1938	5
Projector, Model P-8 Univex (32 vt. DC) - Standard 1" f/3 Lens	P-832	$18.95	1938	5
Projector, Model P-300 Univex - Hi-Lux(Simp) 3/4" f/1.65 Lens	P-301	$23.25	1941	5
Projector, Model P-300 Univex - Hi-Lux(Ilex) 1" f/2 Lens	P-302	$22.25	1941	5
Projector, Model P-300 Univex - Standard 1" f/2.7 Lens	P-303	$18.50	1941	5
Projector, Model P-500 Univex - Hi-Lux(Simp) 1" f/1.6 Lens	P-500	$42.50	1939	2
Projector, Model P-750 Cinematic - Superlux(Univ) 1" f/1.6 Lens	P-750	$135.00	1947	4

259

PRODUCT	CAT NO.	ORIG COST	CIRCA	RATING
Projector, Model P-752 Cinematic - Superlux(Univ) 1" f/1.6 Lens	P-752	$115.00	1948	4
Projector, Model PC-5 Universal - Superlux(Univ) 1" f/2 Lens	PC-005	$75.00	1948	5
Projector, Model PC-10 Univex - Hi-Lux(Univ) 1" f/2 Lens	PC-010	$37.00	1947	4
Projector, Model PC-12 Univex - Superlux(Univ) 1" f/2 Lens	PC-012	$35.00	1946	4
Projector, Model PC-500 Universal - Superlux(Univ) 1" f/2 Lens	PC-500	$63.50	1946	2
Projector, Model PU-8 Univex - Hi-Lux(Simp) ¾" f/1.65 Lens	PU-081	$22.70	1937	3
Projector, Model PU-8 Univex - Hi-Lux(Ilex) 1" f/2 Lens	PU-082	$21.70	1937	3
Projector, Model PU-8 Univex - Standard 1" f/3 Lens	PU-083	$14.50	1937	3
Projector, Model PU-300 Univex - Hi-Lux(Simp) ¾" f/1.65 Lens	PU-301	$25.75	1941	5
Projector, Model PU-300 Univex - Hi-Lux(Ilex) 1" f/2 Lens	PU-302	$24.75	1941	5
Projector, Model PU-300 Univex - Standard 1" f/2.7 Lens	PU-303	$21.00	1941	5
Projector, Tonemaster 16mm Sound - Superlux(Univ or Natco) 2" f/1.6 Lens	P-1000	$350.00	1947	5
Rangefinder, Mercury	M-044	$ 5.95	1939	4
Rapid Winder, Mercury	M-054	$ 2.50	1939	4
Reel, Film - 200 ft.	M-006	$ .40	1936	1
Reel, Film - 400 ft.	M-		1947	5
Reel, Film - 2000 ft.	M-		1947	5
Reflector, Auxiliary 5" Flash	M-032	$ 1.00	1939	5
Screen, Crystalux Deluxe Projection - 22"x30"	SD-2230	$ 9.95	1937	5
Screen, Crystalux Deluxe Projection - 30"x40"	SD-3040	$15.95	1938	5
Screen, Crystalux Projection (30"x40") with Floor Stand	FS-034	$19.95	1940	5
Screen, Crystalux Projection - 22"x30"	S-2230	$ 2.50	1937	5
Screen, Crystalux Projection - 27"x36"	S-2736	$ 4.00	1937	5
Screen, Crystalux Projection - 30"x40"	S-3040	$ 5.00	1937	5
Screen, Crystalux Projection - 36"x48"	S-3648	$ 7.50	1937	5
Screen, Junior Crystal Projection - 18"x24"	S-1824	$ 1.49	1937	5
Screen, Silverlux Projection - 24"x34"	S-2434	$ 1.50	1936	5
Screen, Silverlux Projection - 26"x34"	S-2634	$ 1.95	1940	5
Splicer Kit, Film	M-001	$ 1.00	1937	2
Sunshade, Mercury f/2.0 - No.11	M-053	$ 1.95	1939	3
Sunshade, Mercury f/3.5 - No.9	M-052	$ 1.00	1939	3
Sunshade, Mercury II - No.11	M-053	$ 3.95	1946	3 *
Titler, Automatic	M-031	$ 3.95	1938	5
Titler, Standard	M-009	$ 2.50	1936	2
Tripod Clip, Model AF	M-		1937	5
Tripod, Table	M-080	$ 7.00	1940	5
Viewer, Minute-16 (available light)	M-	$ 1.00	1949	3
Viewer, Steré-All (battery operated)	M-	$12.50	1954	5
Viewfinder, Cine Auxiliary Optical (use with f/1.9 lens)	M-027	$ 2.95	1938	5
Viewfinder, Cine Optical (use with f/5.6, f/3.5, f/2.7 lenses)	M-025	$ 1.95	1936	3
Viewfinder, Mercury Optical (use with 125mm lens)	M-064	$ 2.25	1939	5
Viewfinder, Mercury Optical (use with 75mm lens)	M-081	$ 2.25	1939	3
Winder, Daylight Bulk Film	M-	$ 3.45	1939	5

(*) Postwar Product. The same catalog number was used for both the prewar and postwar versions of this item.

(**) The No.15 filter could also be used on the AF-5, Iris Standard and Zenith cameras and also on the prewar Mercury f/2.7 Wollensak lens.

(***) Not sold as a separate item.

This completely assembled camera with serial number 000000 was very likely a working prototype or demonstration model.

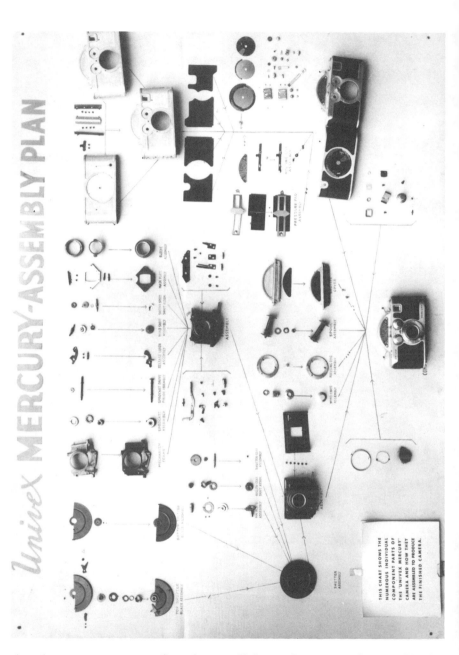

Actual camera parts were configured on a wall chart to demonstrate the assembly plan of the Univex Mercury and Univex Cine "8" camera.

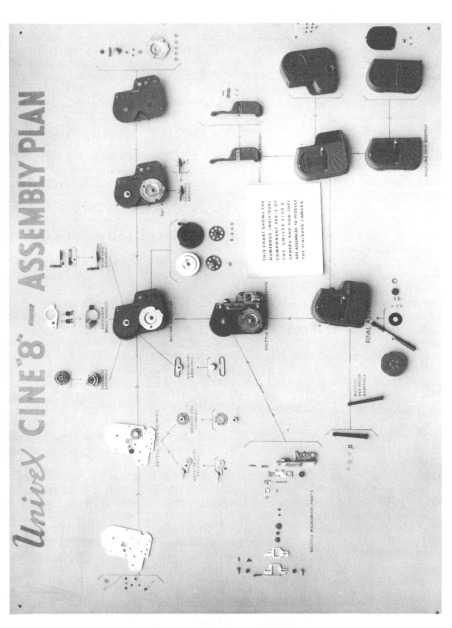

The body shells of the Univex Cine "8" in this display
all carry the serial number 000000.

263

BIBLIOGRAPHY

BOOKS

Abring, H. D., *Von Daguerre bis Heute - Vol. I, II, III.* Herausgeber: Privates Foto-Museum, Hernes, West Germany, 1977, 1981/2, 1985.

Coe, Brian, *Cameras, from Daguerreotypes to Instant Pictures.* A B Nordbok, Gothenburg, Sweden, 1978.

Deschin, Jacob, *Rollei Photography, Handbook of the Rolleiflex and Rolleicord Cameras.* Camera Craft Publishing Co., San Francisco, California, 1952.

Gilbert, George, *Collecting Photographica, The Images and Equipment of the First Hundred Years of Photography.* Hawthorn Books, Inc., New York, New York, 1976.

Gilbert, George (Editor), *Photographic Advertising from A to Z. Vols. I, II, III.* Yesterday's Cameras, New York, New York, 1970, 1972, 1976.

Goldsmith, Arthur, *The Camera and Its Images.* The Ridge Press, Inc. and Newsweek, Inc., 1979.

Gross, Harry I., *Antique and Classic Cameras.* Chilton Books, Philadelphia, Pennsylvania, 1965.

Hicks, Roger, *A History of the 35mm Still Camera.* Focal Press, London, England, 1984.

Hillyer, Whit (Editor), *The Camera Digest.* Paul, Richmond & Co., Chicago, Illinois, 1947.

Holmes, Edward, *An Age of Cameras.* Argus Books, Ltd., King's Langley, England, 1974.

Klamkin, Charles and Isenberg, Matthew R., *Photographica, A Guide to the Value of Historic Cameras and Images.* Funk & Wagnalls, New York, New York, 1978.

Lahue, Kalton C. and Bailey, Joseph A., *Collecting Vintage Cameras. The American 35mm, Vol. I,* American Photographic Book Publishing Co., New York, New York, 1971 or 1972.

Lahue, Kalton C. and Bailey, Joseph A., *Glass, Brass, and Chrome: The American 35mm Miniature Camera.* University of Oklahoma Press, Norman, Oklahoma, 1972.

Lea, Rudolph, *Lea's Register of 35mm SLR Cameras.* Lea's Register, Elkins Park, Pennsylvania, 1981.

Lothrop, Eaton S., Jr., *A Century of Cameras.* Morgan and Morgan, New York, New York, 1974.

McKeown, James M. and Joan C. (Editors), *Price Guide to Antique and Classic Cameras, 1990-1991.* Centennial Photo Service, Grantsburg, Wisconsin, 1989.

Office of Production Management, *Training Within Industry - Precision Lens Grinding.* United States War Production Board, Washington, D.C., 1941.

Office of Scientific Research and Development - Vannevar Bush, Director, *Summary Technical Report of Division 16, NDRC - Volume 4, Image Forming Infrared.* National Defense Research Committee, Washington, D.C., 1946.

Rifkind, Eugene H. and the Delaware Valley Photographic Collectors Association (Editors), *Cameras of the 1930's.* The Delaware Photographic Collectors Association, Delanco, New Jersey, 1977.

Robinson, Jack Fay, *Bell & Howell Company, A 75-Year History.* Bell & Howell Co., Chicago, Illinois, 1982.

Rowe, H. G. and Fairfield, C. T. (Editors), *North Adams and Vicinity Illustrated.* The Transcript Publishing Co., North Adams, Massachusetts, 1898.

Schneider, Jason, *Jason Schneider on Camera Collecting - Book One, Two, Three.* Wallace-Homestead Book Co., Des Moines, Iowa, 1978, 1982, 1985.

Smith, R. C., *Antique Cameras*. David and Charles, Ltd., Newton Abbott, England, 1975.

Taylor, A. Marjorie (Editor), *The Language of World War II*. The H. W. Wilson Co., New York, New York, 1948.

Twyman, F., *Optical Glassworking*. Hilger & Watts Limited, London England, 1955.

Twyman, F., *Prism and Lens Making, A Text Book for Optical Glassworkers*. Hilger & Watts Limited, London, England, 1942.

Tydings, Kenneth S., *Advanced Rolleiflex and Rolleicord Guide*. Chilton Co., Philadelphia, Pennsylvania, 1960.

U.S. Army, Department of, *Technical Manual 9-1580, Ordnance Maintenance: Binoculars, Field Glasses and B.C. Telescopes, All Types*. Washington, D.C., 1945.

U.S. Army, Department of, *Technical Manual 9-1240-372-34P, Direct Support and General Support Maintenance Repair Parts and Special Tools List for Binoculars M3, M7, M13, M13A1, M15A1, M16 and M17A1*. Washington, D.C., 1972.

U.S. Army and U.S. Air Force, Department of, *Technical Manual 9-1580, Ordnance Maintenance: Binoculars M3, M7, M8, M9, M13, M13A1, M15, M15A1, M16, M17 and M17A1 and BC Telescope M65*. Washington, D.C., 1953.

U.S. Army Armament Command, *Depot Maintenance Work Requirements for Overhaul of Binoculars W/E: M3, M7, M13, M13A1, M15A1, M16, and M17A1*. Rock Island Arsenal, Rock Island, Illinois, 1976.

Vial, Bernard, *Histoire des Appareils Francais, Periode 1940-1960*. Fotovic, Paris, France, 1980.

Wahl, Paul, *Subminiature Technique*. Chilton Co., Philadelphia, Pennsylvania, 1960.

Wolf, Myron S., *Directory of Collectible Cameras*. Privately published, Lexington, Massachusetts, 1972.

Wright, Lieut. Col. F.E., *The Manufacture of Optical Glass and of Optical Systems, A War-time Problem*. U.S. Ordnance Department, Washington, D.C., 1921.

PERIODICALS

American Druggist, 1933-1950.
Consumer's Research Bulletin, 1942, 1943, 1944, 1947.
Girl Scouts of the U.S.A. – Official Catalog, 1933-1940.
Master Buying Guide and Directory Issue, Photographic Trade News, 1945-1955.
Mercury Bulletin, Spiratone, Fall 1948.
Modern Photography (Minicam), 1933-1955.
Movie and Photo Merchandising, Universal Camera Corporation, 1937-1939.
Photographic Dealer and Photo Finishers News, September 1939.
Popular Photography, 1933-1955.
Popular Science, 1933-1950.
The American Girl, New York, New York, 1935-1938.
The Camera, 1933-1950.
The New York Times, New York, New York, 1935-1952.
The Transcript, North Adams, Massachusetts, 1952-1960.
The Univex Merchandiser, Universal Camera Corporation, 1940-1942.
U.S. Camera, 1933-1950.

Amateur Photography Booms in Business Week, June 28, 1947.
Bausch & Lomb in Fortune, October 1940.
Binoculars in Mass in Fortune, June 1943.
Boom in Twin Lens Cameras in Science Illustrated, June 1948.

Camera Future in Business Week, August 30, 1947.

Cameras of the Future in Business Week, March 10, 1945.

Canadian Binoculars in Canadian Machinery and Manufacturing News, November 1944.

Cheap Camera Clicks in Business Week, September 14, 1935.

Distinguished Group Honors Edison Entree to Schenectady in Electrical World, June 20, 1936.

Glass Speed - Diamond Charged Lens Grinding Tools for Precision Optics in Scientific American, April 1943.

Ike Likes Realists in Fortune, August 1952.

Japanese Cameras Bid for the Quality Market in Business Week, March 7, 1953.

Leads 10,000 Salesmen in Radio Retailing, April 1936.

Marketing a Camera Revolution in Business Week, June 12, 1954.

New Camera Gives Depth to Picture in New Popular Science Monthly, August 1934.

New Markets for the Camera in Business Week, September 3, 1949.

Off the Record, Univex in Fortune, October 1936.

One-Step Camera in Business Week, March 1, 1947.

Origin of the Navy 'E' in Army and Navy Journal, April 29, 1944.

Out of Focus in Business Week, March 11, 1944.

Plastic Binocular in Journal of Franklin Institute, National Bureau of Standards Notes, November 1944.

The Drug Store Market for Photography in The American Druggist, April 1947.

Twin-Eye Cameras in Business Week, December 8, 1945.

Univex Goes Places in Business Week, May 2, 1936.

Your Position is Well Taken... in Developments, July 1936.

Bailey, W. R., *Covering Binocular Bodies* in Modern Plastics, October 1942.

Bailey, Lt. W. R., *Carrying Cases for Binoculars* in Modern Plastics, December 1943.

Bailey, Lt. W. Russel and Kline, Gordon M., *The 6 x 42 Binocular* in Modern Plastics, October 1944.

Barton, Robert, *Minicams and Minifans* in Dun's Review, October 1937.

Benton, L. R., *Selecting Your New Movie Camera* in Popular Photography, June 1937.

Brown, Donald, *Huge New precision Optics Industry in U.S. built with Aid of Machinery Industry* in Iron Age, December 9, 1943.

Chisholm, Cecil, *How advertising brought in 60,000 binoculars for Britain's armed forces when all other means had failed...* in Printers' Ink, April 25, 1941.

Cookman, Jr., Aubrey O., *Report from Bikini* in Popular Mechanics, August 1946.

Cushman, George and Randall, Curtis, *Biography of an Idea: An Outline of Cine History Tracing Progress of Amateur Movies from 35mm to 8mm* in Home Movies, October 1945.

Goode, Monroe H., *Prismatic Binoculars* in American Rifleman, September/October 1938.

Hammond, Arthur, *For the Beginner, Choice of Apparatus* in American Photographer, April 1947.

Howe, Hartley E., *American Cameras Step Out* in Popular Science, June 1946.

Ingalls, Albert G., *Telescoptics* in Scientific American, August 1944.

Jordan, Donna Lee, *Seventy Years of Girl Scout Souvenirs* in Collectibles Illustrated, September/October 1982.

Kelley, Etna M., *America's Camera-Crazy Millions: A Market That Grows and Grows* in Sales Management, December 15, 1940.

Kende, George, *An Attractive Post War Picture for Precision Equipment* in Die Casting, February 1945.

Klock, F. G., *Learning as It Grows, This Company Builds Volume by Good Advertising* in Printers' Ink, November 1, 1940.

Kuhn, Lt. Col. R.C., *U.S. Small Arms Inspectors* in American Rifleman, December 1961.

Lahue, Kalton C., *Obsolete Cameras? There's no such thing!* in Photographic Quarterly, Fall 1971.

Laughlin, Jess, *Cameras for the Police* in Popular Photography, October 1938.

Mees, C. E., *The Modern Era in Photography* in Popular Photography, August 1939.

Moses, Morris, *A Short Legend in American Camera History: The Universal Camera Company* in The Antique Trader Weekly, December 12, 1980.

Radzinsky, Harry, *What Camera to buy* in American Photographer, April 1944.

Reichert, Robert J. and Elsa, *The 'Inside Story' of Binoculars* in The American Rifleman, April 1948.

Sanders, Gold. V., *Sandless Glass speeds up Lenses* in Popular Science, March 1946.

Simmons, C. R., *Molding Photographic History* in Modern Plastics, April 1940.

Starkman, David, *Inexpensive Stereo for the Masses: The Amazing Duo-Vex 3rd Dimension Camera of the 30's* in Photographist, Spring/Summer 1980.

COMPANY REPORTS

Annual Reports, 1948-1951
Bankruptcy Records, 1952-1964
Statement of Incorporation, 1933
Statement of Incorporation, 1937
Patents and Trademarks, 1932-1955
Prospectus, November 1944
Prospectus, October 1945

INDEX

Page numbers in italics refer to illustrations.

A.A. JAEGER CO: 223
ABE COHEN'S EXCHANGE, INC: *218,*
219
Accessory items, Univex: *19,*25,27,*28,*
42-50,*43-46,48-50,53,57,58,67,68,*67-72,
*70,71,79,80,97,100,*107,*176,177,*176-77,
180,*195,*196,*212-15,*214-216,*217,232,*
233-34,*234,*244-46,256-60
Advertising, Univex: *15,*23,32-34,*33,*40,
57-60,*59,*74,*75,76,*80,*82,*101-2,103,
*103,128,134,171,*172-74,182,*190,202,
203,*204
AFRICAN CONSOLIDATED FILMS,
LTD: 37
AJAX OPTICAL CO: 127
AMERICAN DISTRICT TELEGRAPH
CO: 37
AMERICAN OPTICAL CO: 116
ANCHOR OPTICAL CO: 123,136,156,
*157-59,*159,161
Argus: 71,74,*76*
Argus A: 25
Argus C: 13,64
Argus C 3: 182
ARLEN, RICHARD: 40
Army-Navy "E" Award: 123-27,*123-26*
Assembly plans: *262-63*
Atomic bomb tests: 132
ATOMIC ENERGY COMMISSION: 132
ATWOOD, LT. COL. FRANK J., USA: 141
B.F. GOODRICH CO: 201-4
Baby Brownie Special: 13
Bankruptcy: 112,200-1,208,223,*224,*
225,*226-28,*235-36,*237,*238
Bantam: 25
BASS CAMERA SHOP: 239
BAUSCH & LOMB CO: 122-23,*136-38,*
136-39,141-45,*146,*154,*158,159,*
159-60,161,208
BENNETT, JOAN: 40
BENNETT, RICHARD: 40
BEVERLY HILLS, DEPARTMENT OF
POLICE: 82
BIASI, CHARLES: 241
Binoculars: 91,114,116-17,120,122-27,
*135-49,*135-69,*152-55,157-59,163-65,*
209,211,223,232,244,246,250,256
BLAIR, POLICE CHIEF CHARLES: 82
BLOOMINGDALES: 238
Bombsights: 91,223
BRANDON, COMMDR. T.O., USN: 164
BRITISH GOVERNMENT: 82,117,127,
136,161-62
BROOKLYN DAILY EAGLE: 127
BROWNSCOMBE, PHILIP J: *62,63,*
65-66,102,*111,*244,245,248

BRUNS, JOHN F: *62,63,*241
Buccaneer: *181,*182,*202,*220,245,247,
250,256
Bull's Eye Six-20: 13
Bullet: 25,188
CALDWELL, SAMUEL P: 46
Cameras, Univex: *see individual listings
under model name or number*
CANADIAN GOVERNMENT: 126,*135,*
136,161-62,*163*
Canon: 233
CARL L. NORDEN, INC: 91
CARL ZEISS, INC: 64
CARLISLE, MARY: 40
CASE, PERCIVAL H: 114,141-42,*141,
142,145,146,*241,244,246,248
CASSIDY, JOHN D: 209,*210,*216,*217,*
241,244,246,248
CAZIN, OTTO K: *110,*244,245-46,248
CHARLES BESELER CO: 91
CHASE NATIONAL BANK: 223
CHEMICAL BANK & TRUST: 223
CHRISTMAS, LT. COL. JOHN K, USA:
141,*141*
CHROMEX FILM LABORATORIES: 242
Cinemaster: 10,55,*104-6,*105-7,142,
172,*182,*182-84,*221,*221-223,232,
246,247,250,254
Clarus 35: 182
COHEN, ISAAC B: 241
COLLIER'S: 40
COLUMBIA UNIVERSITY: 84
CONSOLIDATED FILM INDUSTRIES,
INC: 37
Contax: 64,71,74,*76,*233
Contax II: 79
Contax S: 83
Copy Stand: 71,*71,*176,257
Coronograph, Solar: *73,*74,*75*
Corsair I & II: *69,*77,*98,*98-101,*101,*182,
187,220,244,245,250,256
COSMOPOLITAN: 40
DAVEGA STORES CORP: 219-20,*219,220*
DAVID WHITE INSTRUMENT CO: 207
Defective cameras: *201,*201-4
Defense work: 91,106,113-34,*128,134,*
135-69,*171,*223
DEFOREST PHONO FILMS: 37
Dufaycolor film: *69,*69,100
Duo-Vex: 14-16,*14,16*
E. LEITZ, INC: 64
EASTMAN KODAK CO: 13,25,32,42,69,
102,122,123,142,172,188
Editor/Viewer: 45-46,257
ELECTRICAL TESTING LABORA-
TORIES: 74,*76*
ELISON, ELI: 117,*118,*245-46,248
Enlarger: *70,*71-72,82,142,176,245,257

Exhibits, Univex: *53,55,80,81*
EXPOSITION, SAN FRANCISCO: 53-55
Exposure meter, candid: 97,*97*,257
Exposure meter, cine: *46*,46-47,97-98, 257
Exposure meter, Mercury: 68,*80,176*, 176-77,257-58
Falcon Junior: 13
Falcon Press Flash: 13
FALKOFF, ADIN D: *149,150*,151,168, 246,248
Film processing: 32,42,64,180,211,214, 220,232,235,*236*,238,242,243
Film winder, Daylight bulk: *100*,100,260
Film, #00: *18*,18-22,31-32,41,70,92,99, 102,214,*222*,245,250,258
Film, #100: 41-42,99,214,*222*,245,250, 258
Film, #200: 66,69,*69*,98,100,174,180, 214,*222*,245,250,258
Film, Minute-16: *210,211*,211,212-14, *222*,232,235,*236*,246,250,258
Film, UniveX Feature: 51,251-53,259
Filters: 77,97,176,258,260
Flash unit, Mercury: *67,68*
FORESTAL, UNDER SECRETARY OF NAVY JAMES V: 126
FORTUNE: 114
FRANKFORD ARSENAL: 116,122-23, 126,145
FRIER, JOSEPH H: 223
FROST, GEORGE: 233
G. GENNERT, INC: 14
GaMi: 233
GENERAL ELECTRIC CO: 11,31,33,98, 102,103,*110*,166,182
GENERAL ELECTRIC TOPPERS CLUB: 31
GENERAL FINANCE CO: 9
GENERAL PLASTICS, INC: 12
GENERAL TALKING PICTURES CORP: 37
GEVAERT CO.: 18,22,41,69,99,*99*,105, 127,214,227-31,*229*,233,234
GIRL SCOUTS OF AMERICA: 28-29, *29,30*
GITHENS, OTTO W: 9,11,17,20-21,25, 32,35-39,40,*60*,64,87,91,102, 126-27,*126*,132,172,176,187,208-9, 241,244,245-46,248
GRAND UNION TEA CO: 238
GREIST MANUFACTURING CO: 45
HARPERS BAZAAR: 84
HARRISON W. ROGERS, INC: 37
HARVARD UNIVERSITY: 72-74,*73,75*
HAYWARD MANUFACTURING CO: 123
HIRSCHHHORN, L: 241
HOOD RUBBER CO: 160,201
HOOK DRUG CO: 238
HOOSAC MILLS: 227-31,*229*,234
House organ, Universal: 60

Icaroscopes: 127-32,*129,130*
ILEX OPTICAL CO: 55,77,87,113,*183*
Incorporation: 9
INTERNATIONAL CAMERA CONVENTION: 55
Iris: 77,92-95,*93,94*,101,103,*103*,244, 245-46,247,250,256,260
J.C. PENNEY CO: 238
JACKSON, F. FRANCIS: 80
Jiffy Vest Pocket: 25
JOHANSON, STEN: 117,*118*,142,*142*, *146*,168,244,245-46,248
JOHNSON SMITH & CO: 24
JOHNSON, FRANK: 205,246,248
KAY JEWELRY CO: 239
KENDE, GEORGE: *36*,37-40,*60,62,63*, 64-66,95,102,*109,110*,111,114,115, *116*,117,*118*,124,127,*164,165*,166, 168,176,205,*206*,208,241,244-46,248
KERSHAW CO: 162
KERTESZ, CARL: 244,248
KIRSCHSTEIN, ATTY. MORRIS: 18
KLEINBERG, LAWRENCE: 223
KLOCK, F.G: *60*,241
Kodachrome film: 25,69,105,172
Kodak 35: 64
Kodaprinter: 32
Kodocolor film: 172
KOLLSMAN INSTRUMENT CORP/ SQUARE D: 123,208
KOSKEN, WILHO A: 245,248
LAND, DR. EDWIN H: 207
LAWSON, WILLIAM L: 245,248
Leica: 64,71,74,*76*,233
Lenses & Prisms, Manufacture of conventional: 113-16,*116*,121-22
Lenses & Prisms, Manufacture of Universal: 55-56,108,113-22,*116,118*, *119,121*,123-27,132,142,156,170, 174-75,246
Lenses, Cine: 40,*41*,47,*49,54*,55,*56*, *104-6*,107,113,*182,183*,184,*221*,247, 259
Lenses, Mercury: *61*,77,*77-80,172*, 174-75,*175*,176,180,247,259
Lenses, Projection: *51,52,57*,108,*108*, 170,*184-86,189,191*,194,259
LIBERTY: 40
LIFE: 40,102
Liquidation of assets: 225,231,235
LOOK: 40
LOTZ, RICHARD: 102,245,248
LUPINO, IDA: 40
MANNERBERG, EDWARD G: 25,35, 244,245,248
MARKS, JOSEPH DAVID: *210,215*,216, *217*,241,244,246,248
MARSHALL FIELD & CO: 238
MASLANSKY, PHILIP: 23
MASTER PHOTO FINISHERS OF AMERICA: 32,*33*

MCKESSON AND ROBBINS: 238
MECHANICS & HANDICRAFTS: 84
MENZEL, DR. DONALD H: 74
Mercury (CC) I: 6,*61-63*,64,*65*,65-82,*69*,
   76,78,79,81,82,91,92,95,98,*103,111*,
   112,172-80,182,232,244,245,247,
   250,256,*262*
Mercury (CC-1500) I: 79,*80*,250,256
Mercury (CX) II: 6,172-80,*172,173,175,
   178,179,202*,232,250,256
Mercury exposure meter: 68,*80,176*,
   176-77,258
Mercury flash unit: 67,*67,68*,82,*103*,176,
   196,244,245,258
Mercury lenses: *61*,77,*77-80,172*,174-75,
   175,176,180,259,260
Mercury rangefinder: 68-69,*80*,176,
   180,245,260
Mercury rapidwinder: 68,*80*,177,245,
   260
Mercury shutter: 72,*72,73*,74,*75,76*,79,
   175,245
Mercury shutter speed tester: 80-81
Mercury viewfinders: *79*,176,260
Meteor: 187-88,*187,188*,197,244,247,
   250,256
Meteor II: 188
Microflex: 83-86,*84,86*
MILLSTEIN, HARRY: 208
MILNE, DR. GORDON G: 130
MILNE, JAMES D: 14,244,248
Minicord: 233
Minox: 233
Minute-16: *209*,211-16,*212,214*,223,
   231-32,235,244,246,247,250,256,
   258,259,260
MOCK & BLUM ATTYS: 18
Model A: 11-17,*11,13*,20,22-24,29,35,
   60,92,102,209,239,244,245,250,256
Model A, 1933-34 Century of Progress:
   20
Model A, Girl Scout: 29
Model A, Johnson Smith & Co: 24
Model A, Lone Ranger: 24
Model AF: *24,25*,25-31,35,92,95,244,
   245,250,256
Model AF, GE Toppers Club
   Convention: 31,*31*,
Model AF, Girl Scout: 28-29,*29,30*
Model AF, Hollywood: 31,*32*
Model AF-2: *26*,27,250,256
Model AF-3: *26*,27,250,256
Model AF-4: 27,*27*,250,256
Model AF-5, Minicam: 27-28,*28*,77,250,
   256,260
Model A-8, Standard: *38,39,41*,42,*43*,47,
   49,54,109,244,245,250,255,256
Model B-8, Trueview: 50,53-55,*54*,250,
   256
Model C-8, Turret: 56,*56*,244,245,250,
   256

Model C-8, World's Fair/Exposition:
   53-58,*54*,80,106,250,256
Model D-8, Cinemaster: *104*,105-7,250,
   256
Model E-8, Cinemaster: *105*,105-7,250,
   256
Model F-8, Cinemaster: 105-7,*106*,183,
   250,256-57
Model G-8, Cinemaster II: 106,182-84,
   182,221,250,257
Model H-8, Cinemaster: 221-223,*221*,
   250,257
Model P-8: *44,51*,51-52,*53,59*,244,
   245-46,250,254,259
Model P-300: 107-8,*108*,186,250,254,
   259
Model P-500: 56-57,*57,58*,108,184-85,
   244,250,254,259
Model P-750, Cinematic: 188-92,*189,
   190*,247,250,254,259
Model P-752, Cinematic: *190,191*,192,
   247,250,254,260
Model P-1000, Tonemaster: 188-94,
   189,250,254,260
Model PC-5: 185,*185*,250,254,260
Model PC-10: 186,*186*,250,254,260
Model PC-12: 186,250,254,260
Model PC-500: *184*,184-85,250,254,260
Model PU-8: 52,*52*,250,254,260
Model PU-300: 107-8,186,250,254,260
Monocular: 169,*169*,223
MONTGOMERY WARD & CO: 238
MONTGOMERY, DOUGLAS: 40
MOVIE & PHOTO MERCHANDISING: 60
Murder/suicide scandal: 208
Namco Midget: 13
NASH/KELVINATOR: 123,146
NATIONAL GEOGRAPHIC: 40
NATIONAL INSTRUMENT CORP: 123,
   127,156,*157*
NATIONAL PARK SERVICE: 162
NATIONAL TEA CO: 238
NEW YORK MERCHANDISE CO:
   23-24,132,200,208,211
NEW YORK MIRROR: 102
NEW YORK TIMES: 35,60
NEWMAN, WILLIAM B: 241
NIKON: 233
Norad Mill: 235
NORCA CO: 22
Norca Pin-up: 23
Norca Rower: *22,23*
NORDEN, JESSE: 25,35,241,244,245,
   248
Norton: *12*,12-13,20-22,244,245
NORTON LABS: 11-13,20-21,244
Norton, 1933-34 Century of Progress:
   20,*20*
Norton-Univex: *21*,22,250,257
O'BRIEN, DR. BRIAN: 130
O'NEILL, HENRY: 81-82,*82*

270

OLIVER, COMMDR. E.B., USN: 127
OPTICAL FILM & SUPPLY CO: 123
Optical plant: 56,64,108,113-134,*116,*
    *118,119,121,*175
OWL DRUG CO: 238
PACIFIC COAST MERCHANDISE CO: 14
PARSONS INSTITUTE OF ART: 84
Patents & trademarks matters: 13-18,
    22,25,39-40,45,46,50,67,87-88,91,
    102,117,*146,*151,166,168-69,188,
    207,208,233,*240,*244-48
Patents drawings: *17,62,63,65,72,88,109,*
    142,145,150,164,165,206,210,217
PATHE: 42
PATTERSON, UNDER SECRETARY OF
    WAR ROBERT: 126
Perfex 44: 64
Perfex 55: 182
Phonograph: 205-07,*206,*244,246
Pignone Reflex design: 83,*85,*86-87,89
Pignone Speedflex design: 89-91,*90*
PIGNONE, JOSEPH: 89-91,*111,190,*
    191,246,248
PLATT, SAMUEL C: *17,*18,245,248
POLAROID CORP: 207
Polaroid Land: 207
Police, Use of cameras: 82
POLYGRAPHIC COMPANY OF
    AMERICA: 227
POPULAR MECHANICS: 102
POPULAR SCIENCE: 114
PORTER, EVERETT M: 35-40,244,
    245-46,248
Prisms & Lenses, Manufacture of
    conventional: 113-16,*116,*121-22
Prisms & Lenses, Manufacture of
    Universal: 55-56,108,113-22,*116,118,*
    *119,121,*123-27,132,142,156,170,
    174-75,246
Profits and losses: 112,132,170,201,
    216,*234,*249
Projectors, Univex: *see individual listings
    under model name or number*
PROVSKY, L: 241
R.H. MACY & CO: 238
Radio/Phonograph: 205,244
RADIOCRAFT: 84
Record changer: 205
Rectaflex: 83
REMINGTON RAND CO: 231
RESEARCH ENTERPRISES LTD: 123,
    162
RICH, IRENE: 81
Roamer I, II & 63: *192-95,*196-97,201,
    *201,203,*220,232,247,250,257
ROBERTS, DR. WALTER ORR: 74
ROBINTON, FRANK A: 244,245,248
ROLLEICORD: 205
RUBIN, LEWIS JAY: 244,248
SALES TALK: 114
SALVATORE, ROLAND: 244,248

SATURDAY EVENING POST: 40
SCHWARTZ, MORTON M: 241
Screens, Projection: 47,*48,*260
SEARS ROEBUCK & CO: 238
SHAPIRO, HARRY L: *60,*241
SHAPIRO, JACOB J: 9,11,17,32,35,39,
    *60,*64,65,87,91,102,126,132,172,
    176,209,211,231,241
SHAW, MILTON M: *60,*208,241
Single lens reflex, eyelevel: 83,87,89,
    *111,*170-72,191
Single lens reflex, waist level: 87-88,*88,*
    91,170-72,191,246
Slide projector designs: *109,*111,216,
    *217,*244,245-46
SPENCER OPTICAL CO: 123
SPINATELLI, C.J: 241
SPIRATONE FINE GRAIN LABS: 177,
    *178,179,*180
Splicer: *45,*46,260
SPRAGUE ELECTRIC CO: 234
SQUARE D/KOLLSMAN
    INSTRUMENT: 123
STEINER CO: 234
Steré-All: *232,*233-34,247,250,257,
    258,260
Stereo Realist: 207
Stocks & Stockholders: 24,132-34,*133,*
    201
Strikes, labor: 200
STUCKENS, LEO J: 233,241
TATKIN, MICHAEL: 241
TEAGUE, WALTER DORWIN: 188
Telescopes, Sun: 127-32
THOMAS A. EDISON, INC: 91
Titlers: 42-45,*43,*260
Tonemaster: 188,*189,*192-94,247,250,
    254,260
Trade paper, Universal: 60
TROPP, VICTOR: 241
Twinflex: 103-5,*104,*244,245,247,250,
    257
U.S. FORESTRY SERVICE: 162
U.S. GOVERNMENT: 82,117,121,122,
    145,148,162,165,168,170,216
Uniflash: *101,*102-5,*103,*186,245-46,
    247,250,257
Uniflex I, II & III: *196-98,*197-98,201,*201,*
    *203-5,*204-5,*220,*221,232,244,247,
    250,257
UNITED CIGAR WHELAN CO: 238
UNITED RESEARCH CORP: 37
UNIVERSAL CAMERA CORP.,
    Managers: *60,*241
UNIVERSAL CAMERA CORP., Offices
    & Facilities: *8,9,9,227,229,230,*231,
    235,242,243
UNIVERSAL CAMERA CORP., Tool
    & Model Shop Employees: *199*
UNIVERSAL MANAGEMENT GROUP:
    127,*157*

271

UNIVERSITY OF CALIFORNIA-
  BERKELEY: 37
UNIVERSITY OF PENNSYLVANIA: 167
UNIVERSITY OF ROCHESTER: 130
UNIVEX MERCHANDISER, THE: 60
VICTOR ANIMATOGRAPH CO: 42
Viewer/Editor: *44*,45-46,257
Viewfinders, Cine: 47,*49*,53-55,260
Viewfinders, Mercury: *79*,176,260
Viewing filter: *240*
Vitar: *219*,220-21,247,250,257
Vokar: 13
WABASH PHOTOFLASH CO: 127
WAIN, SIMON: 241
WALDORF-ASTORIA: 123,*123,124*
WALGREEN DRUG CO: 238
WALTER, SEYMOUR: 241
War contract work: 91,106,113-34,*128*,
  134,135-69,*171*,223
WARD, WALLACE W: *215*,216,244,248
WARNER BROS: 37,81-82,*82*
WATERMAN, W.V.A: 241
WEIL, SIMON: *222*,231,241
WELCH, COL. GORDON B., USA: 126,
  126
WERBLOW, D. HENRY: 225-27,
  231-32,241
WERBLOW, ROBERT: 225-27,232
WESTINGHOUSE ELECTRIC &
  MANUFACTURING CO: 123,146
WHITAKER, DAVID C: 187-88,244,248
WHITLOCK, CARL H: 12,20-21,244,
  245,248
WILLOUGHBY'S: 127,239
WINS RADIO: 127
WITHERSPOON, CHARLES S: 31
WOLLENSAK OPTICAL CO: 55,77,113,
  123,*183*,208
World's Fair, 1933/34 Chicago: 20
World's Fair, 1939/40 New York: 53,*53*,
  55,*80,81* ·
YALE UNIVERSITY: 72
YEVICK, WILLIAM E: 244,248
Zenith: 77,95-97,*96*,103,*103*,247,250,
  257,260